Also by Thomas C. Renner

My Life in the Mafia (with Vincent Teresa)
Vincent Teresa's Mafia (with Vincent Teresa)
Wall Street Swindler (with Michael Hellerman)
Mafia Princess (with Antoinette Giancana)
Mafia Enforcer (with Cecil Kirby)

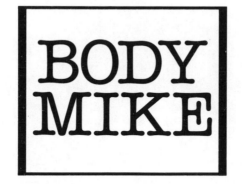

BODY MIKE

AN UNSPARING EXPOSÉ BY THE MAFIA INSIDER WHO TURNED ON THE MOB

JOSEPH CANTALUPO
and
THOMAS C. RENNER

Villard Books  New York 1990

Library of Congress Cataloging-in-Publication Data
Cantalupo, Joseph.
    Body Mike / Joseph Cantalupo and Thomas C.
    Renner.
        p.   cm.
    Includes index.
    ISBN 0-394-56371-9
    1. Cantalupo, Joseph. 2. Informers—United
States—Biography. 3. Mafia—United States.
4. Witnesses—United States—Biography.
I. Renner, Thomas C. II. Title.
HV6248.C165A3   1990
363.2'52—dc20
[B]   89-35463

Manufactured in the United States of America
9 8 7 6 5 4 3 2
First Edition
Book design by J. Vandeventer

To Nancy, for all the years and all the love
T.C.R.

To my greatest loves
J.C.

CONTENTS

INTRODUCTION

When I first met Joseph Cantalupo in a Queens FBI office in 1979 at a meeting arranged by an FBI agent, I wasn't certain he had a story that was important enough to turn into a book . . . but that was before he had begun to testify against the mob in Brooklyn and Rhode Island.

At that time, I was the coauthor of two books on the Mafia, including the best-seller, *My Life in the Mafia*, with Vincent Teresa. I had reported on organized crime for a decade for *Newsday*, writing stories about many of the criminals Cantalupo had dealt with, including crime bosses Joseph Colombo and Carlo Gambino. Because of my background, agents I knew arranged for my preliminary meeting with Cantalupo in Queens.

While we reached no agreement at that first meeting, I found Cantalupo to be brash, cocky, sometimes arrogant, often humorous and always streetwise. He was a fascinating character, always on the con, always trying to extract something extra out of those he knew and was close to. He had potential.

Agents and prosecutors were impressed by his depth of knowledge and his virtual total recall. His ability to tell anecdotes, little inside takes on the mob and its members, was reminiscent of other remarkable mob turncoats—Joseph Valachi, Vincent Teresa, and James Fratianno. Still, he was untested by a courtroom and I wanted to see how he would stand up as a witness. I wanted to see just how valuable he would be to the government.

I quickly learned in a succession of major Mafia trials that ended in the convictions of accused mob assassins in Rhode Island, Colombo family acting boss Alphonse Persico, Genovese family boss Frank Tieri, and in a major effort in Arizona to stop the expansion of a liquor distributorship that had hidden Colombo crime-family ties.

"Without Joe Cantalupo," recalled Arizona Attorney General Robert Corbin, "we wouldn't have gotten the settlement we did. He was invaluable. His information, together with other evidence we compiled with the help of the FBI and the U.S. Department of Justice, was devastating."

In September 1973, when Cantalupo succumbed to the years of foreplay of the calculated mind games played by a cunning FBI agent, he took the step that would forever alter his life and that of his family. He became a professional paid informer for the FBI and wore a body mike to record the conversations of the criminals he worked and dealt with.

No one, least of all the Mafia men he came in daily contact with, would have considered his betrayal a possibility. Cantalupo was like a son to crime leader Joseph Colombo, so close that the late Mafia boss sponsored him for membership in his Masonic Lodge, planned the creation of the Italian-American Civil Rights League in his office, and trusted him to collect the weekly vigorish on a $100,000 shylock loan.

While at the side of Colombo and his own father, Cantalupo more than simply rubbed elbows with the high and mighty of the world of the Mafia. He became the personal notary for then chairman of the board of New York's Mafia Commission, Carlo Gambino. He organized a flea market in partnership with the boss of the Genovese crime family, the late Frank "Funzi" Tieri.

There is little doubt that had Colombo lived, Cantalupo would have been sponsored for the Mafia. When an assassin's bullet intervened to change the course of leadership control in the Colombo crime family, FBI agent Raymond Tallia shrewdly played on the uncertainty, turmoil, and fear that gripped Cantalupo's mind. With exquisite patience, he turned that mind into a weapon against the mob—a devious, cunning, dangerous paid informer who has wreaked havoc against those who once trusted him because he sat at the right hand of Colombo.

Edward McDonald, former director of the Brooklyn Federal Strike Force observed: "Joe has been an outstanding witness . . . a guy with a remarkable memory for detail, who has been the key in important cases." Among those cases McDonald cited were the convictions of jailed former Colombo crime family boss Alphonse "Allie Boy" Persico, who died in prison last September, and Tieri, deceased boss of the Genovese crime family.

When New York's federal crime buster Rudolph Giuliani launched his campaign to break the control of the Mafia and its ruling body, the Commission, one of the first men his staff secretly sought as a witness was Cantalupo, who as a young married man had hosted a Commission meeting in his small apartment as a favor to Colombo. Giuliani's office used him not only in the Commission trial, but in the Colombo crime family racketeering trial that ended in the conviction and imprisonment of most of the experienced leadership of that criminal enterprise.

Long before the Mafia star cases pursued by Giuliani's offices surfaced in 1986, Cantalupo's talent as an informer-witness was tested in a Providence, Rhode Island, courtroom. In 1979 Rhode Island state prosecutors turned Cantalupo loose for the first time in court when they sought a solution to the strange disappearance of another informer—one who provided information to state police on members of the New England crime family of Raymond Patriarca.

Cantalupo became the first witness in that state's history to convince a jury to convict two mobsters for murder without the police ever having produced a body or weapon.

Six years later, after successful major trials against Persico and Tieri in New York, Cantalupo surfaced in Arizona as a vital informant, a valuable resource in state Attorney General Robert Corbin's fight to prevent what he considered an attempted takeover of the state's liquor industry by a suspected Mafia-connected, New York–based liquor distributor. The man he said was crucial to halting that 1985 takeover was Cantalupo.

"Joe is a jewel among witnesses," explained one of the Arizona agents who knew him and worked with him. "You may not love him, but you know he possesses a storehouse of information about the mob and its bosses that no other witness can duplicate."

Cantalupo, unlike most federal informers and protected witnesses, is not a convicted felon. That is not to say he has not committed a variety of criminal acts while he maneuvered his way through the catacombs of organized crime. He has been a bookmaker, a loan shark, a burglar, a safecracker, a fence, a stick-up artist, the director of a crime crew, a drug dealer . . . all while he was a paid federal informer.

Cantalupo was a consummate professional insider. When he was at work, no one was safe—not loan sharks, not crime bosses, not federal agents, not even prosecutors. He has become a legend in his own time among federal law enforcement authorities who both praise and vilify him for his informer role.

To survive, informers use the system to their advantage. They manipulate people, twist the truth, take advantage of internal communication failures to gain the security and advantages they desire. They steal, they lie, they cheat. They are aware of the lack of communication in the bureaucracies they serve and the desire within those bureaucracies to achieve success, and they use both to their advantage.

Cantalupo was a master of manipulation. To insure his survival and that of his family, he stole and cheated and committed crimes while he was working for the FBI. When Cantalupo became a witness, he turned on those whose job it was to protect him, manipulating some for financial advantage, denouncing others when he felt they had endangered him. The result was that some deputy federal marshals lost their jobs or careers in the Witness Protection Program, FBI agents were admonished for being suckered, and prosecutors were reprimanded—all in the cause of keeping Cantalupo as a viable and valuable witness.

"When I first met Joe, I was naive about him," explained McDonald. "I was a young prosecutor. He was my key witness in my first big Mafia case. I had never handled a case like that or met someone like him.

"Joe was a real dapper dan, like John Gotti. He would come in with the coat across his shoulders and sharp clothes and a line that would con anyone out of his shoes and I found myself liking him and that was the problem. Since then, and for the rest of my life, I'll never get that close to a witness again."

Although I had decided to write books about others, including Antoinette Giancana's *Mafia Princess*, I found our lives intertwined all too frequently. Cantalupo sought out advice, pressed for my commitment to work with him on a book as he became more and more deeply involved in informer-witness activities. Bookmaking in Minnesota, drug and gun smuggling in Idaho and Iowa, corruption and the mob in Kansas, problems with witness security, and eventual desertion by federal authorities . . . a never ending chain of crises swirled around Joe Cantalupo.

Too often, I found myself personally caught up in the Cantalupo whirlwind—something I tried not to let happen when I dealt with and wrote about organized crime witnesses and informers during the last twenty-five years. With Cantalupo it was difficult to keep that arms-length posture. He is, as McDonald says, likeable, a charmer, and above all, a con man par excellence.

When George Weisz, an investigator friend of mine in Arizona's Attorney General's Office, sought out Cantalupo as a potential witness against a New York–based liquor distributor, he asked me to have Cantalupo contact him, which I did.

Cantalupo's subsequent testimony and knowledge was a major factor in stopping that liquor distributor from operating in the Southwest and West Coast.

"His knowledge of the players in the company and his ability to pinpoint what they were doing enabled us to gather valuable evidence that would not have otherwise been obtained," said Weisz. "Cantalupo is just an incredible witness."

More than a year later, while Weisz was vacationing in Alaska, he was tracked down by federal prosecutors Michael Chertoff and Frank Sherman, both of whom were working for Giuliani. They were trying to locate Cantalupo.

In August 1985, I found myself spending endless hours reasoning with Cantalupo, attempting to allay his fears, listening to his arguments against testifying in the two most important cases of his life—the Commission and Colombo racketeering cases—before he finally realized he had no choice but to agree to testify.

As the years passed, I found his story impossible to ignore any longer. Joe Cantalupo's life before and after he became a federal witness provides remarkable insight into the unsettling, often terrifying world of the informer.

Cantalupo lived by his wits and cunning on the street, but with that came a state of constant fear and stress. Had he been seen with his agent contact? Would those he talked to suspect his questions and his delays in paying loan shark debts? Would mob superiors discover his microphones?

Familiar social clubs and restaurants, telephone calls, suggested meetings, payoffs, planned heists . . . all were potential death traps. Lying became routine, but the slightest deviation, the smallest error, could raise suspicions and end in discovery of the bugs he wore, resulting in instant death.

Cantalupo became the master of deceit and deception, flim-flamming loan sharks and bosses alike, yet his full potential was never tapped. As much as Cantalupo accomplished as an informer, McDonald conceded that he could have done more had the Justice Department and the FBI then shown the vision and creativity recently evident in stinging the mob's leadership.

"We really blew it with Cantalupo," McDonald said. "If we [the strike force] had used him as some agents wanted to to set up a sting, and legally bugged and monitored his real estate office, we could have nailed almost everyone in Brooklyn . . . all the mob families. They would have all gone to him for bank loans . . . for hiding their money. It would have been a bonanza and he could have played it to the hilt. Joey was that good."

He still is.

Thomas C. Renner
June 1989

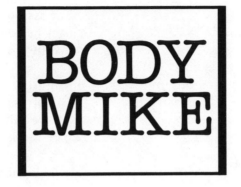

1

SINGING WOLF

My gut was churning as I stared out through the bars of the partially opened window and looked down into the enclosed courtyard from a small, drab witness waiting room located on the fourth floor of the federal courthouse at Foley Square in Manhattan. I puffed nervously on my cigarette, watching the smoke curl up and out through the window, and wondered what the hell I was doing there. What made me crazy enough to come to New York and testify against the godfathers . . . the Commission . . . the Mafia chiefs and their wiseguys who ran New York's organized crime?

I didn't have any answers as I peered through the bars. All I could see outside was an empty courtyard. For an instant, the emptiness was broken when in the distance I saw Alfie McNeil, a deputy federal marshal I knew, darting from the courthouse into another building. Good-natured Alfie. I always liked the guy. There had been days when we laughed together and drank together. Now, that was impossible. Alfie was good people, but he was part of another life, another time—and there was no going back . . . just remembering.

I was alone with my mind playing tricks, waiting . . . waiting to testify against the most powerful and ruthless mob bosses in America, and I remember feeling terribly alone. I shivered for a moment from a chill that raced through my body. The palms of my hands were clammy, and cold sweat dripped from my armpits, soaking my shirt. I looked at the hard wooden bench and the bare walls of the tiny, cold room, and I felt lonelier than I'd ever felt in my life. For an instant, just for an instant, I wanted to run—someplace, anywhere, just run. But there was no place to run. There never was.

The marshals were no longer my friends. They were supposed to be the good guys, but years earlier I'd had to testify against some deputies, and now I could no longer depend on them. Once they were my protectors, now I had to view them as I viewed the Mafia Commission I was about to testify against . . . as potential enemies.

There were marshals in the courtroom and in the corridors providing protection for jurors and witnesses in three major Mafia trials—the Commission case, the Colombo crime-family RICO trial (which I'd already testified in), and the Pizza Connection–Sicilian Mafia trial. The courthouse was crawling with feds—deputies, FBI agents, drug agents, IRS, you name them, they were there. And across the river in Brooklyn, deputies were providing the security for jurors and witnesses at trials of the Bonanno family bosses, who were running the movers union, for Lucchese wiseguys controlling Kennedy Airport, and for the Gambino family's flashy new leader, John Gotti.

But outside my witness room, immediately behind the packed courtroom where the trial of trials, the Commission trial, was taking place, it was the FBI who provided my protection. The FBI had brought me to the courthouse, hidden secretly in a van, while more than a dozen agents stopped traffic on Foley Square and provided protection as our caravan of two cars and the van roared across the square of justice, down a side street, and into the underground garage that early September morning in 1986. And the same band of heavily armed FBI agents would take me away from the courthouse later that afternoon to my Holiday Inn hideaway in Rahway, New Jersey.

"If you do this thing, Joey, they are gonna get you . . . and they're gonna hurt me. There's gonna be no place for you to hide–no place!"

It was September 14, 1985, and the voice was that of my father, Anthony Cantalupo. Somehow he had just learned that the federal government was planning to call me as a witness in two of its most important organized-crime cases, the Colombo crime-family trial and the Mafia Commission trial, both scheduled to take place in the Southern District of New York in the months ahead.

I don't know how my father learned about it. I had not yet agreed to become a witness, and I hadn't been declared a witness by the feds. I never asked him, and until now I've never told the FBI or prosecutors Michael Chertoff, John Savarese, or Frank Sherman—or anyone in the government—that I had talked to my father about testifying or that I had considered not testifying, considered going into hiding until the trials were over.

"Go away, Joey," my father was saying. "Just go away for as long as it takes . . . just go away until the trials are over."

In the old days, when wiseguys were tipped that subpoenas were about to come out to bring them before grand juries or to trial, they would disappear until everything blew over. They called that "going away." It was mobese for going into hiding— ducking subpoenas and federal investigators, staying under wraps until the heat was off. Only I had no money to do that. I barely had two dimes to rub together. My father wasn't about to give me any dough. The feds would turn the country upside down to find me, and when they did, I'd wind up in jail for contempt of court—prime meat for the jailhouse assassins the mob would have waiting, eager, and able, to kill me.

In the summer and fall of 1985, I was living in an apartment with my wife and daughter in the quiet little suburban town of Overland Park, Kansas, under one of the half-dozen phony names I've had to use as a federal witness as I've moved from town to town and state to state to hide from the dozens of Mafia men I've testified against. There was a price on my head then, just as there is now, but no one would ever live to collect the two hundred or three hundred grand that was supposed to have been put up to kill me. Nobody ever collects that kind of money. The guy who informs on you, the guy who whacks you, just gets buried along with the guy he kills. That's mob justice and mob gratitude.

For the first time in years, I was living a relatively quiet life—if the life of a Mafia informer and witness can ever be quiet—selling Italian ice to neighborhood supermarkets and Italian specialty stores in Kansas City and its suburbs.

Neither the federal prosecutors, the FBI, nor the federal marshals who once protected me under the Witness Protection Program were certain of where I lived. I had long since been dumped from the Witness Protection Program by the marshals when the feds thought they didn't need me anymore. But when the government decided to build these racketeering cases against the crime families and against the Mafia Commission, the government reached out to talk to me, and I made arrangements to see them through a friend. But with all the talk, no one knew if I would testify. I hadn't made up my mind. We were still negotiating—talking about what the feds would do to take care of me and my family during the time I had to leave my business and testify in New York, and what they would do for my wife and kids if I got knocked off.

When I heard my father's familiar voice, I was in a public phone booth near a public golf course in Missouri, where I had gone to play golf and to call my father at a specific time. It was all prearranged. I had gotten a message to call him from someone whom I trusted and who had heard from my father. The arrangement was simple and safe for me. I was to go to a public phone booth of my own choosing, and call the number of another public phone booth in Brooklyn, a number that had been provided for me.

So here I was in Missouri, in the heat of the day, standing in the phone booth like any golfer, in my loud Hawaiian shorts and shirt and golf shoes, with my bag of clubs leaning against the booth and a large stack of quarters on the phone-booth shelf, ready to pump into the phone whenever the operator asked for them.

My father was deadly serious as he spoke. "Joey . . . you can't do this thing," he said. "This is worse than before. This is the world you're gettin' ready to do in."

My father knew what he was talking about . . . and I knew. He was close to a lot of important people in the mob, not just street wiseguys, but bosses. I never knew if he was a made member of the Mafia or not, but he knew a lot of bosses, and I had met or dealt with some of them because of him over the years.

Carl Gambino and Joe Colombo, both family bosses when they were alive, talked to him and trusted him like he were a brother, and they had treated me almost like a son. He was close to Paul Castellano, who had succeeded Gambino and who I'd gotten in trouble with during my early years—trouble that the government might have tried to exploit and capitalize on as part of a conspiracy case they planned against him later. Carmine Persico, who in 1985 was boss of the Colombo family, and Christy Tick (Christopher Furnari), who was the *consigliere*, the adviser to the Lucchese family—they all knew my father, and they knew and hated me for what I'd become . . . Joey the Rat, a federal stool pigeon and witness.

"Look, Pa," I answered, "I don't want to do this thing, but I don't have a choice. You gotta understand . . . I'm between a rock and a hard place. Who's to stop these people? What am I gonna do? If they subpoena me and I'm on my own—if I don't agree to testify for them—then I'm dead meat."

"You gotta go away, Joey," he said. "If you do, everything will be taken care of. If you don't, you don't even make it to the first trial. Do it, Joey. I love you, son."

He hung up. I stood there for an instant, paralyzed, holding the receiver, unable to move. Then I stumbled from the booth, and I fell back on my golf cart. It wasn't like my father to say things like that. I hadn't heard the words "I love you" since I was a kid. I was stunned, but only for the moment. There were other events, other moments, other conversations, that were to affect my decision to testify.

The sharp rap on the door jogged me from my daydreams. I turned from the window and looked back at the door. The air was heavy with the smell of cigarette smoke, and butts lay all over the floor. The door opened slowly, and a dapperly dressed, balding man with a big smile entered the room.

"Jesus . . . Ray Tallia!" I shouted as he walked briskly toward me and embraced me. "It's been a lifetime since I saw you. You look terrific!"

He was grinning like a Cheshire cat as he grabbed my hand, pumped it, and gave me a bear hug. "Looking good, Joey . . . you're looking good."

Tallia was an FBI agent, but he was like family. Agents come and agents go, but the Tallias of the Bureau are few and far between. Ray was about 5'10", brown eyes, carefully dressed in a relatively expensive dark suit with a flashy tie Windsor-knotted into the collar of a clean white shirt.

He was still trim and athletic-looking, maybe 160 pounds at the most. His shiny, nearly bald head was slightly oversized, giving him a rather scholarly appearance, something like a professor or a lawyer, and yet there was a slick side of him that would have let him pass as a hustler and a con man. He looked like someone who'd made it . . . and he had.

Ray was boss in the Bureau's special section on organized crime in Washington. As I looked at him, I saw only a remote glimmer of the fast-talking street agent who hassled me in the mid-sixties and early seventies, dogging me and rousting me, putting me on the road to the Commission trial.

When I first met Tallia, he was half a rookie . . . or so I thought. He was brash, young—in his early twenties—fresh out of the army paratroopers, like me. The mark of the Bureau's academy was stamped on his forehead. He was the stereotype of the Bureau street corps of the sixties. The agents then all dressed alike. The suits, the ties, the shoes—even the same sunglasses and the same briefcases. They stood out like sore thumbs. They might as well have worn an army or navy uniform. Any street kid in Brooklyn could spot them a mile away.

But Ray had something extra. He had the personality, the endurance, and the patience that paid off on the street. Christ, did he have patience! I learned later that he spent weeks researching my background, learning how I thought, whom I looked up to, what made me tick. He almost knew how and when I breathed.

Ray had found out what I did in the paratroopers and the military police, what schools I went to and how I did—he knew my family, he knew everything about me, and he used it.

For nine years, he worked on my head . . . turning my mind upside down, inside out, and around and around. Week after week, year after year, Ray and other agents were on my tail, dogging me, turning up when I least expected it, embarrassing me, giving me a sense of insecurity. Night or day, in broad daylight or in front of my father's real estate office at night, he would drive up out of nowhere, easing up to the curb with a partner, and roll down the window as I walked along the street.

"Hiya, Joey," he'd say with a smile. "How are you today? Whaddaya doing with these bums you're working with? Don't you know you're a cut above these clowns?"

I remember how frustrated I'd get with his talking to me at streetside while Joe Colombo, or half a dozen other mob guys I knew, were watching. "Ray . . . why are doing this to me? Why are you bothering me?" I'd ask. "I'm nobody. I just work for my father."

But he was working on my brain, working . . . working, and I started to think. He's right. What *am* I working for these guys for? Then, one day in 1973, I crossed the over the line. I turned against everything I believed in and became a Tallia, a Bureau informer.

There were a lot of us. Tallia had a reputation for coming up with informers. At one time, he had twenty top active informants in the mob feeding him information, more than any agent in the Bureau.

Now, twenty-three years later, we stood face-to-face, greeting each other, waiting to testify against the supermen of the Mafia . . . the Commission . . . twenty-three years from the time I began running errands for Joe Colombo and notarizing affidavits for Carl Gambino . . . twenty-three years from the time I was first hassled by this bulldog of an agent.

"Joey, I've been watching your escapades for years," Tallia said. "You've done great."

"Sure, Ray," I said. "I'm doing great. Look at me . . . and look at you. You're a boss now, and me—well, I'm still living on the edge."

We hardly had time to get reacquainted when I heard someone say, "You're on, Joey . . . showtime."

I turned and walked toward the door leading to the courtroom. I looked back at Ray before I started to walk in.

"See ya, Ray," I said softly. "Thanks for stopping by."

"Break a leg, Joey," he said as he stepped out of the room into the corridor.

At that moment, I felt a surge of energy, like a jolt of electricity, race through my body. Tallia had shocked me back to the business at hand. This was the day of Singing Wolf, the name that my grandfather had told me Cantalupo was based on. Then I turned toward the inner door to the courtroom and walked in, looking straight at the jury as I stepped up to the witness chair and took my seat behind the microphone. I nodded to the judge and looked at Savarese and Chertoff, and then at the three defense tables shaped in an L where all the bosses—the godfathers and their flunkies—sat. For a moment, my eyes locked onto those of Persico and Christy Tick, and then it was time to tell my story.

2

THE HOMECOMING

I looked out from the cab as we passed Christy Tick Furnari's restaurant and bar, the 19th Hole, made a right turn, and pulled up to the two-story white stucco-brick office building at 1434 Eighty-sixth Street in Bensonhurst. Bold black illuminated letters identified the familiar street-level office—CANTALUPO REALTY CO.—and I grinned from ear to ear as I handed the cabbie a ten-dollar bill and thanked him for the quick, if short trip from Fort Hamilton.

"I'm home," I half-shouted as I pulled my army duffel bag from the cab's trunk, hoisted it to my shoulder, and marched smartly up to the front door, peering into the large front office window plastered with real estate listings and pictures for some sign of activity. There was none. I tried the door; it was locked. Then I knocked, and got no answer. In frustration, I looked at my watch and realized I was too early for business. It was only 9:30 A.M., and no one was in for work yet. I looked across the street at Caplan's Buick, past Vinnie Buffa's Pisa Caterers, toward Fourteenth Avenue, noticing a familiar landmark, Scarpaci's Funeral Home. It too was quiet on this hot August morning of 1964. For once, they weren't burying someone.

I dropped the duffel bag on the front walk, took off my army cap, and sat on the bag to wait for someone to open the office.

It wasn't long—maybe fifteen minutes—before the man who was to alter my life irrevocably stopped his shiny four-door maroon Cadillac close to the front door of the building. As he stepped from the car, he looked like a bank executive, with his carefully tailored pin-striped blue suit. It fit him like a second skin, and I remember thinking the suit probably cost him more than my entire year's salary as a corporal. I learned later it was one of three suits he would wear that day and every day that I saw him in the eight years I was to know him, and each of the suits cost him more than one thousand dollars apiece.

He was immaculate. He wore absolutely speck free, freshly shined handmade shoes that matched the lining of his jacket, and I noticed he wore color-coordinated shirt, tie, and socks that were monogrammed with the letters J. C. On his left hand was a giant diamond pinky ring that he also changed two to three times daily, to match the color of his suit.

There was one other thing that I noticed, and that was his eyes . . . his deep, expressive brown eyes. They seemed to dart from side to side, taking in everything on either side of the street and in the buildings as he strode briskly toward where I was standing.

I was a brash and cocky young soldier fresh out of Germany, and hungry to get out of uniform. But when I saw the man approach, there was something about him that made me stand up smartly to greet him. He was a small man, maybe 5'6", weighing 160 pounds, and I towered over him by at least four inches, maybe more. Still, there was a presence about him that made me feel small as I looked down at him.

"Hiya, I'm Joe Cantalupo," I said, extending my hand.

"Hello . . . I'm Joe Colombo," he answered, looking at the hand like a dead fish before shaking it. "You gonna work here?"

"Yeah," I said, with something of a smirk. "I'm gonna start at the top."

He shook his head. "You're better off, you start at the bottom and work your way to the top," he answered. Then he stepped past me, opened the office door, let me in, and walked through the foyer across the marble floor and past the carved marble lettering, CANTALUPO REALTY COMPANY, ESTABLISHED 1929, a company seal placed there by my grandfather.

For a moment, I felt like an interloper, like a stranger in my father's office, as we walked briskly through the waiting room, toward some salesmen's desks where Colombo told me to wait and then disappeared into a private office, closing the door behind him. I heard him call my father. It was a week before I saw Joe Colombo again, and by then I would know he wasn't just a salesman for my father; he was the boss of one of Brooklyn's most violent crime families—but he wasn't my father's boss!

From the time I was a kid and old enough to think, I always dreamed of working in my father's real estate office, carrying on a family tradition that had been started by my grandfather, Joseph Cantalupo.

Grandfather was tough, fair, loving, and caring. He wasn't particularly ambitious, flashy, debonair, or a ladies' man or like my father. Grandpa was all those things I wanted my father to be; he had all those emotions I wanted my father to show that he never could. As I think about it now, Grandpa was my best friend, more like a father to me than my father was. My father was more like a swinging older brother who knew all the angles instead of a father I could go to for advice. Still, I looked up to my father, idolized him, tried to please and be like him . . . at least for a while.

In the short fourteen years that I knew him, Grandpa was always ready to pay attention to me, play with me, talk to me. I remember when I was thirteen, my mother and father were divorced, and my sister, Maryann, and I seldom did anything but stay home with my mother and our stepfather in West Islip. But I vividly remember taking the train to Valley Stream to see my grandparents and my father, with my mother's last words echoing in my ears. "Now don't forget to get the twenty dollars from your father," she'd say as we boarded the train. "And show him those shoes of yours." I'd look down, ashamed at the scuffed old shoes with the holes in the soles, and the pants that sometimes had tears in them. It was her way of trying to squeeze extra bucks from my dad for child support, but it made me feel ashamed and cheap and unwanted, particularly when she would send us back to my grandfather's if I didn't return with the money. "Don't come back without the money!" she'd shout, and we'd board the train once again.

My deep sense of low self-esteem would quickly disappear when Grandpa met us at the train station. He had an old Buick, and he would hop out laughing, with his arms outstretched, and give us a big hug and kiss. Then he'd hoist me onto his lap, start up the car, and drive us to his house.

When we got there, he'd put my hands on the wheel and say, "Drive, Joey, drive it, boy," and I'd drive around the big circular driveway, while everyone from the Cantalupo family who was there for a get-together laughed and clapped. I'd shout loudly with pride, "Look at me, Pa, look at me!"—only he was usually too busy doing something else to look at what I was doing. Only Grandpa would be there, saying, "You're doing great, Joey, great."

After a few trips like that, Grandpa Cantalupo let me drive the car around the driveway by myself, while he got everything ready for the barbecue feast. When I wasn't driving, I'd watch as he cut off the tails of the steaks, ground them up, and made delicious hamburgers for my sister and me to go with our french fries while he and Grandma and the other adults sat down to have their steaks and macaroni or whatever had been prepared.

I remember thinking of those days as I waited in the office of Cantalupo Realty for my father to show up. It was typical of him to make me wait.

It was nearly 1:00 P.M. before my father came into the office. It was almost like seeing my reflection in a mirror as I looked at him. We looked so much alike . . . almost like twin brothers, except for his gray hair and age. He smiled broadly, gave me a perfunctory hug and kiss, and then noticed I was scratching the side of my crotch.

"What's the matter with you?" he asked.

"I got the crabs—got 'em on the ship—and they're driving me crazy," I said.

He drew back from me. "Stay away from me, Joey," he said. "You go see Doc Vesce . . . he'll take care of them for you. Then you hole up at the Golden Gate until you're cured before you come back here to go to work."

Joe Vesce was a doctor that my father and his friends had used for years to take care of various problems. He had an office on Fourteenth Avenue, so with some money my father gave me, I went to see him and then went to the Golden Gate Motel, a motel that for years was a hangout—although I didn't know it then—for a lot of wiseguys from Brooklyn. I almost didn't make it through the first day at the Golden Gate Motel. My whole life very nearly ended that night.

I was bored, sitting at the bar in the Golden Gate Lounge between showers and treatments, taking a drink in uniform. Sitting at the same bar was this good-looking blonde with a body that wouldn't quit, giving me the eye, fooling around. As she was eyeing me and giving me the come-on, one of my father's salesmen, Jerry Marinelli, walked in, and sat down next to me to have a drink with me and welcome me home. At the same time, a short, thin, gaunt-looking guy with curly hair and expensive threads and a big diamond pinky ring comes in with a monster of a guy behind him and sits down at a table in the lounge.

Marinelli nudged me. "Do you know who that is?" he said excitedly.

"Nah," I said. "Never saw him before."

"That's Carmine Lombardozzi . . . he's a goodfellow* in the Gambino family," Marinelli continued.

I was still pretty naive and cocky, and what he said didn't mean diddle to me at the time, because I didn't know who was who or what was what. I was just a big, happy discharged army corporal who was glad to be out but not flush enough to have new civilian clothes yet. I was also very horny, and this gal who had been giving me the eye was still giving me a look while she was dancing with this Lombardozzi.

What do I know? I get up from the bar, walk to the dance

*Goodfellow: an indoctrinated member of the Mafia, a made man.

floor, look down at this little guy, and tap him on the shoulder to cut in. "You mind?" I asked.

Now as I do that, I see this guy's face turn first white and then sort of livid as he storms off the dance floor to his table and this big ape he has sitting with him. I swear this guy looked like something out of a caveman movie with clothes.

I think Marinelli saw my future flash before his eyes when I walked onto the dance floor, and what he saw was the government sending a neatly folded flag and pine box to Scarpaci's for my funeral.

At that very moment, my uncle Sal Palotta, my mother's brother, who also worked as a salesman for my father, walked in. By this time, I've sat down with Marinelli, who is white as a sheet, and the girl is back sitting with Lombardozzi, who is by now ready to kill me.

Marinelli tells Uncle Sal what I've done, what a cardinal sin I've committed. I've dishonored one of the most powerful members of the Gambino crime family. I have made a fool out of a wiseguy who I learned later was one of Brooklyn's most powerful loan sharks, a powerhouse behind a lot of crooked Wall Street brokers, and feared even by some in law enforcement because of his violent temper. I was "in deep, deep shit," as Marinelli put it.

Uncle Sal patted me on the shoulder. I wasn't thinking so much about getting laid as I was about getting laid out after Marinelli spelled it out for me.

"He's a friend, Joey," Uncle Sal said to me. "Let me talk to him."

Without another word, he gets up from the bar, walks to Lombardozzi's table, and talks to him. Then he motions to me to come over to the table, where he introduces me to Lombardozzi and his Neanderthal bodyguard, whose name I can't remember.

"So you're Cantalupo's kid," Lombardozzi said stonily.

"Yes, sir," I said meekly.

"She's a real looker, ain't she?" he said, nodding to the blonde, who was smiling at my obvious discomfort.

I stuttered a bit before I confirmed what was obvious, and he told me good luck before I walked back to the bar. Ten minutes later, he sent the blonde over to me.

"Have a good time," he said as he and Neanderthal man walked out the door.

Here I am—I probably just escaped with my life, I got the crabs . . . and I don't give a damn. I just want to get into the sack with the broad . . . and I did, for two days. She probably got them—the crabs—and she probably gave them to him. He never said a word about it in the years that followed.

When I was sixteen, my father gave me my first car—a flashy 1952 Ford convertible that he had owned with a Continental wheel on the back and a Mobil credit card to pay for the gas and oil. It made me a half-assed big shot at West Islip High School. It also infuriated my mother and didn't make my stepfather too happy either, but in his own way, my father was trying to make up for not being with me while I was in school. He tried to do that by buying me things that he knew my mother wouldn't have the money to give me. But when it came to being there— standing up for me, personally being there to help—he couldn't handle that. He sent others to do his work.

Within six months, he took the card back because I abused it so much running up charges, and I began piling up speeding tickets with the car. At the time, I was working at a local King Kullen supermarket to help pay my expenses and ten dollars a week rent to my mother while I finished school.

One day, while I was working at the supermarket, a Suffolk cop came up to me, asked me my name, and, when I gave it, put me under arrest for failure to answer a speeding ticket. He took me off to the Third Precinct lockup, where they held me on three hundred dollars bail. It was my first experience with the law, and at first I was cocky, unafraid, certain my old man would buy my way out of trouble.

When my mother was called, she blamed it on a girl I was running around with and threatened to go to court herself and ask the judge to pull my license. She wouldn't lift a finger to get me out of jail.

I sat there for hours while my father let me stew and worry

about it, get a taste of what the can was like. The cops made it worse. They made me feel like a murderer, and they treated me like dirt. It didn't take long for me to become afraid, and I never forgot that early scare. My father finally sent a lawyer out from Brooklyn to post my bail, and the next day the judge let me off with a ten dollar fine after a tongue-lashing.

When I graduated from high school in West Islip in June 1961, my father gave me a diamond pinky ring and told me he was proud of me for finishing school. That's when I told him I couldn't take living with my mother anymore, that I was going to join the army and be a paratrooper before I got drafted. He didn't like that idea too much, and he arranged through a friend of his who was an official of the Maritime Union to get me a union card as a seaman first class.

Now I didn't know the first thing about ships. At eighteen, the largest boat I'd ever been on was probably a cabin cruiser, and all I did then was lean back and enjoy the sun and do some fishing. But my father and his union buddy said that wouldn't matter.

"You'll learn all you have to at sea . . . and you'll get to see the sights," my father said. "When you get back, after six months, you'll forget about the army and you won't have to worry about no draft. Then you can go back to school, learn some more, and maybe come to work for me."

So I went down to the union hall to sign up for a trip to Hong Kong. It took me just half an hour to figure out that a sailor's life wasn't for me. What I saw at the union hall was the ugliest crew of toughs I'd ever seen. Guys with peg legs and beards, others with a hook for a hand and slashes across their mouths where they'd been cut by some guy's knife. I thought I was with Long John Silver and his pirates getting ready to sail for Treasure Island, so I turned tail, got my ass into gear, and got the hell out of there.

I joined the army. Two days before I was supposed to leave, Uncle Sal—my godfather and my mother's brother—and my father decided to take me and a cousin out on the town. After dinner we went to a nightclub, and then my father and my uncle introduced us to two good-looking hookers and told us to have a great time that night at the hotel. I did, my cousin didn't. He was in and out in a half hour and never said why. Uncle Sal told me later the hooker told him what was wrong. The kid turned out to be gay and begged the hooker not to tell Sal, but she did. It took a long time for Sal to get over that.

A day later, I was on my way to the paratroopers. My first stop, in September 1961, was Fort Dix, New Jersey, where I soaked up eight weeks' infantry training and another eight weeks' advanced infantry training with periodic one-day visits from friends and relatives. My next stop was Fort Benning, Georgia.

I was a good soldier. I finished a rigorous six-week jump-school course and was good enough to become a squad leader. I was one of 220 who graduated from the jump school out of 400 who went, but I'd be lying to you if I didn't say I was scared to death.

I joined the paratroopers because I was afraid of heights. It doesn't make much sense, but I figured I could conquer that fear by driving myself to finish the school. From my first to my last jump and every one in between, I shook like a leaf and felt as if I were walking with death. My worst time was that last week of school, when I had to make five jumps from 1,250 feet. I was sure every jump was my last jump, but somehow I forced myself to make it, and I earned my paratroop wings. From school I was reassigned to the 82nd Airborne at Fayetteville, North Carolina. That's where the trouble began.

In the airborne, you're taught—they brainwash you to believe—that any one paratrooper is tougher than any four marines and or a half-dozen local pansies. It's a lot of crap, but you get to think that way and believe it. So when a member of my squad, a kid named Billy, was attacked in a wooded area while he was with his girlfriend, he did what any paratrooper would do—he beat and cut the hell out of his attackers.

Billy was jumped by three locals who didn't like seeing local girls with a paratrooper. To handle them all, Billy pulled out a small pocketknife, with only an inch-long blade, and fought them off. He was charged with assault with a deadly weapon.

I went to see Billy with members of the squad, and when we

found out he needed some things, we went back to the base and got the things he needed, and I decided, like a jerk, to smuggle a knife in to him in a pack of cigarettes so he could take care of himself in jail. Within minutes after we gave Billy his supplies, sheriff's deputies were holding the squad and warning us that we were all going to be arrested. Then they left.

The faces of my friends were ashen. All they could think of was spending three years rotting on some Carolina chain gang or getting a dishonorable discharge. I thought the best thing to do was keep our mouths shut, they thought different, and it was in that instant as we argued about it that I knew that we were being watched through a one-way mirror-window and that the room we were sitting in was bugged. When the deputies returned, I confessed putting the knife in the cigarettes, and I was charged with aiding and abetting a criminal.

I was scared, but I didn't implicate my friends. I said I did it on my own. Then I got permission to call my father, explained the situation, and asked him to send his lawyer.

"No, Joe, no lawyer," he said. "I'll send you one thousand dollars, and you get a lawyer. You get out of your own scrapes now."

So I went to my company commander, who arranged for a retired colonel to defend me. After about five or six meetings with him, he got me off. It cost me five hundred dollars, but he got me off. It wasn't long afterward that I got out of the paratroopers. I just couldn't handle the fear of jumping. The more I jumped, the more I was afraid. It just got worse and worse.

I called it a day after my tenth jump. We had just made one of those mass jumps, a big army training exercise with hundreds of troopers bailing out. One of us didn't make it that day. I still see him in a dream every now and then. I'm on the ground, pulling in my chute, and I look up, and there he is, banging up against the side of the plane. Banging . . . banging . . . I can still see him bouncing off the back of the plane until crew members finally stick a big hook out the door and drag him along the plane's frame, back to the open door. He was a squad leader I knew. At that moment, I decided I wasn't going to jump anymore. Shortly after that, I was shipped to Germany and assigned to the military police.

In Würzburg, I met Ilse. She was a beautiful blue-eyed nineteen-year-old—blond, busty, with fantastic long legs, a soft, sexy voice . . . a really gorgeous girl whom I fell head over heels in love with.

We met in a bar called the Kleine Stuben (Little House). She had just returned to Würzburg after spending six months in the can for passing bad checks, and she had broken up with a German boyfriend.

It took me three days of heavy attention, but by then we were making love where and when we could . . . in the Catholic church on Franz Schubertstrasse, in her mother's small apartment, and even once or twice in the summer months in a cemetery filled with headstones pockmarked by bullets from World War II. I just couldn't get enough of her.

Her mother was good to me. She didn't speak much English, but she understood our needs. Her apartment had only one heated room, the living room. The bedroom was unheated, but you kept warm . . . so warm in the goose-down feather beds.

Ilse's mother, bless her, came to me one night and told me that Ilse and I could have her bedroom to stay in. She slept in the living room. When she wasn't out working or shopping, she was in their small kitchen preparing food for us . . . stews and mouthwatering salads and sandwiches, one slice of dark bread covered with sliced German sausages and spiced meats. To repay her for what she provided, I would bring all kinds of food and coffee from the base for her, foodstuffs she couldn't afford or find in the German shops.

Occasionally, Ilse and I would have a fight, and she'd run off to see her former boyfriend. She'd be gone for a couple of days and I'd go wild. But our separations were short, and more and more I thought about marrying Ilse. But the thought didn't finally gel to reality until 1964, when Ilse told me she was pregnant.

At first I panicked and called my father. "Dad, I'm in trouble with a girl," I said.

He was laughing. "Not again," he said.

"It's serious, Dad," I said. "She's pregnant."

"Okay, okay," he answered. "I'll send you something to take care of it, all right?"

What he sent was quinine pills, which an army friend had told me would abort the pregnancy if it's early. The trouble was, my father gave the package of pills to Frankie the Beast Falanga to send to me. Now Frankie the Beast, who was a mob shylock and the cash bank for Joe Colombo, decides to send the pills regular mail to save money, and it takes more than a month to reach me in Germany. By then Ilse was too far along in the pregnancy to abort.

I was frantic. I wanted to stay with Ilse. I wanted to marry her and bring her home with me. But I didn't have the money, and I was nearing the time for discharge. I wrote my father and told him I wanted to marry her and bring her home.

That didn't sit well with my old man. He didn't want any *Fräulein* in his family, particularly married to his firstborn son. "You marry this girl, Joey," he wrote, "don't come here. Forget going into business with me." With the letter, he sent one thousand dollars, the equivalent of four thousand German marks in those days.

My biggest dream was going to work for my father. I couldn't give that up. So I gave Ilse the one thousand dollars and told her it was a wedding present from my father. Then I told her and her mother I had to go on maneuvers. It was one of the hardest things I ever had to do. I felt like a true rat. She was seven months pregnant, and I kissed her good-bye and boarded the troopship *Darby* to go home to Fort Hamilton, New York, to get discharged.

It took ten days in the hold of the *Darby* to get home. I was seasick all the way back, just as I was sick going to Germany on the same ship. It was on that ship I got the crabs. When we got to New York, we anchored for the night under the Verrazano Bridge before passing the Statue of Liberty and docking. When I debarked, I was shocked. There were no bands, no banners, no well-wishers, no Anthony Cantalupo. Just my mother and sister, who wanted me to come home to West Islip. I was still mad at my mother for not accepting a collect call from me on Christmas Eve.

"Go home, Ma," I said. "Thanks for coming, but go home. I'm going to work with Dad at the office." I kissed her and my sister and left.

I never saw Ilse again. Months later, I heard from some buddies that she had given birth in October 1964 to a beautiful girl and married some officer. They moved to the States. She was better off. So was my daughter, who would try and fail to see me in New York seventeen years later, when I was living in a world she could never reach, under a name she could never find.

But in 1964, I never thought about the consequences of my actions or what would happen to Ilse and our child. All I thought about was myself . . . fulfilling my dream of working for my father. And now the dream was about to become a reality.

3

THE MONEY MACHINE

I quickly learned that Cantalupo Realty was more than just your friendly neighborhood real estate office. It was a kind of nerve center for organized crime, where a lot of the mob's elite met to decide the fate of many of its victims, where the Brooklyn mob operated their version of a federal reserve bank for the collection, distribution, and circulation of money by and for organized crime. And the man directing that particular mob money machine was Joe Colombo.

I didn't learn all that in the first week or even the first few months that I was back from the service, and it wasn't something my father spelled out for me as he trained me to work in the office. It was something I learned gradually, day by day, as the high and the mighty as well as the victims of organized crime were buzzed in daily through the small gate at the office waiting room, past what was my desk, down a short corridor to the private office on the left where Colombo sat directing the traffic of his crime family.

Some came to confer about the high-level problems of the Mafia, leaders like Carl Gambino, a small, deceptively mild-mannered man who wielded so much power that Colombo, a family leader in his own right, owed his power, his money, his stature as a boss, his very existence, to Gambino. There was Frank "Funzi" Tieri, an aging, almost decrepit-looking leader of

the Genovese crime family, whose ironfisted rule made underlings cringe and one crime captain I later worked with literally
whimper in fear. There was also "Christy Tick" Furnari, who
ran the 19th Hole Restaurant on Eighty-sixth Street and Fourteenth Avenue, just a stone's throw away from Scarpaci's Funeral Home. When I first met him, Christy was a captain in the
Lucchese crime family, a normally powerful position. Christy,
however, also had a reputation as a negotiator, a talent that
quickly earned him the respected position as family adviser or
consigliere for the Lucchese mob. In that job, he negotiated disputes between members of various crime groups both in and out
of his family. One of those sitdowns, a dispute between members of the Colombo and Lucchese families, took place at his
restaurant on March 31, 1981, the day they carried Tieri's casket
out of Scarpaci's.

Others came quietly to pay their dues and take their orders
. . . men like Carmine Persico, Thomas DiBella, and Vincent
Aloi, powerful men, *caporegimes* who would one day succeed
Colombo as boss, but who then saw to it that his rule was
enforced and that cheaters or family dissidents were snuffed out.
And then there were the leg-breakers, the arm-twisters, loan
sharks like Frankie the Beast and Frank "Peewee" Campagna,
men who collected suitcases full of money every day from the
longshoremen, dressmakers, salesmen, and gamblers on Brooklyn's waterfront and Manhattan's garment center.

I watched and I listened and I occasionally asked questions.
Just as occasionally, I got some answers from my father, my
uncles, or some of the salesmen. But for the most part, I learned
more from what I saw than what I was told.

I was still in uniform when I first noticed the cars that constantly drove around the area, east and west along Eighty-sixth
Street, or north and south on Bay Seventh, Bay Eighth Streets
and Fourteenth Avenue. Round and round, up and down, circling, stopping, parking, taking pictures. They were all the
same. Gray, tan, or black sedans, each with two men dressed in
business suits and ties who looked as out of place as Arabs in
front of a Jewish temple.

Whenever I arrived, one or more of the cars would be parked

across the street in front of Scarpaci's, Caplan's Buick, or the Pisa Caterers. Occasionally, they would cross over and park in front of our office or next door in front of D'Onofrio's Pork Store. Now and then, one of the agents would step from the car, walk up to the big office window, and peer in to see who was inside or what was going on.

"Who the hell are they?" I asked Uncle Sal one day, pointing to a car with two men parked across the street, snapping pictures.

"They're fuckin' feebs," he growled. "They're always around, giving everyone a hard time, particularly Joe Colombo. Wherever he goes, they're on his ass."

"Jesus, why?" I asked, showing how new to everything I was, as well as how dumb.

"If your father wants you to know, he'll tell ya," he answered. "Just keep your eyes open and your mouth shut, and you'll learn what you have to."

In the beginning, my father didn't offer me much of an explanation either. "They're just out here harassing people, Joey," he said. "Just watch the salesmen and learn . . . forget them."

I did what I was told, but from office chatter I found out that the feebs circling the area were members of the FBI's Colombo Squad, a special group of agents assigned to watch and report on the activities of Joe Colombo, his friends, his business associates, and the rackets he controlled.

One of those leading the teams of agents was Ray Tallia. The big guy who frequently peered in the front window was an agent named Bernie Welch who often rode with Tallia. I met them while I was still in uniform, leaving the office to return to the motel. As I walked east down Eighty-sixth Street, a gray sedan pulled up to the curb next to me and Tallia leaned out.

"Hey, kid, I hear you used to be a paratrooper," he said.

I kept walking, trying to ignore him.

"We should talk sometime," he said, laughing. "I was a paratrooper myself."

As he drove off with a wave, I wondered how the hell he knew I'd been a paratrooper. I wasn't wearing a paratrooper uniform, and it had been nearly two years since I'd jumped with the 82nd

Airborne Division in North Carolina. I turned on my heel and returned to the office to see my father. He'd seen the agents stop and talk to me.

"What was that all about?" he asked.

"They knew I was in the paratroopers," I said. "How do they know that?"

"Never mind," he answered. "It's time you got out of that uniform. Let's get you some clothes."

We later went to his tailor, F & F Tailors on Broadway in Manhattan, where he laid out more than five hundred dollars for suits, shirts, ties . . . all the essentials. But before he did, he introduced me to Alexander Wasserman, a wealthy real estate investor who owned apartment houses and other properties and was a close friend of my father's.

"This is my son, Joey, Al," my father said. "He's joining me in the business."

"That's good . . . that's good," Wasserman said, shaking my hand. "Now, so you should make a good impression, here's something to replace that uniform with. You can't sell real estate in an army suit." Then he pressed a hundred-dollar bill into my hand.

The hundred dollars bought my first suit, and a year later Wasserman gave me my first business property, a brick two-family building at 2400 Stillwell Avenue, under the elevated subway. He gave it to me for the mortgage, thirteen thousand dollars, complete with gypsy tenants who I collected rent from for a year before I sold the place for twenty-five thousand dollars.

Friend that he was, Wasserman would also in future years become the victim of a $100,000 shakedown scheme I initiated—a scheme that very nearly cost me my life, almost destroyed my informant role with the FBI, and resulted in a serious territorial dispute between the leaders of the Colombo and Gambino crime families.

But in 1964, Al Wasserman was just a nice Jewish businessman, and the FBI and its agents were like a plague to be avoided at all costs.

• • •

The rules of the business were simple. Make money any way you can, legally or illegally, and, above all, protect Joe Colombo from any tax raps by the IRS or the FBI—and do it right under the noses of the surveilling agents. It was like giving mice a smell of cheese, then hiding it where they couldn't get at it.

My father spelled some of it out to me as he taught me the ropes of real estate as it was practiced at Cantalupo Realty Company. Part of that explanation was the fact that Colombo, a friend since they'd caddied together in Bensonhurst as teenagers in 1938, was the boss of a Brooklyn crime family. He didn't say "Joe's a crime boss," he just said, "Joe runs things around Brooklyn, and he has a lot of friends." He also said Joe brought in a lot of business—big-bucks business.

Colombo came to "work" for my father in 1960, a couple of years before he became a boss. His sponsor, the man who gave him permission to work in my father's office and use it as a legitimate business front, was Gambino. What the godfather permits is like a command for men like my father. Since Colombo was an old friend, and my father was an associate of Gambino and his family, he was obligated to give Colombo the job. Of course, there was a price for such a favor, a price neither Colombo nor my father put a figure to, but it was considerable—enough so that Colombo used to complain about my father's spending habits.

"Joey . . . your father must bury his money in shoe boxes somewhere," he'd say, shaking his head after my father would come to him to borrow ten thousand dollars, fifteen thousand dollars, or more in cash. "No matter how much he gets, he never has enough."

As much as he complained, Colombo would always have the money for him, it was always there, and my father never paid more than half a point a week for that money—maybe fifty or seventy-five dollars a week to borrow it instantly. That was part of the arrangement, part of the deal that Gambino made possible. For my father, instant, almost unlimited cash was always available on easy terms. Colombo's own loan sharks paid two to three points a week on the money they got from him, and they charged four or five a week in the streets.

The decision to bring Colombo in as a salesman almost over-night changed the friendly neighborhood real estate office image my grandfather had taken decades to build. From a quiet, if successful neighborhood business, it became a hub of activity and hustle and the center of unsolicited attention.

To become a licensed real estate salesman in New York, you have to take a state test. Colombo couldn't and didn't. He was too busy running a mob and moving millions of dollars to bother with taking the time to study and pass a salesman's test. The mob had a better and quicker solution. They had a connec-tion in the New York Secretary of State's Office then, and through that connection they arranged for a stand-in to take the salesman's test for Colombo. The stand-in was my uncle Severino Palotta, Uncle Sal, as I called him. He was a partner of my father's in business, and he was associated with Colombo, so he did what he had to do. He went in, took the test, and signed for Colombo, and that's how Colombo got his license. I didn't have that kind of clout. I had to take the test and pass it.

"Joe's got to show some legitimate business income to keep the tax men off his back, and we help him do that," my father explained. He didn't bother to tell me what he was doing that wasn't legitimate. I found that out from the salesmen, from running errands for some of Colombo's hoods, from business-men and bankers who came in to pay their shylock bills, and from Colombo himself as time went on.

The method used to give Colombo "legitimate" income was through commissions salesmen earned when they sold real es-tate out of the office.

We had a dozen salesmen employed in the office, including Colombo, and we handled 100 to 150 sales a year, with a gross value of up to $4 million. But only a limited amount of those real estate sales were diverted to Colombo, allowing him show a legitimate income of up to twenty-five thousand dollars a year.

What we did was relatively simple, and, we thought, almost impossible for the feds to make a case on. When office salesmen sold a house, an office building, or some landed property, they would collect a commission that they were required to split with the office. But when Uncle Sal, or myself, or some other selected salesman closed a deal, instead of being credited for that sale and receiving a check for our commission from my father, the sale would be credited to Colombo.

Colombo would receive a check for the sale, bank it, and show an income from the office through his bank account. At the same time, he would pay us in cash the amount of the commission we were entitled to. That way he had a source of "legitimate" income to show the IRS and the FBI for his "work" as a salesman, and we had hidden cash income that we didn't have to declare and pay taxes on.

It would work this way. One of us might sell a house for fifty thousand dollars. The commission for that was 6 percent. Half went to Cantalupo Realty Company, the other 50 percent, or fifteen hundred dollars, would normally go to the salesman who made the sale. Instead, it was credited to Colombo, who would get a check for fifteen hundred dollars. He, in turn, would give the salesman—me or Uncle Sal, whoever it was—the same amount in cash. The cash he paid us came from his "banker," Frank Falanga, who always had cash available for him . . . cash from shylocking, gambling, payoffs, whatever, that Colombo could launder in part through the office.

One particular transaction I handled in 1969—a fairly big one—was the sale of some land that had been a former dump and landfill. Wasserman had it up for sale. It was on the ocean, but it was filthy, covered with garbage, rats, and sea gulls, and located off the Belt Parkway next to a city incinerator.

Campagna, through some friends of his in the garment center, arranged for me to handle the sale, which I made for $750,000, to a rabbi and Bob Knapp, the owner of a restaurant chain known as Big Daddy that had branches in the Bahamas, Florida, and Coney Island. My commission—actually it was credited to Colombo—was for $13,333. The office got the same amount. Colombo paid me the cash. That land then became the site of the Brooklyn Hebrew School for Retarded Children.

In 1966, to broaden his so-called legitimate-income base, Colombo filed a state application for a broker's license. It was a terrible mistake, bringing unnecessary public attention to Cantalupo Realty Company and more headlines about his activities, headlines that from a mob point of view are always bad for business.

Colombo had a salesman's license that permitted him to buy and sell property, arrange for appraisals, and set up the financing for those sales or purchases for other clients. The salesman's license, however, had restrictions that limited the deals he could make.

A licensed broker with the right connections has a money machine at his command. He can employ whom he wants and, as Colombo did, arrange for his employees to get licenses with a minimal of work and knowledge. He can arrange for mortgages with banks and bankers whom he controls. He can wash rackets money—money from gambling, shylocking, extortion, hijacking, even narcotics—through the office as inflated property sales or rentals. Shylock loans can become bank loans and second mortgages. There are just a million ways to make big bucks and thumb your nose at the federal and state tax men with a real estate office, and Colombo recognized that. He also recognized that as long as he had to work for someone like my father and get permission from Carl Gambino to do it, he wasn't his own man, boss or no boss. He would always owe favors to Gambino and my father. His operation would always be under surveillance, not just by the feds but by Gambino. It was like having a spy in the bedroom.

Colombo saw the broker's license was his way out. With that he could set up his own office, put in his own salesmen, and wash millions in rackets money that came by the carload to him daily, and he wouldn't have to cut Gambino in to a piece of that pie.

To get such a license, Colombo had to go public. It was no longer a situation where someone could be reached and arrange to have someone else sit in for him and pass his tests. The game had changed, and so had the players. There had to be public hearings—testimony by friends, including my father. I don't think Colombo realized just how much trouble he was letting himself in for.

One of the first things Colombo had to do was make an appearance of legitimacy by disclosing his income and his assets to the New York Secretary of State's Office. Part of that disclosure detailed income of real estate sales income of over $95,000 from 1960 to 1966 that he claimed he received from commissions at Cantalupo Realty. Of course, that kind of income doesn't explain away the perks Colombo enjoyed, and it gave state and federal tax agents as well as curious legislative committees ammunition that made headlines.

It wasn't long before there were stories about all the extras Colombo had—extras and assets that a salesman with an income of $95,000 can't explain away—things like a big estate in Blooming Grove, New York, with tennis and handball courts and a swimming pool; an expensive home in Brooklyn with an interior fit for a king; a separate private apartment with closets full of thousand-dollar suits where he changed two and three times daily, not to mention his top-of-the-line Cadillacs, one of which he'd given my father.

Along with those assets, which the FBI and tax agents picked up on, he admitted to partnerships in apartment and office buildings with my father and a 55 percent interest in the Prospero Funeral Home in Brooklyn, an interest shared equally with Carl Gambino.

In just those few years, Colombo had also become too visible, attracting too many headlines with grand-jury investigations and public appearances. That began to cause problems not only for his family and himself, but also for other families and other bosses.

On September 22, 1966, Colombo and twelve other members of the mob's Who's Who were rousted at what was described as a national Mafia meeting, a "Little Apalachin," with twelve other mob bigwigs, including Gambino, at the La Stella restaurant in Forest Hills, Queens. The arrests made headlines across the country. It started grand juries buzzing, and it made life uncomfortable and very inconvenient for bosses like Carlos Marcello of Louisiana, Santo Trafficante of Florida, as well Tommy Eboli and Mike Miranda of the Genovese family.

There were some that blamed Colombo. They claimed he had been the cause of the raid because of his federal tagalongs, Tallia and other agents who were always buzzing around our office, tailing Colombo wherever he went. While the raid was handled by the Queens District Attorney's Office and city police, some in the mob believed that they had been tipped to the meeting by federal agents watching and bugging Colombo.

The state hearings on his broker's license made things just that much worse. They came in November and December of 1966, and again in January 1967. My father was questioned at length; so was Colombo. It was very embarrassing for a lot of people, and in the end the hearing officer used the headlines of the La Stella meeting and his associations with those he met with against him. He was denied the license, but not until he and the people he had to deal with in organized crime got a lot of undesirable and unnecessary publicity.

Giving Colombo a legitimate source of income was only one of the scams that I had to learn about. Another money-maker was the raised contract. It was a swindle designed to increase the value of a home and allow clients to buy homes without putting up a dime. Some clients didn't have the cash to put up, and others, usually friends and associates of Colombo, couldn't show they had cash to put up. Our answer to their problems was to draw up a contract inflating the value of the house or property we wanted to sell and using the bank's mortgage money to pay the down payment as well as the sale price. We got commissions on both ends that way—for selling the house and as an under-the-table kickback for the inflated house value.

To operate the scheme, we used an appraiser from the Metropolitan Savings and Loan Bank. We would call him and tell him we had a contract for the sale of a house at fifty thousand dollars and were applying for a mortgage for that amount from his bank. He would come out and look at the property and fill out an appraisal for the amount we wanted the property valued at to get the mortgage approved—say, sixty thousand dollars. The appraiser got fifty dollars to one hundred dollars for his trouble. We collected a 6 percent commission for the sale of the house and maybe another thousand to fifteen hundred dollars in cash under the table for the raised contract. The buyer got the mortgage and the house, the seller got his money, and we got money above and under the table. The under-the-table money, of course, was not taxable, because it was never declared. In fact, the records showed no such transaction as having taken place.

We also had a reverse version of the scheme for wiseguys and goodfellows in the mob. For example, if Rocky Miraglia, a leg-breaker loan shark and bodyguard for Colombo, wanted to buy a house that was worth $100,000 but he wanted to hide the cash he was paying, we arranged a "lowered contract."

To work that scam, we would work out a contract with the seller to show a sale price on the house for sixty thousand dollars to the wiseguy who would get a mortgage or some other form of loan to cover the "listed price" on the contract. At the same time, the wiseguy would funnel forty thousand dollars in cash under the table to the seller. That worked out great for every-one. The wiseguy was able to show he had bought a house within his "legitimate" income means if IRS or state taxmen took a look. He was also able to unload forty thousand dollars in rackets cash he had hidden in his shoeboxes to the seller who, in turn, was able to pocket forty thousand dollars in cash with-out paying a nickel in tax because he didn't have to declare the income on his tax returns. At the same time we got a piece of that forty thousand dollars as a fee and whatever we got was never declared as part of the office income. More hidden fees, more hidden cash . . . the money machine kept grinding it out for everyone with the right connections.

A lot of Brooklyn's goodfellows and wiseguys bought their homes and business properties that way, building mini-empires in real estate assets while laundering mob money through legiti-mate people who weren't too inquisitive about where the money was coming from as long as they could keep it from Uncle Sam's clutches.

Probably the biggest money-maker outside of loan-sharking was our second mortgage business. The second mortgage busi-ness was geared, my father used to say, "to the suckers who need money so bad they practically drool from the mouth."

They would come to our office almost in a panic. They had shylocks to pay off, gambling debts, or schemes to make money that were suckers' pipedreams. All these money harvesters weren't interested in whether they could pay the money they borrowed, and their wives and families either didn't know what they were up to or were too scared to say no to the contracts. All these borrowers wanted was hard cash.

A borrower might come in who had a house or rental property worth eighty thousand dollars. He had a mortgage of maybe forty thousand dollars but he needed ten thousand dollars in a hurry. He had the equity. If he went to a bank he'd never get the loan by himself or it would take too long. We'd give him the second mortgage but he'd have to pay us 20 percent—two thousand dollars—under the table right off the top before he got the balance. We'd then arrange for him to get the second mortgage at the prevailing rate of interest for a three-year period. At the end of three years, if the borrower hadn't paid the ten thousand dollars in full, he'd have to refinance it again through our office with another 20 percent taken off the top. It was an absolute gold mine.

The majority of the people who came in for the second mortgage loans were loan-shark victims—longshoremen and garment workers steered to Cantalupo Realty by Colombo's shylocks, men like Falanga, Miraglia, Peewee Campagna, or Mike Savino. They owed five to ten thousand, sometimes more, and they were told to either put up their houses for second mortgages or wind up in an alley with broken legs or arms . . . even worse, violence was threatened against their wives and kids.

In the long run it was cheaper to get and pay off the second mortgage than pay street loan-shark rates. The borrower might pay three thousand dollars in interest and commissions to us for the loan but to the loan shark, at loan-shark rates, he would have to pay three hundred dollars a week in vig, interest, just to stay even, without paying off a dime in principal. So I sort of looked at the second mortgage scheme as a kind of insurance plan to help the loan-shark victims stay out of the hospital. Of course, he probably went right back in hock to some other shylock after falling short on some other sports bets.

I remember one in particular sent to me by Michael Bolino, who was himself a real estate salesman and a Colombo loan shark, and Salvatore Albanese, a family thug who later disappeared. I arranged for the borrower to close the mortgage deal in a lawyer's office on Eighty-sixth Street. The borrower owed five thousand dollars but he wanted to keep some of the money he got . . . he didn't want to pay off his whole debt to them. They grabbed him as he came out of the lawyer's office, dragged him around the corner, whacked him around a bit and sent him back to the office with a new outlook. He decided it was better to pay up in full as soon as he got the cash and he did.

By 1968, we had our own banker at what was then the Kings County Lafayette Trust Company to funnel money to the street and pay off the waterfront loan sharks. I'll call him Herbie. He was a nervous little guy who I wined and dined until I finally got him in my pocket, convincing him that he could make a bundle with me arranging for quick loans. He had the authority and he saw the potential. He was a loan officer who could arrange for loans of up to five thousand dollars on just a signature.

Once he was convinced, I went to some of Colombo's loan sharks who I knew and who would jump at the chance to get more of their money working the piers. Falanga and Savino were sort of office bankers for Colombo but they also worked the piers shylocking longshoremen. Campagna had borrowers both on the waterfront and in the garment center.

"Here's what we can do," I told them in meetings I had with them at the office. "I got this banker over here. You bring your borrowers down to the bank, no questions asked, and get them a loan for three years. For that I am going to charge you a nominal fee . . . one hundred dollars for each one thousand dollars in loans I arrange." It was a beautiful deal. This group had hundreds of loan-shark victims they could send to us, and they did. They would bring them to the real estate office and I would bring them to Herbie at the bank where he would fill out their loan applications, approve the loans of two thousand dollars, three thousand dollars, four thousand dollars, issue a check, have them sign it, cash it, deducting the money due us and send them on their way. As they walked out of the bank, Frankie the Beast or Peewee or one of the other shylocks would be waiting to take the cash from them.

We must have had thirty or more loans issued before the bank caught on to the scheme. All of the loans defaulted and when bank examiners checked the origin of the bad loans they found that all of them came out of the Eighty-sixth Street office of the bank far away from where the borrowers lived and worked.

Herbie was fired as loan officer and moved out of state. And all the money he and I collected? Herbie lost it playing some penny stocks while I was out of town. He bought thousands of shares of some penny stock that went belly up before I returned. If I'd have been able to find him then, I think I would have strangled him.

4

THE MAKING OF A BOSS

I didn't have the advantage of having a stand-in take my state real estate salesman's test. It's probably why I flunked the first two tests I took. I finally passed it on the third try in the fall of 1964. If I hadn't, I'd have had to wait six months to qualify to take the next test. That would have been an embarrassment for my father, who shocked me by not lifting a finger to help me. His attitude was, "If you want to work for me, get a license, pass the test."

He made it equally clear that if I was to work for him, I had to pass the state test for notaries. "I need someone who can notarize some confidential documents for some important friends," he said, "and they want someone they can trust. The only one I can guarantee is you . . . so you better pass the test."

I didn't learn until later in 1964 that among the "important friends" was Carl Gambino. I was introduced to Gambino in the office by my father. Several weeks later, after I passed the notary test, I became his personal notary, frequently going to his home on Ocean Parkway, where I would notarize documents and, on rare occasions, seek his personal advice.

While I couldn't sell real estate or put my stamp on documents until I passed the tests, I could sweep out the office and wash the bathroom, keep the desks clean and run errands for the salesmen or Colombo's gofers. I was also assigned to keep the light burning bright over my grandfather's portrait behind my father's desk. I had to keep a supply of bulbs in my desk, and at the slightest flicker of the portrait light replace it so the portrait would remain illuminated.

I was the low man on the totem pole, and my father made sure I realized it. I'd go for the pizzas, go for the sandwiches, go for this and go for that. I got the menial tasks at the beginning because I think Colombo had told my father that I was too cocky, too sure of myself. My father was, at Colombo's suggestion, making sure I wasn't "starting at the top," as I predicted I would be when I first met him. I was being taught some humility, and I learned fast because I didn't like cleaning up other people's dirt.

There was one concession my father made to my ego. He gave me the front desk, the first desk in the office, and I loved it. It was like having a front-row seat at the Latin Quarter. I got to see all the players. I had a vantage point few people get in the world of organized crime.

To see my father, to get to Colombo, to get to any salesman, customers and hoodlums alike had to sit in a waiting room, wait to be buzzed through the electrically controlled gate and then walk past my desk. The buzzer controls for the gate were located in Colombo's private office, where they could be viewed from behind a one-way glass, my father's and the secretary's desk, and later at my desk.

At first I saw it as a position of importance. It wasn't long before I realized it could be a liability a position of danger. While I could see everything that moved into our office, anyone coming to the office could see me, through the front window, from the waiting room, and at the gate.

On October 21, 1964, the streets of Brooklyn were alive with excitement, particularly the predominantly Italian neighborhoods from Sixty-fifth Street all the way up to Eighty-sixth Street over to Shore Parkway, from Tenth Avenue to Eighteenth Avenue. Two men had dared to grab a legendary Mafia godfather . . . a man whose name was only whispered in the kitchens and shops of the area. Family boss Joseph Bonanno had been snatched in broad daylight, with his attorney watching, at Thirty-seventh Street and Park Avenue in Manhattan by a couple of thugs. He was shoved into a waiting car hours before he was scheduled to appear before a federal grand jury.

The kidnapping, which Bonanno later said was engineered by his cousin, the mob boss of Buffalo, Stefano Magaddino, sent shock waves rippling through Brooklyn's underworld, particularly through the world I watched and the one Colombo ruled.

Newspapers, television, and radio speculated on the danger, the probability of violence, and the possibility that the kidnapping somehow connected to both Colombo and his mentor, Carl Gambino, or that Bonanno had staged the disappearance to avoid the grand jury.

Our office reflected some of those shock waves as dozens of mob friends of Colombo's beat a trail to and from his private office while his bodyguards, men like Rocco Miraglia, kept a wary eye on everyone approaching the office.

With all the speculation in the media and the hushed conversations that were taking place in Colombo's private office, I still didn't understand how serious things might get for me personally until the return of Bonanno in May of 1965. That's when my father decided to move me. I didn't particularly like it.

"Why do I have to move?" I asked. "I like it where I am."

"Because I don't want you to get killed," he said.

"What are you talking about?" I asked. "Who's gonna kill me, for Chrissakes?"

My father shook his head in frustration. "Things could get violent around here," he answered. "This Bonanno thing could explode. Some of his people could come here to take some potshots through the front windows or toss a grenade. Where you're sitting now, you'd be the first one they'd hit. I don't want you in the line of fire."

So my desk was moved from the front to the rear and center of the office, directly in front of my father's desk. Above his desk was my grandfather's portrait with the light I had to keep lit.

My new desk had been that of my uncle Sal, who had split up with my father and ended their partnership to open his own real estate office. So I had been removed from what I was told was a position of direct danger from outside gunners or bombers. In reality, I was moved closer to the volcano—the core of organized crime and the men who ran it.

Joe Colombo and my father had grown up together, as I explained earlier, caddying for golfers at Dyker Park in Brooklyn when they were teenagers. They became close friends, but they followed different paths, largely, I think, because of their heritage, and their family environment.

Both Colombo's father and my grandfather were immigrants who came to this country and were swallowed up by the power of tradition from their homelands. My grandfather came to this country from Italy, and Colombo's father came here from Brazil, although he was born of Italian parents.

To my knowledge, my grandfather was not directly involved in what is now called Cosa Nostra, or the American Mafia. He did know, as did my father, some of the crime figures who had migrated from Sicily and southern Italy. One of those they knew was Joseph Profaci, who, with Bonanno, was one of the original crime bosses of the American Mafia. Known as "the olive-oil king" because of the olive-oil companies he and his sons controlled in Brooklyn and New York, Profaci was powerful and ruthless, a man not to be crossed.

Colombo's father, Anthony, was a Brazilian-born immigrant of Italian parents who, I was told, worked for Joseph Profaci in the 1930's. My grandfather provided real estate services, as did my father, for Profaci, and later for his son, Salvatore. They and their families went to the same church, St. Bernadette's, where Bonanno's son, Salvatore, married Profaci's daughter, Rosalie. But the similarities ended there. Colombo's father was killed in 1938. He was found strangled, with his genitals stuffed in his mouth, in a car in Brooklyn. He'd broken the old law of the Mafia—he'd been screwing the wife of a wiseguy. Worse, he'd been caught. I'm told Profaci was tough on rules like that.

Colombo, like his father, became a member of the Profaci mob and later its boss after serving a couple of years in the Coast Guard during World War II. My father followed the path of my grandfather; he took over his real estate business and maintained his friendships and alliances with people he came to know in the underworld. His closest alliance was with Gambino, who he was responsible to and an associate of, but he maintained his friendship with Colombo as he rose through the ranks of the Profaci mob.

So they were close, and the last thing in the world that I would think about was that Colombo or anyone could or would pose a danger to my father. He knew too many people . . . he had too many powerful friends and too many serious high-level connections, or so I thought.

I think my first inkling of how powerful and deadly Joe Colombo was came in a seemingly kidding exchange between my father and Colombo. Up to that moment, I knew Colombo was important because of the thugs and politicians and associates who came in daily to confer with him or take orders from him. But that was something distant, remote. I never heard their conversations. I never saw them quake in his presence. I never saw the violence in his manner, not personally. All that changed one day when my father got too personal in front of the office peons, myself included.

They were laughing, horsing around, and suddenly my father pointed to Colombo and shouted something like, "Hey, Porky . . . who are you shitting?" It was a nickname Colombo had when they were caddies together, but it wasn't a name you call a crime boss by, not even in jest, and especially not in front of others.

Colombo's face turned red with fury, and he yelled at my father in such a way as to make my father literally quake. His face turned pale, and he didn't say a word as Colombo screamed, "Don't you ever fuckin' call me that name . . . you hear?" I couldn't hear what else he said, but everyone in the office froze where they were standing.

I remember thinking, as I watched the color drain from my father's face, that he seemed to be honestly frightened. Colombo never lost his temper like that again in all the time I knew him and his kids, but I never forgot it. It was at that moment I first realized who and what Colombo was.

Colombo had only been a family boss a short time when I

came to the office. He had survived the gang war between Joe Gallo and his brothers and Profaci, who died of natural causes on June 7, 1962.

I never met Profaci, but I did meet his son, Salvatore, who ran the old man's olive-oil and garment businesses and was identified by police as the Colombo family's major capo in New Jersey. Because of his father and his business activities, Salvatore had friends from New York to Kansas, and those friendships, on at least two occasions, almost compromised my security as a witness.

Salvatore frequently came to the office or to the Pisa Caterers across the street to meet with Colombo. But in the mid-1960's, after his father died, he had a lot of property to liquidate, including a very large home on Fifteenth Avenue, and I had to help my father inspect and appraise those properties before they were sold.

From the 1930's into the 1960's, many of the homes built in the Bay Ridge area of Brooklyn were two-story brick buildings with large basements. The Profacis had three houses on adjoining properties, and all three houses were connected by underground tunnels because Profaci used to hold major meetings with crime bosses in the main house. It was at that house, a beautiful solid-brick house built like a fortress on a 100' × 100' plot, that I got my first taste of how organized-crime bosses hold their "sitdowns" to make the decisions that keep the rackets ticking.

We had the houses up for sale. At the old man's main house, there was a large meeting room with a huge wood table, I think it was hand-carved and hand-polished mahogany with eight or ten high-backed carved wood chairs with big arms. I was looking at Mafia history and didn't realize how much. The lives of a lot of men and the direction of Mafia crime in New York had been decided in that room.

At one end of the table, which must have been at least thirty feet long, was a huge high-back Italian Provincial chair for the head honcho of the meetings. The table itself was what they called the "round table" for crime Commission meetings, only the table wasn't exactly round, but more rectangular in shape. The tables and chairs alone were worth more than fifty thousand dollars, and that was back in the sixties.

In the basement, I was informed, had been a private altar, erected for special services Profaci wanted conducted by selected priests who he called to the house. There also had been hidden tunnels connecting the main house to other houses, so those attending the high-level meetings had ways to escape from the main house without ever being seen. I never inspected the basement where the tunnels and the altar had been located, but I suspect they were probably built during Prohibition and then bricked over after Profaci's death. Such are the legends of the Mafia.

Profaci's immediate successor was Joseph Magliocco, but he didn't last too long. Loan shark Frank "Peewee" Campagna, who, like my father, had grown up on the golf links with Colombo, told me that Magliocco couldn't control the Gallos, who wouldn't accept him as boss. Peewee had the ear and trust of Colombo, and thus knew many of the inner secrets of the mob.

Because he was facing more violence with the Gallos and was getting no support from the Commission, Magliocco turned to Bonanno, who tried to make a case for his selection as boss before the Gambino-dominated Commission. They didn't like Magliocco either and didn't accept him, so he and Bonanno plotted to eliminate Gambino and Tommy Lucchese, the boss of the Lucchese crime family, and take over their lucrative rackets on New York's waterfront, the construction industry, and the garment center.

According to secret tape recordings made by the FBI and according to Campagna, the fly in that ointment was Colombo. He was one of those who Magliocco and Bonanno recruited to do the eliminating because he had ready access to Gambino. Instead of doing what they wanted him to, Colombo went to Gambino and Lucchese and told them what his boss Magliocco was plotting with Bonanno.

The bosses who were targets of the pilot turned the tables. With the help of Buffalo's Magaddino, they pulled together enough muscle to scare the hell out of Magliocco, who, the secret recordings say, knuckled under and confessed all. That led to the successful plan by Magaddino to kidnap Bonanno and force him out as a member of the Commission and as the boss of his New York family.

Instead of killing Magliocco, Gambino—and the Commission he controlled as a sort of unofficial chairman of the board—allowed Magliocco to step down as boss. On December 30, 1963, he died at Good Samaritan Hospital in West Islip. The cause of his death was listed as heart disease, but because of a conversation recorded by the FBI between two New Jersey mobsters, crime boss Sam the Plumber DeCavalcante and his capo Joseph LaSelva, doubts were raised about the cause of death. Their conversation suggested he had been fed a "poison pill," and in 1969 his body was exhumed to see if he had been murdered. The Suffolk medical examiner found no evidence of poison, and if there were any lingering doubts, they weren't reflected by some of Magliocco's relatives, who remained in the Colombo family and paid their tribute to him at the Cantalupo Realty Company office.

With Magliocco out, Gambino repaid Colombo for his loyalty by arranging to have him named as the new boss of what had been the Profaci family. But to be a boss, you need money, lots of it, because with money you have power to buy the strength and protection you need. Colombo needed money to fulfill his promises to both the Gallos and other members of the Profaci family that, unlike Profaci and Magliocco, he would share the wealth that he accumulated. But he didn't have immediate wealth to share, and that's where Gambino came in.

"The old man [Gambino] set up Colombo with the money," Campagna told me. "He gave Joey a million, two hundred thousand dollars to get him started as a boss. At a point a week on the street, that's twelve thousand dollars a week . . . six hundred twenty-four thousand dollars in yearly vig alone to Joe." In five years, Joe had made well over $3 million by collecting from one to three points a week, and he had repaid Gambino in full plus a half-point-a-week vig. At the same time, that money was put to work by his capos and loan sharks, like Campagna. Colombo charged them one to two points, and they charged their customers anywhere from two to five points a week, so that the original $1.2 million was actually pulling in about $3 million a year. In five years, that's over $18 million just in shylock returns, and that quadruples and more when the capos and soldiers get the debtors to pull dock thefts, Wall Street bond thefts, burglaries, and dozens of other types of scores.

That's how bosses are made. That's how they get power, and that, explained Campagna, was what brought him back from Chicago to work for Colombo.

After they had grown up on the golf links together—Peewee, my father, and Colombo—Peewee went to Chicago, where his uncle had been a member of the old Al Capone mob and was a man of some importance in the area. That's where Peewee would have stayed and probably died instead of New York but for a phone call.

"I got this call from Joey," Campagna told me. "He wanted me to come east and work for him. 'It'll be like old times,' he said, 'you and me and Anthony. I'll make you a millionaire,' he said, and he did."

When Gambino made Colombo the boss, Colombo reached out for his old friend and got permission from the Chicago mob to bring him back to the coast. He made Peewee his most trusted shylock in the garment center, an extremely important and profitable place in the family scheme of things. He put Campagna in a union where he had a lot of clout, and in a garment-center trucking company where he had a front to explain his income to the tax people.

That's when I met Peewee. He had come to work for Colombo in 1964, and he had a seat in our office; he was brought in temporarily as a salesman by Colombo and my father. For a while, he worked in the office with Colombo to get a handle on things and to learn the business, but he didn't handle any real estate sales or rentals. He was a figurehead like Colombo, and he was given commissions from the sales of the regular salesmen in the same manner Colombo got them. The books showed he made sales, and he kicked back the cash he received from the checks paid by Cantalupo Realty to him for sales others made.

The salesmen were able to pocket the cash and never declare it as income, and Peewee could show the tax people he had legit income.

When an opening turned up in the garment center, Colombo sent Campagna there to handle some of his important union connections and loan-shark collections. He was assigned to work under Anthony Abbatemarco and Sally Albanese, but he reported to Colombo directly, even though he wasn't a made member of the family.

While Peewee was in our office, he worked as a loan shark, and I used to go with him on his collections, take a ride with him and provide him with a sort of show of force to those he was collecting from. Peewee got his name because he was small in stature, but there was nothing small about how he operated. I learned a lot about loan-sharking from him.

One of the most important lessons I learned—but didn't pay attention to, unfortunately—was that in making money, friend-ship don't mean shit . . . not when it comes to the mob and its members. In the mob, everyone pays.

Peewee went to Colombo one day to borrow ten thousand dollars. He had a sucker lined up who would pay him three or four points a week. To get the money from Joe, he had to pay a point a week. He couldn't get the money for the half-point that capos got—that would have caused trouble in the ranks.

5

JOE THE BOSS

Hollywood's old movie studios would never have selected someone like Joe Colombo to play the role of a mob boss. He was too suave, too much of a gentleman's gentleman to be a boss. He was well mannered and well spoken—not a college-graduate type, but he could pass in the best of dinner company. That was to the outsider. To those who knew him, who worked with him and watched him, Colombo and the role of the boss went together like lox and cream cheese, like tomato sauce and spaghetti.

Colombo had it all. When he walked, he had an air about him that made you think "boss." It wasn't a swagger, it was a presence. He didn't look down on those who worked for him. He was, in fact, always very respectful, very humble, in front of others, but he made it clear he wasn't a man to screw around with. His word was his bond, and that was the way he expected those around him to be—to do their jobs without excuses. You just knew that when you were in his presence you were in the presence of a man of respect, a man of immense power and controlled violence, who with the wink of an eye or the snap of his fingers could have anyone he chose eliminated.

He could rub elbows with the elite of crime and politics or he could scramble to his knees, hike up his shirtsleeves, and throw dice with the best of the crapshooters. He could make men tremble with a change of tone or awaken hidden passions and emotions in women who he just met. He was streetwise, the top fox in the business of the streets. Ask him about real estate, stocks, banking, things like that, he wasn't too worldly; but he knew the ways of organized crime in the streets, and that was where he had to have the smarts.

I admired Colombo. I don't care what people say about him, I thought he was a wonderful man. He was always polite to me, always treated me with respect. Who the hell was I? I was just a smart-ass kid out of the army trying to hustle a buck and make a place for myself in Brooklyn, but he still treated me special.

I looked up to him like a father, and at times I was jealous of his sons, not because of what they got, like clothes and cars and jewelry, but because he treated them with love and respect. When they came into the office to see him, whether it was Joe Junior, Anthony, or Vincent—any of his kids, no matter what time of day—they would walk up to him, hug him, kiss him hello and good-bye, always show their love and respect. He would do the same thing with them. I'd try to show my love for my father with a kiss and he'd wipe his face.

Colombo liked and enjoyed the expensive things in life that I wanted when I first met him. He had a new Cadillac every year. He would go to the barber once a week to have his thinning hair trimmed and his nails manicured whether he needed to or not. He maintained an apartment on New Utrecht Avenue that was really nothing but a huge closet where he would go three times a day to change his entire wardrobe, from twenty-thousand-dollar diamond, sapphire, and ruby pinky rings to thousand-dollar specially tailored suits and five-hundred-dollar shoes. A couple of the rings, a four-carat diamond, and a three-carat blue star sapphire, were gifts he'd received, the proceeds of a robbery by one of his flunkies. He rarely went home to change, and he had a beautiful home at Eighty-third Street and Eleventh Avenue, where his wife, Lucille, a really beautiful and wonderful woman whom they called JoJo, lived with their kids.

• • •

In a way, Colombo became a teacher for me, a sort of professor of the college of street smarts. When he gave advice, I always learned and almost always listened. Like the time he advised me not to take a car from Carl Gambino.

I had become a notary public, as I explained earlier, at the insistence of my father, to notarize the documents of a number of special people. One of those special people was Gambino. Now Gambino, unlike Colombo, was very low key, very quiet, and very private. He's been called "the nodding Don" by some, "the nose" by others, but not to his face, at least not while he was alive.

He didn't wear a lot of different rings like Colombo, or drive a flashy Cadillac, and his clothes were moderate in cost. In fact, he usually had Jimmy Brown Failla, a capo in his family who ran Manhattan's garbage rackets, drive him around in an inexpensive Buick or Chevrolet sedan. He in fact gave no appearance of the enormous wealth and power that he controlled. But he was, like Colombo, very even tempered, very polite, very much the gentleman in the presence of others.

In the mid-sixties, Gambino was constantly receiving subpoenas to appear before state and federal grand juries investigating organized crime or in courts where prosecutors wanted to use his associations and his past as a reason to deport him to his native Sicily.

To avoid those appearances, he would remain home and have his doctors and lawyers fill out documents certifying that he was too ill—that his heart was too weak—to make such appearances. Those documents had to be notarized, and I was the one called in to certify that the signature on those documents was his.

Gambino's son Joseph, who worked like an immigrant laborer in a garment-factory sweatshop, would usually be the one to call me, generally in the evening at my grandmother's home in Valley Stream, where I was living temporarily.

"Joey, my father needs a notary tomorrow morning," he'd say. "Can you come early?"

My answer was always a polite yes, and when I'd arrive at Gambino's two-story home on Ocean Parkway, either his son or his black maid would be there waiting to lead me to his room.

There was nothing elaborate about Gambino's house from the outside. It blended into the neighborhood. It looked like and was a very simple two-family brick house, with six rooms on the first floor and seven rooms on the second floor, and a detached garage at the rear of the home and a driveway along the side. The interior was quite different, decorated in expensive but tasteful Italian Provincial furniture with a lot of marble and antique Italian figurines, china, and glassware.

Whenever I arrived, I always entered through the side entrance—I guess to avoid being spotted by the police and the federal agents who constantly watched the house—and I would be led upstairs to the kitchen-dinette, where I would be invited to sit and have a demitasse of espresso with Gambino and whoever was there with him at the time. The ground-floor apartment wasn't rented out—I don't know who stayed there, but Gambino lived and held meetings on the second floor.

Now on the occasion Colombo advised me about, I had been called to the home by the son. It was raining that morning when I left for Brooklyn, driving a brand-new blue Buick Skylark that I had just bought from Caplan Buick. My first stop was my office, to pick up the notary stamp. Then, in the early morning downpour, I was headed down Cropsy Avenue to get to Gambino's house when some guy skidded on the wet pavement, slid through a stop sign, and plowed into me. He totaled my car, and I was taken to Coney Island Hospital in an ambulance. When I awoke, standing by my bedside were Gambino and his son Joe.

There was real concern in his voice and in his eyes when he asked me if I was all right. "If there's is anything you need, Joey, tell me and it is yours," he said.

I thanked him for his concern and for coming to the hospital to see me, and I assured him I wasn't hurt too bad. "I just have a few bumps and bruises and I'm a little groggy . . . that's all," I said. "I'm just mad that the guy totaled my new car."

"Ah . . . you are not to worry about the car," he answered. "When you are well enough and are out of the hospital, I will provide you with a new car."

When I left the hospital, I told Colombo what Gambino had offered to do.

"My advice to you, Joey," he said, "is don't take the new car. You are young, you have insurance, let the insurance take care of the car. If you don't take the car, he will owe you a favor, and that can be very important later on in your life."

I followed Colombo's advice. I wound up with an expensive new Buick Riviera. The insurance paid for the car, and Caplan Buick gave me a deal. It was years later that I went to Gambino and sought his help—a favor that he unhesitatingly returned.

Colombo had died by then—it was in 1975—and I was a heavy gambler. I loved playing the numbers, and I played for big bucks. One day, after years of losing, I hit the number big with a numbers racketeer named Joe the Book, who is no longer around. When I came to collect, Joe the Book said I hadn't played the number.

"You couldn't have played it, 'cause I don't have it," he said.

"You son of a bitch!" I shouted. "I been playing that number with you for more than a year, and now you say you never got it from me?"

"That's what I said," he snarled, "and what are you gonna do about it?"

"I want what I got coming!" I yelled.

"Fuck you," he said. "You ain't gettin' squat, and if you don't get outta here now, you'll have a broken head."

I don't know why I did it, what made me seek out his help, but I made an appointment through his son to see Gambino. He was sick in bed, but I was allowed to come to his house to see him.

"I'm embarrassed that I am here bothering you when you are sick," I said. "I didn't realize you were ill."

"I am always ready to see a friend who has a problem," he said. "You are welcome, and I am glad to see you. Now what is the trouble?"

"I play numbers," I explained. "Not a great deal, but I play regularly, and when I lose, I pay without question. The other day, I hit the number with this numbers guy, Joe the Book.

I continued, "This bum says I didn't play the number after I played it every day for a year. I wouldn't say anything, but it gives the game a bad name. If he does something like that to me, he does it to others, and people lose faith. I was upset by it, and I thought you should know."

Gambino nodded and patted me on the hand. "Do not worry, Joey, I will take care of everything," he said. "Thank you for coming."

"Thank you for listening to me," I said. "I hope you feel better tomorrow. I would not have come had I known you were sick."

"You were right to come," he said.

The next day, Joe the Book came looking for me at the office. He was white as a sheet, and his hands were actually shaking. He handed me an envelope with more than twelve thousand dollars, and apologized for not paying as he was supposed to.

"I'm sorry," he said. "I made a mistake . . . I found the number you bet."

It was the last time I saw Joe the Book in the neighborhood. After that, someone else picked up the numbers in that area. I never learned what happened to him after that. He just sort of disappeared.

Colombo always looked for an edge, a way to make money with the minimum risk and the least amount of work. Whether it was loan-sharking personally for very special customers, like corporate executives, or dealing in stolen goods, he liked the challenge of driving a hard bargain and making a big profit.

As I got to know him better and became closer and closer to him, Colombo encouraged me to bring special deals to him no matter the time, the day, or the circumstance. There was only one caveat: I always had to act as the buffer in the action, the go-between, so that he could rarely be connected directly to any particular deal.

I became a pretty good salesman and an even better hustler, learning to deal and interact with the street people. What's more, I was known as someone the street people could trust, I guess because I was always seen hanging around with Colombo and his people and I never stiffed those I was dealing with. Those on the street figured I had to be trustworthy to be a confidant of Colombo's. It was an impression, not altogether accurate or inaccurate. There were some things Colombo did talk to me about, but never about things like the Mafia or the family or the Commission that he answered to. He talked about shylock loans and bad debtors or stupid flunkies, but not really about mob business as it involved him or as he ran it.

Regardless, that association attracted an element to me who had quick deals—money-making schemes they wanted to run by me or by Colombo through me. One of those schemes was a jewelry burglary that a bunch of hyped-up young teenagers, one of them a young female relative of Colombo's, had gotten involved in.

The kids, it seems, had broken into a house in Brooklyn and come out with a load of jewelry. One of them came to me and asked me to look at the stuff and see what I could get for it. They showed me a small suitcase full of diamond rings and bracelets and necklaces—jewelry that must have been worth $100,000 or more. They wanted ten thousand dollars, but I had the feeling they'd settle for less. The trouble was, I didn't have that kind of money and it was a Sunday.

When you need money on a Sunday and you are someone like me, you go to someone with the bucks who you can trust. While my father might have had money, he'd never had parted with it in any deal with me. The one person I knew I could talk to about it was Colombo, who I knew was home recovering from an infection, Bell's palsy, that had paralyzed one side of his face. I also knew he wouldn't be home alone. He'd be with his kids and with some of his capos who always gathered at his home in Brooklyn or upstate New York on Sundays because they figured the FBI wouldn't be working and watching on a Sunday.

So I took the suitcase filled with jewels, and I drove over to Colombo's, and who's there but his kids, Joe Junior and Anthony, and members of his crew, Miraglia, Vinnie Aloi, Greg Scarpa, Joe Notch (Iannacci), Charlie Moose (Panarella), and Nicky Bianco. It was like a gathering of the clan.

I went straight to Colombo, who was lying in bed recovering from the face paralysis, and put the suitcase on a chair next to him and opened it up. "Joe, here's the situation I'm in," I explained. "Some kids have come to me to unload this stuff."

As I'm explaining things to him, his crew members are oohing and aahing, and fingering the baubles.

"These kids want ten thousand dollars for all this stuff," I continued. "It's stolen goods, but it's cool—no one's looking for it yet, and it's worth a helluva lot more than ten grand, maybe a hundred or two hundred grand."

Joe nodded very slowly, and then he said, sort of slurring his words as he spoke because of the facial paralysis, "Okay . . . here's what you do, Joey. You take the ten grand I'm gonna give you. You put five grand in one pocket, two thousand in this pocket, a thousand in another pocket, and two thousand more someplace else. You separate the money, and you try and make a deal. You negotiate . . . you try and get it for less than the ten grand. But if you gotta pay the ten, pay it . . . but negotiate first."

He signaled Rocky, and a few minutes later there were ten thousand dollars in my hot hand, and off I went to negotiate . . . but not alone. Bianco and Miraglia drove me back to the apartment where the kids were waiting, a dingy, smoke-filled apartment with open liquor and beer bottles and a stench from pot-smoking that made me choke.

I pull out the five thousand dollars and offer it to them. Their eyes light up, but they shake their heads. "Jeez, that's not enough, Joe . . . can't you come up with a few more bucks?" one of them pleaded. "There are six of us . . . we need more."

I stood there scratching my head, in deep thought, then I offered them two thousand dollars more. "But that's it, that's all I can get for you," I said. "Take it or forget it."

They took it, and I went back to Colombo with Bianco and Miraglia, who had waited in the car downstairs, and when I walked back into his bedroom, I handed him the three thousand dollars that was left. Now I feel great, I'd made a good deal, I'd saved him three thousand dollars. He just smiled and said, "Thank you very much."

The next day I ran into Peewee Campagna at a local Chinese restaurant where we all hung out. "What did you do yesterday?" he asked.

When I told him the sequence of events and the savings I had made for Colombo, he just shook his head. "You gotta understand, Joe, you weren't too smart," he said. "He gave you ten grand, and you got it for seven. You should have kept the three thousand dollars and kept your mouth shut. This is how it works . . . this is how it's expected to be."

"Gee, Peewee," I said, "I didn't know that."

"Well, now you know," he said.

A couple of weeks went by, and Colombo comes back to me and hands me one thousand dollars. "Here's a thousand bucks, Joe," he says.

"What's this for?" I asked.

"That's your end," he said. "That's what you made on the deal."

"How come, Joe?" I asked.

"Well, you made a thousand, and I made a thousand, all right?" he said. "Nicky Bianco I gave five hundred dollars . . . Joe Notch I gave five hundred dollars . . . Rocky got five hundred dollars, and Greg Scarpa got five hundred dollars."

I thought, I'll be a son of a bitch. Everybody got a piece. The profit was maybe eight or ten thousand, and everybody got a piece. I should have put the three grand in my pocket, and then I would have gotten a bigger piece. But just for being there, they all got a piece, and I found out that Peewee was pissed off because he wasn't there and he didn't get a piece.

Time goes by—a few weeks, maybe—and these kids come to me with another jewelry deal. This time they want five thousand dollars, only I chisel them down to three thousand dollars and pocket the remaining two thousand dollars instead of giving the balance to Colombo.

Colombo takes the jewelry I give him, has it taken to the fence, and a few days later comes back and wants his five thousand dollars back, only I've spent the money . . . I don't have it. Now, I'm in the hot spot because of this advice I got from Peewee, so

I go to a close friend and adviser—my goomba*—and ask to borrow so I can pay back Colombo, which I do.

Here I am with the jewelry, I don't know how to get rid of it, and everyone in the Colombo crew at the office knows I'm stuck with it. It's not something that you can keep secret.

After a few days, one of the low-level members of Colombo's crew, a guy I hated called Fat Philly, came to me and offered to sell it for me.

"I know a fence, Joey," he said. "He can handle it."

I didn't have many options, so I agreed to let him handle it. "I want five thousand dollars," I said. "Whatever else you get is yours."

A day later, he comes back. "Joey, I went to this friend in this jewelry store," he said. "I showed him the stuff. He looked at it and he said, 'Hey, thanks for bringing it back . . . these people robbed my store of it.' "

According to Fat Philly, the jewelry belonged to this jewelry store, and they took it back without paying a dime. Now I'm out five thousand dollars, and I've got no jewelry. I wanted to kill Fat Philly, but I couldn't, so I went to Colombo . . . humble Joe Colombo.

"You wanna dance, you gotta pay the fiddler," he said with sort of a twinkle in his eye. But he was nice enough about the whole thing. The jewelry guy made an insurance claim and got twenty-five-hundred dollars, which Colombo made sure I got because I'd paid him back the five thousand dollars. But he'd taught me another lesson. If you want to make money in the mob, you don't bite the hand that feeds you, you keep that hand filled with goodies, and that keeps your pockets full.

There was nothing Colombo liked more than a good fight, a good street brawl, especially when the odds were stacked in his favor, and that was almost always.

I remember particularly one event in 1967 when Colombo didn't hesitate to get into a brawl with a couple of guys.

*Goomba: a godfather-like figure to whom one goes for advice.

It all started when one of our salesmen got a call that there was a house for sale and the seller needed a real estate office to handle the sale. So the salesman, whom I'll call Tony, went with another salesman to look at the house. Now Tony was sort of a showman, a good-looking guy who made the best of every situation. The best of this situation was two good-looking women in the house, both of them married, whom he played up to while looking the house over. In fact, he not only played up to them, but he entertained them with his piano-playing talents and, I suppose, some other talents.

Later that afternoon, two big guys come to the office, slam the door, and start yelling . . . looking for Tony. Colombo was in his office and heard them, and came outside to see what was going on.

"You Tony?" shouted one of the guys at Colombo.

"What if I am?" he said, winking at Rocky Miraglia.

"Then let's step outside," the loudmouth shouted. "I want a few words with you."

So Joe, the boss of Brooklyn, steps outside, and motions to Tony to stay where he is, not to move.

While Tony and I watch, Colombo and Miraglia walk up to these two, and the next thing I know Colombo hauls off and belts the loudmouth. Rocky, who is an animal when it comes to violence, knocks out the second guy and comes running back into the office to grab a cigarette stand. He runs back outside and begins pounding this unconscious guy lying on the ground with this metal cigarette stand until he's bleeding like a pig. Finally, Colombo stops him and they come back inside.

The two bleeding guys were cops. They had come looking for Tony because he had made a play for their wives. They took a terrible beating, but nothing happened. There wasn't a whisper from the cops, and the FBI agents who were always hanging around were nowhere to be seen. No one filed any charges, and the two cops stumbled away without any help, licking their wounds. And Tony, he kept on doing his thing with females he thought he could come on to.

Rocky and Colombo were at ground zero of another brawl, one that landed me in a doctor's office where I had to get taped up and drew the attention of a Nick Pileggi article in *New York* magazine.

It all started when Joey Gallo got out of jail. There was a lot of bad blood between Colombo and Joe Gallo and his brothers. The Gallos had tried to take over the Brooklyn mob from Profaci and had gone to war over it. They wanted to run the family, or at the very least they didn't want Joe Magliocco, Profaci's brother-in-law, to become heir to the throne.

A lot has been written about that gang war, and there isn't much I could add to it, particularly since I was either in the army or in school when it was going on. But Joe Gallo went to prison during the war and made a lot of noise about pushing Colombo around when he got out of prison.

In May 1971, Colombo, my father, Rocky, and myself were standing outside our office when this truck drives by with five guys in it, and a couple of them yell at Rocky, calling him a queer and a few other names suggesting that he did things that no manly Italian would do with his mother.

Rocky has a short fuse, and before you could say his name, he was off and running down the street toward a luncheonette where he meets with Nate Marcone, who was then the president of the Italian-American Civil Rights League, and another guy named Pete.

While I'm standing there talking to Colombo, out of the corner of my eye I see the three of them fighting with three other guys, apparently from the truck that had just passed us. Across the street, Nicky Bianco, a capo from the New England mob who was at the time working for Colombo, and a couple of other members of the mob were sitting in Caplan Buick, ignoring what was happening a short distance from all of us.

Not Colombo. He ignored nothing. "Come on, Joe," he said, "I haven't hit anyone in a long time."

So off we went, dressed in our expensive suits and shoes, to join Rocky, Marcone, and Pete. As we come running down the street to help, two guys come out from an alley between two homes. One jumps Colombo and starts fighting with him, and the other I knock to the ground and start beating when a sixth guy comes out of nowhere with a golf club and hits Marcone in the chest. Pete sees him coming and swinging and puts up his hand. For his effort, he lost two fingers—the guy takes two fingers off his hand with the head of the golf club. Colombo and Rocky are now running the other way, and out of the corner of my eye I see this golf club come down toward my back. It hits me on the spine, and I roll off the guy I've been hitting, and I'm seeing stars, nothing else, as I lie there, bleeding.

I was lucky this guy didn't hit me twice. The guy with the golf clubs rolls me over on the street, and then he and his friends take off. With everyone running in different directions, I'm lying there in agony, trying to get my wind back. Slowly, I start crawling to the other side of the street, where I find a wallet. It took a lot of effort, but I pocketed the wallet, crawled to a telephone pole, and slowly, all the while bleeding down my neck and back, pulled myself up and staggered to the luncheonette a short distance away.

When I got there, the people inside pulled me into the bath-room, washed and bandaged me, and while they are doing that, Colombo comes back. As he does, I see two cars take off from Caplan with Colombo's son Anthony and a bunch of guys in one car and Bianco and another group in the second car, and they are roaring down the streets after the truck with the five guys.

Now I want a piece of those guys, as bad as I feel and as much pain as I'm in, but Colombo won't let me go; none of them will let me go because I'm in such bad shape. I reached into my jacket and gave Colombo the wallet I'd found.

While everyone hunted for the guys who jumped us, I was taken to a doctor who took X rays and bandaged me up. He told me that if the club, which hit me on the knuckle of the spine, had struck a fraction of an inch closer, I would have been para-lyzed from the waist down for the rest of my life.

That night the FBI paid me a visit. I was alone in my apart-ment when there was a banging at the door. Standing at the door were two FBI agents.

I'm in a lot of pain, all taped up, and I didn't feel like arguing, so I told them to come in and sit down.

"We heard there was a big fight on Eighty-sixth Street," one of them said. "You want to tell us about it?"

"I don't know what you're talking about," I answered.

"Well, then, what happened to your back?" the other asked.

"I just had a cyst removed," I said.

That was the end of it. Later, I heard that Colombo's men found some of Gallo's hoods who were involved and got rid of them. They were found through information discovered in the wallet. I never did find out who they were, and Pileggi's story, which reported our attackers were "housepainters," never identified them. Pileggi did suggest that there were rumors that Joe Gallo was behind the beating and that Colombo's leadership had been challenged that day. He was close. A little over a month later, Colombo was gunned down with a shot that shook the mob world.

6

THE ERRAND BOY

In the beginning, I was little more than an errand boy for Colombo and a sometimes escort for his thugs when they went out to make shylock collections. Because I was big and looked threatening, I suppose, Peewee Campagna and Frankie the Beast Falanga would asked me to go with them when they went out to shake up late-paying borrowers. I never had to do much except make the muscles in my face twitch a bit to look tough. If they wanted to beat up someone, I just stood there, looking menacing, as though I were ready to join in and help them do what they had to do. They didn't want me to use my hands, and I never volunteered. "Just look tough," Peewee would say. "I'll take care of what has to be done."

The operation became so smooth that borrowers would come to the real estate office weekly, ask to see me, and drop off their envelopes with whatever they owed for that week. I made sure the money got to Colombo, or Falanga, or Peewee.

One of the surest ways to be sure that the money got to Colombo and that it was safe from surprise raiders was to put the envelopes in a secret wall panel in Colombo's office located behind a coatrack my uncle Jimmy Cantalupo put in.

The coatrack could hold up to seven coats or jackets and

appeared to be part of the wall with a metal-plate base. But the metal plate could be moved up, and behind it, in the wall, was a large compartment where Colombo could stash his numbers and slips and other paraphernalia, including money.

When there was about to be a raid, we'd get tipped by people in Colombo's crew or friends in the neighborhood who'd signal us that there were strangers around. One of the tipsters was a guy named Joe Iannacci. We called him Joe Notch or "Joe Nazadabeep," a big guy with a big nose. Joe wasn't just big, he was huge. He'd put a gorilla to shame, and his nose . . . it would give Durante competition.

Joe's job was to sort of patrol the area, act as a lookout by walking in front of the office or Caplan's Buick. He'd immediately spot strangers, the FBI, or strange cops in the area. When he saw them, Joe Notch would hit the side of his nose, meaning "The feds are here, driving around."

Colombo could see Joe give the signal, or he'd get a high sign from someone who did. Sometimes he would send me out to take pictures of the feds with a Polaroid instant camera that Peewee had given me to make appraisals on the property and homes of his loan-shark clients.

I'd take the picture and give it to him to go with a stack of photos of agents he said were harassing him. He used those pictures in a court appearance one day to show he was being hounded.

When there was a clear danger that a raid was about to take place, Colombo would watch through the one-way mirror-window in his office, and if Joe Notch or someone else gave him the high sign, he'd clear his pockets and his desk, push up the metal plate, dump his stuff in, and pull the panel down. When the cops or FBI came into his office with their search warrants, they went through his desk, files, and office with a fine-tooth comb, but they never found the hidden compartment built by Uncle Jimmy.

Uncle Jimmy became something of a lush after my grandfather died. I think he felt lost without Grandpa. He used to drink a quart of scotch every night, like clockwork. He also had a reputation as a fighter, something he earned when he was middleweight champion on a Coast Guard ship during World War II.

He loved a good fight, and there wasn't anyone he wouldn't take on just for the hell of it. I remember a night at the San SuSan, a Nassau County nightclub that used to attract the name entertainers and the mob back in the fifties and sixties. Uncle Jimmy got smashed, and when it was time to leave, he decided to pick a fight with a parking valet.

The valet was a midget who assigned attendants to park customer cars. Uncle Jimmy said the midget was too slow and threatened to pulverize him. But he wouldn't do it from his towering vantage point. To fight the midget, Uncle Jimmy got down on his hands and knees in the dirt. He was so drunk, he lost the fight.

My grandfather loved Uncle Jimmy and his other sons and his daughter, but he'd fume when he heard about Jimmy fighting or when he had an argument with my father. More than once his anger would prompt him to say to me, "I should have raised pigs instead of children . . . that way I could have cooked them and had them for dinner."

Sometimes when shylock loans were made in the office, Colombo would send his cash banker, Frankie the Beast, out to get the money from someplace he had it stashed. When Frankie the Beast would return, Colombo would call me into the office, hand me the money, and tell me to count it.

"Go count it, Joe," he'd say. "Make sure it's a full count."

There were no adding machines or money-counting machines around in those days, and this wasn't something to be done with others watching anyhow, so I'd take the money to the office bathroom, close the door, and start counting. Whoosha, whoosha, whoosha . . . counting as fast as I could. Sometimes I wasn't as fast a counter as Frankie the Beast or Peewee or someone else wanted me to be, but Colombo never complained. He knew I wasn't going to make a mistake, not with his money. There were occasions when a lot of money was involved and it took me hours, counting and straightening each bill and putting them into stacks. I remember having to count out $100,000 for a loan by Colombo to the owner of a Brooklyn trucking company who needed cash in a hurry.

The trucker was a friend of Al Wasserman, and he had a serious cash-flow problem. He had lots of assets, like property and the trucking company, but he needed cash.

So Wasserman calls me about the guy and says he needs the $100,000. Now I knew the trucker when Al mentioned his name, and my father knew him well. I knew the guy would make good on any loan he had because he had so many real estate assets.

I didn't have the kind of clout to arrange that hefty a loan with anyone, but I figured my father did, so I called him. He, in turn, talked to Colombo. The next thing I knew, I was in the bathroom counting out the cash that Frankie the Beast had delivered. When I was through, Colombo sent me to the trucker's office on Sixteenth Avenue with the cash. That was in 1967.

For the next year and a half, Colombo had me collect the vig each week from the trucker. Every week, without fail, the trucker paid three thousand dollars to cover the three-point vig that Colombo charged. Only the vig didn't just go to Colombo. A thousand a week went to my father, a thousand to Colombo, and another thousand went to Carl Gambino. Colombo had covered his ass by getting a third of the $100,000 from Gambino at one point a week. My father got a piece of the interest, I suppose because he steered the loan to Colombo.

There were weeks when I'd deliver the money to my father when Colombo was out. Colombo would come back after a couple of weeks and ask my father, "Anthony . . . where's the envelope?"

"Oh, I needed some cash," my father would explain, and Colombo would mark down on a piece of paper, "Anthony, $6,000." Then he'd remark, "Anthony, what the hell do you do with all your money?"

More than once he told me my father had a hiding place where he stashed his money. "Joey, let me tell you something," he said. "Your father has a shoe box at home. He could put the money in, but if he goes to take it out, the rattrap snaps on his hand. With him it's money, money, money."

The truth was, my father liked to live well, and he spent money as fast as it came in for whatever he wanted. He also invested well, owning most of the business fronts around and near Cantalupo Realty as well as a score or more rental apartment houses.

Somehow Bureau agents got wind of the loan and tried to squeeze the trucker into talking. He was hauled before a grand jury and, when he refused to talk, was sentenced to six months in jail for contempt of court. He still kept his mouth shut. That's when they stopped the clock on the loan. I never made a collection from him again. After Colombo was shot in 1971 at an Italian-American Unity Day rally in Manhattan, Gambino came to see my father.

"Remember that hundred-thousand-dollar loan to the trucker?" Gambino asked.

"Yeah, what about it?" my father told me he said.

"Well, part of the money was mine," he said. "You owe me thirty-three thousand dollars."

My father paid what Gambino said he owed without question, but by then he, Colombo, and Gambino had collected more than $156,000 in interest, and my father hadn't put up a dime, just arranged for the loan. But from Gambino's point of view, the loan was a bad loan; the principal was never paid off, and my father was responsible in his eyes. Since he got a third of the profits, he also shared a third of the loan loss. As far as I know, the trucker never had to pay the outstanding $100,000 principal on the loan because he'd kept his mouth shut and everyone was convinced that the feds would come down on them like a ton of bricks if they went near him.

And me? I never got a dime. I steered the trucker to my father, who turned it over to Colombo. I also collected the vig every week for a year and a half. But no one gave me a red penny. It's just as well. I'd have got stuck for a piece of the loss if I had.

There were other debtors who showed up at the office who weren't as lucky as my trucker friend. The trucker always paid what he owed on time, week in, week out. Colombo liked that. What he didn't like was someone who didn't pay and didn't have the guts to come to see him face-to-face and give him an explanation.

One of those debtors was a Staten Island builder who had borrowed heavily from Colombo and came to the office weekly to pay his vig. A week went by, and he didn't show up. Then it was two weeks. Finally, he showed up on the third week. Colombo was livid.

"You should have come to me the first week and said, 'Joe, I don't have it.' But you went a second week, like you was evading me," he said angrily. Then he motioned to Rocky Miraglia. "Rocky . . . take our friend downstairs to the basement and educate him."

Rocky took the builder past my desk to the basement of the office. There was no struggle, but the builder's face was chalk white with fear. I could hear some banging around for a short while, and then the builder and Rocky returned to the main floor. The builder's face was all puffy and swollen. He was never late again on his payments.

There were others who made the same mistake—showed bad faith by not showing up with their payments and then not telling the loan shark why they were behind in payment—and they usually wound up in the basement getting a beating from Rocky or Frankie the Beast.

They didn't yell much. Most of them took their beatings like men. Some of them may have groaned a bit or even whimpered down in the basement, but when they came up to the main floor, their mouths were shut. Only their eyes showed their fear. They were apologetic to Colombo, and they promised to pay on time in the future. None of them were really hurt so bad they couldn't walk or write. No legs or arms were broken there that I can remember. Loan sharks normally don't want to damage their property too badly. If they do, they don't get paid, and the main rule for all loan sharks is get the money above all else. There are exceptions, but the kind of people Colombo and the people in the office were dealing with got the message real quick with some whacks in the face and belts in the belly and groin. It was just as effective.

I had to handle other collections for Colombo and my father. One of their more profitable business ventures was in the handling of rental property. Some of it fell directly under the umbrella of Cantalupo Realty, but in instances where Colombo was a joint property owner and was sharing in the rental proceeds, another corporate front had to be established so as not to endanger the real estate brokerage license of my father.

The corporate front they chose was a company called UCAL Holding Corporation. Its officers included a former banker who had once turned down Colombo for a loan because he was a bad risk, my father, Colombo, and myself. The banker was listed as the president, and I was listed as the treasurer. My father and Colombo were vice-president and secretary.

Under the corporate front, we managed three major properties that Colombo, my father, and I owned—a factory and five-room apartment on Sixty-seventh Street and Thirteenth Avenue; a two-family apartment house on Stillwell Avenue; and Sbarro's, a six-family apartment building with four stores. We owned them together, but eventually we wound up selling the properties to Colombo outright except for Sbarro's. That property we jointly parted with for a mere ten-thousand-dollar profit at Colombo's suggestion after Frank Tieri, then the boss of the Genovese crime family, came to the office and paid him a visit.

Would he please, Tieri asked, do him an important favor by selling the property to Sbarro, who was a relative of his?

Colombo, always eager to curry favor with another boss and place it in his favors library for use when he really needed help before the Mafia Commission or support in interfamily disputes, convinced my father it would be important to agree to such a request. We did. Today, the building is worth hundreds of thousands of dollars, and Sbarro's, then a small Italian delicatessen, went on to become a major Italian chain food store and chain pizza eatery.

My job as treasurer was to collect rents for UCAL. I also had to physically collect most of the rents for Cantalupo Realty. One day I questioned why I had to make monthly trips to collect the rents.

"Why do I have to go to every place and personally collect the rents?" I asked. "Why can't we send them an envelope and let them send us back the rent? Collecting rents is time-consuming. It costs us money and time."

My father shook his head. "No . . . you go in and you collect the rents personally, and where the Jewish families are, and you see a mezuzah, a holy scroll in a case hanging on the outside doorknob, you rub that before you go in for good luck."

I did it for months before I complained again. "Dad . . . it's ridiculous," I said. "I mean, why the hell do I rub this Jewish mezuzah, or whatever they call it? Why do I have to go into all these apartments? I lose valuable time doing this."

"Joey, you gotta understand something," he said with a sigh. "When Grandpa was here, I worked for him collecting the rents from a hundred different families. I used to go and collect the rents at every place on the first of the month, and in every place except one I would see the people personally and talk to them. The exception was an apartment where I would knock and the door would open and a hand would pass the money to me. I never saw who was paying. One day the place blew up. Grandpa was furious.

" 'You stupid bastard,' he said. 'I told you, you gotta go in these places and see the people and see how they live. If you had done what I told you, the place would have never blown up.'

"The man in the apartment had installed a still, and it blew up. He was making illegal whiskey, and he destroyed the apartment. That's why I have you go into every apartment and check on every tenant. Then we don't have trouble. That's what Grandpa taught me, and that's what you gotta learn."

Tradition. There's a lot to be said for it, and there is a lot that those of us who are young do not understand. But a lot of that tradition is based on past experience and is designed to prevent the same mistakes in the future.

So that's what I had to do month in, month out as long as I worked there and collected rents for my father and for Colombo. I had to see every tenant and collect personally from each one inside their apartments to be sure that nothing illegal was going on. By doing it Grandpa's way, I guess I probably prevented problems not only for my father, but for Colombo and the corporation he was part of. If there had been illegal activities going on in the rental locations and the feds had learned of them, they could have caused Colombo embarrassment and trouble he didn't want.

• • •

Since I was with Colombo and his people almost daily and he was so highly regarded by my father, I quite naturally threw in my lot with him and those who supported him. He was the boss of the family. He had the power and money. He had the support of Gambino. Who the hell else would someone like myself support?

In the Colombo family, there were three principal factions: the Gallo gang, the Persico crew, and Colombo's own crew.

The Gallo gang was a small but unruly and violent crew that had challenged the leadership of Profaci but lacked the strength and will to directly take on Colombo. In the sixties, Colombo had them pretty much under his thumb, and in fact they never really gathered sufficient strength in and out of the family to position themselves for a run at the family leadership even after the death of Colombo.

The second and more powerful crew was the Persico faction. It was led by Carmine "the Snake" Persico, who had been the person most responsible for putting down the Gallo rebellion against Profaci. It was his crew of hitters, people like Jerry Langella, Hugh "Apples" McIntosh, Alphonse "Allie Boy" Persico, and others who were the core of enforcement within the family. They didn't challenge Colombo's authority—in fact, they supported him—but when he fell from power, when he was shot, they were in a position to move in quickly and take over the leadership of the family. They were the power within the family.

Within the Persico group was a young ex-army veteran named Michael Bolino who I met within weeks after beginning work as a salesman in Cantalupo Realty Company. Bolino was two years older than I was, he had served a couple of years in Germany just as I had, and he had married a German girl and brought her back to the States. He was also a real estate salesman, only he worked in the office of Aldo Girasole, a major real estate broker who competed with and was close friends with my father. So there was a lot of common ground between us. We had shared similar problems in Germany, and we were sharing some similar problems in Brooklyn.

There is an old saying among Italians: "The fruit never falls far from the tree." There was a ring of truth to that saying in Michael's case. His father was John Bolino, a former soldier in the Colombo family who is now dead. He grew up in the time of Profaci and survived the gang wars, and Michael sort of followed in his footsteps.

Michael was, in addition to being a real estate salesman, a loan shark and sometimes enforcer for the Persico crew. He was, in fact, very close to Alphonse Persico and Jerry Lang (Langella), men his father knew well. Now that didn't put him outside the Colombo family. It just put him in the inner circle of the Persico crew, and that alignment—that association and closeness with the Persicos—caused me some serious complications and problems later. But early on, we became good friends, almost like brothers.

My problem with Bolino didn't surface until after November 3, 1968. That was the day I got married to a gorgeous blond Brooklyn girl named Veronica who I'd met through her grandparents in 1964.

She was the daughter of a Polish father and Italian mother, and her mother's parents came to the real estate office looking for an apartment. One of my main jobs in the office until I got my license was handling apartment rentals, so I took them out and showed them around. They finally took an apartment around Eighty-third Street, and the whole family moved there from the Prospect Park area.

Veronica's grandparents were typically Italian. They wanted their granddaughter to meet a nice Italian boy, and I impressed them, so they asked would I be interested in meeting a nice girl?

I played the good salesman role and said sure, but I honestly didn't hold out much hope for anything until I met her. I was stunned by her good looks, and for nearly three years we dated on and off. In 1967, we became engaged, and a year later we were married.

Before I could get married, I had to be confirmed in the Catholic church, St. Bernadette's, where my grandparents and their children went to church and where my grandfather regularly played pinochle every week at the rectory office with the monsignor.

I had made my first communion while my father and mother were still together, but they separated and were divorced before I was old enough to be confirmed. As a result, I never thought about it much until the time came to get married.

Veronica and her parents, as well as my father and mother, wanted this to be a wedding to be remembered—a full-blown church ceremony with all the trimmings.

To get married in the Church and receive communion at the altar in those days, the couple had to be confirmed Catholics. So I had to have lessons in Catholic doctrine and have a sponsor stand up for me when I was ready to be confirmed. The man I chose was Michael Bolino, who had become one of my closest friends.

While Bolino and I were close, I also became very close to Colombo's two oldest sons, Anthony and Joseph Junior. I met them in the office, and almost immediately we began going out together, partying at the Copacabana and the Latin Quarter, any and every nightclub worth a damn in New York.

The relationship between the Colombo kids and myself got tighter in 1966. That was when Colombo asked me and Bolino to become Masons with his two sons in the Columbus Lodge 872.

Crime boss or no, Colombo was very, very serious about the Masons and its secret society. Colombo was a member and it was like a religion with him. He used to say that 90 percent of the nation's presidents had been Masons, and that no Mason had ever been convicted of murder.

I didn't know if it was true or not, but I sure as hell wasn't going to question him or antagonize him by saying I wasn't interested in becoming a Mason. For me, it was an honor to be asked and to have him sponsor me. It was almost like being sponsored for membership in the mob—it was that important in his eyes.

So he sponsored me, his sons, and Bolino, and he raised me. Now being raised in the Masons is special. When you appear for your first-degree training, you're pricked with a compass to draw blood. When you reach the third degree, after three months, you are hit, not hard, but symbolically, with a soft mallet, and you fall to the floor. You are then raised from the floor by the man who sponsors you, and Colombo raised me. That made us extremely close, and it made his boys very close because they were raised with me. He never raised Bolino, because Boline never completed the three degrees of indoctrination.

We became so close, in fact, that when the time came for me to become an informer and later a witness for the FBI, I told agents that I would never testify against Anthony and Joe Junior, or any of Colombo's immediate family. It was a promise I kept and the agents kept, although federal prosecutors did attempt to force me to testify against Anthony and Joe Junior when they got in trouble years later for running a burglary and robbery ring.

While the Masons were a fraternal order of men, they were viewed by the Catholic Church as antireligious, which wasn't true. In the middle of the insignia of the Masons is a G, which stands for God. All the members I knew in Lodge 872 were old Italian Catholics who wouldn't dream of denouncing their religion but were fierce supporters of the Masons.

Now there are a number of degrees of Masons, but to become a full member in good standing you have to reach the third degree by passing tests for all three degrees. It took about three months. Anthony, Joe Junior, and myself went through all three degrees and became full-fledged members. That made Colombo very proud. Bolino quit after the second degree; he got bored I guess, had better things to do, and never finished the training for the third degree, in which you learn certain secret signs.

Michael tried passing himself off as a Mason in the business community, but he wasn't a member, and it upset Colombo. To Colombo, Bolino had shown a flaw in his character that he didn't like. By not finishing as a Mason with all of us, he had lost face. As a result, Colombo didn't trust him, didn't take him under his wing as he had me and his sons. That put Bolino at the bottom of the crime-family wheel . . . for the time being. As long as Colombo was alive and boss of the family, it was highly unlikely that Bolino would be made as a member of the family, despite his friendship with the Persicos.

Membership in the Masons for me meant business contacts, a strong relationship with buyers and sellers and leasers of land who were Masons and preferred doing business with people they could relate to and trust, fellow Masons.

Anthony and Joe Colombo, Jr., never took the Masons—or anything else, for that matter—very seriously. They were pretty wild, out for a good time, and they were always broke. So was I, but I didn't own the catering halls, the rental properties, and the funeral parlors and other businesses that their father provided for them.

Silver spoon or not, we were still buddies, like brothers, from the time we started going out together. We drank together, we whored together, and we bet together. That was how I first got in hock to a shylock . . . because of Joe Junior.

Joe Junior loved the ponies, but he wasn't about to tell his father how much his "hobby" was costing him. He was always going to the track, always betting on a "sure thing." I knew nothing about horses, but I went along with him. One day Joe Junior had a tip about a horse running at Aqueduct, but he didn't have any money and he couldn't go to his father for money—not for something like the track—and he couldn't go to Campagna or Frankie the Beast or Greg Scarpa or any of the loan sharks. Colombo from the beginning told him he couldn't, and he warned his shylocks that lending money to his kids was a serious, serious no-no.

So Joe Junior turns to me, since I'm no shylock, just a collector, and his father never told me never to lend him money, and he says, "Hey, Joey, how about borrowing some money for us from Peewee? He'll give it to you, and he'll keep it quiet."

Dumb schmuck that I was, I said, "Sure . . . how much you need?"

"Get a thousand," Joe Junior answered. "We'll make a bundle . . . we'll clean up. We'll put five hundred dollars to win and five hundred dollars to show. Its a sure thing. We'll make thousands."

So I borrowed the thousand from Peewee without telling him

that Colombo's son was involved. The price to me was three points . . . thirty bucks in vig a week on one thousand dollars.

I give the money to Joe, and we go to the track and he bets the bundle. Now I knew better, and I knew that there were always tips about horses that were sure things, but I went along with him. What the hell, if Colombo's son doesn't know, who does? What happens? What else. This dog of a horse finishes last in a field of six. I mean, I thought this nag was going to fall on its face and maim the jockey before it reached the finish line. Joe Junior had a long look on his face, but he didn't offer to pay a dime of the vig . . . not five bucks' worth. I paid the loan off with vig in a month or so.

You would think I'd have learned, but I didn't. It wasn't too long before I got a call from upstate from Anthony and Joe Junior. They want to party, and they got this whorehouse in Newburgh, New York, with all these beautiful black broads. The trouble is, they don't have money.

Now it's the middle of the night, and they are calling me at my grandma's home in Valley Stream. Where the hell am I going to get the bread? I ask them. You'll find a way, they say, just meet us.

I did. I found a way by taking a giant Seagram's jar that I used to stash quarters in, breaking it, emptying it out, and then spending hours rolling up ten-dollar stacks of quarters until I had five hundred dollars. Then I drove like hell to Newburgh, where I met them at this whorehouse.

I can't remember the street name, but it was a big house, a beautiful old mansion with two big black guys at the door with shotguns. You had to know them to get in, and Anthony knew them. Inside was this big bar, a huge living room, and all the food and drink you could consume. And around it were these gorgeous black girls, like in the old-time bordellos . . . just fabulous. We had a hellava party, but I went home broke. Joe Junior put the quarters in a shoe box in his car trunk, and somehow arranged for our party to be paid. It was his gig of keeping silver—dimes and quarters and whatever—that later caused the downfall of his old man, but that's another story I'll get to later.

I never understood what the hell the Colombo kids did with

all their money. They never had to get involved in criminal things, and while I was with them, they never did. They had the world by the balls.

Because of their father, they owned limousine services, florist shops, wedding-favor stores, catering halls, liquor distributorships, wedding-gown shops, bakeries, travel agencies . . . you name it, the Colombos had it. Joe Junior was pulling down more than $200,000 a year, but he was always broke. I couldn't believe how broke he always was. It got so bad that they even chiseled the hookers we partied with.

There were times when they would organize a hooker party with five or six guys at a hookers' penthouse where there would be two or three good-looking girls.

The Colombos would come up with six hundred dollars to pay the girls for balling the five or six guys who were at the party. Then Anthony and Joe Junior would organize a straw selection—we'd draw straws to see who got first choice, second choice, and so on.

While two of the five or six guys were balling the broads, the Colombos would have the other guys search the hookers' penthouse, looking for money stashes. We'd leave the party laughing, having had a helluva time, and when we left, the Colombo kids would produce rolls of bills big enough to choke a horse— money that had been stolen from the hookers' penthouse stashes. So we'd have the hookers for free, and they never knew they'd been ripped off until long after we were gone.

A lot of the hooker parties took place when the three of us were going to Brooklyn College in 1967 to study for and get our insurance brokers' license. Colombo had one of the top academics in his pocket through a guy who was known as Tony Lap. He arranged with one of the administrators for us to take the course, one of the toughest classes in the business school, and he guaranteed our graduation. Sign up we did, but we weren't about to stick around and attend classes. We paid our tuition, and then for the three-month semester we would go in every night, sign in, and take off to party with some hookers or some other people. At the end of the semester, we got our diploma, our certificate, and we never had to take a test or attend a class.

In the summer of 1968, a lot of the partying ended. I was about to get married, and the wedding was set for November 3. I was between a rock and a hard place in trying to figure out who I should pick as my best man. Bolino was like a brother to me, but so were Joe Junior and Anthony, and I had been invited to be in Anthony's wedding party before I got married. What to do? I went to my father and asked him how to make the selection.

"Who do you think I should make my best man, Dad?" I asked.

"Make Joe Junior," he said without hesitation. "It's the right thing to do. It'll make Joe Senior very happy."

That was what I did. I named Joe Junior my best man. Anthony and Michael Bolino were in the wedding party, but Joe Junior was my best man. That decision turned what would have been a fair-sized wedding of maybe 150 into a regular Mafia event with more than 350 attending.

We were married at St. Bernadette's, a church familiar to many in the mob who lived in the immediate vicinity. The reception was held at the Queens Terrace, a catering hall run by Michael Savino but controlled at the time by Colombo.

Carlo Gambino, his sons, Joe and Tommy, and their wives had a table and were a star attraction, as were Colombo and all his family. And because the bosses accepted the invitation, many of the elite capos and soldiers who were invited turned out for the affair—people I had met, worked with, or run errands for at my father's office. It was really a tribute to my father's influence and his reputation in the families, very unusual for a man who was not a made member of the Mafia.

The singer and the comedian were provided by John (Sonny) Franzese of Roslyn Heights. They may not have been Jimmy Roselli or Don Rickles, but they were great, and Franzese had provided them gratis. Unfortunately, Franzese was unable to attend in person. He was in jail at the time, serving a fifty-year federal jail term for conspiracy and bank robbery that to this day everyone believes was a phony rap set up by someone in the mob who wanted to eliminate his influence in the family.

Sonny was a Colombo loyalist, an old-line traditional capo who commanded a dangerous and powerful army of enforcers, shylocks, and gamblers on Long Island and in Queens. He had enormous influence in the entertainment world, including the fight rackets, and he was one of the few leaders who could have successfully challenged Persico's later move to the leadership. He was a man I think Persico feared, and I've always wondered if Persico had something to do with setting up the informers who testified that Sonny had directed the operations of some low-level bank robbers. Franzese and bank robberies just never rang true with me or with other people who knew him, because that wasn't Sonny's style; we all thought he was too careful and made much too much money to get involved in crap like that.

There were others attending the reception who had considerable influence and power, people like Vinnie Aloi, who used to be at Colombo's home in Brooklyn or upstate almost every weekend and who, for a time, reluctantly held the job of temporary boss after Colombo was shot. Vinnie was a nice guy, and he hated being forced to become a boss. I remember running into him when I'd go to the movies at night around 7:00 P.M., and he'd be coming out of the theater. "Why are you here so early?" I'd ask.

Vinnie would just shrug. "I go to the movies in the daytime," he explained, "because this way when I come out at night, I don't have to worry about being followed." But he did. Becoming a temporary boss put a lot of heat on him that he didn't need. He had a trucking business in the garment center, a big shylocking operation, so why bother being a boss? Who needed it? But he had to take it, and that gave the feds more reason to turn the heat up on him and put him in jail on a stock-fraud case for nine years. The stock fraud was a scheme dreamed up by stock swindler Michael Hellerman, who turned informer rather than be killed or go to jail.

It wasn't hard for me to remember Vinnie's first and last name, but there were others at the reception whom I knew only by their reputations and nicknames, names that had been used at the office. One of the most embarrassing moments I can recall about the reception was when my wife and I made the traditional rounds of all the tables to collect the envelopes, and all I could remember about some guests I introduced her to were their nicknames—people like Johnny Bath Beach, who I knew ran the Bath Beach section of Brooklyn but about whom I knew little else. His real name was John Oddo. There was Tutti, a cousin of Sonny's, whose real name was Carmine Franzese, and there were a half-dozen others who I knew by street names only. I stumbled a lot in the introductions, but I got through them without insulting anyone.

Most of them I knew, like James Muce, a real quiet and likable capo who ran a carting business and some nursing homes; Greg Scarpa, who was a major loan shark; Carmine Persico and John Bolino, all of them capos from the Colombo family. We also had outsiders, people like Buddy Sciandria, who is now the acting boss of a Pennsylvania Bufalino family; James (Jimmy the Blond) Corrao, who later became the underboss of the Gambino family; and Nicky Bianco from the New England Patriarca family.

While it may have looked like a Mafia gathering, there were a lot of nonmember associates, politicians, lawyers, businessmen, and just plain legitimate people, friends, and family.

By the time my wife and I had worked our way through all the tables and collected all the envelopes, we had more than twenty thousand dollars. Now that wouldn't compare with what Anthony or Joe Junior got at their weddings—more than $100,000—but for me it wasn't Swiss cheese. Interestingly enough, the biggest contributors were the nonmember associates of the crime families who had legitimate businesses.

It was a helluva blast, but it had a price.

I didn't realize, but I had managed to insult Michael Bolino. He was angered by the fact that I had named Joe Colombo, Jr., as my best man instead of him, and he harbored that grudge for years. When Colombo died following an assassination attempt several years later, the Persicos took control of the family and loan-shark debts. In that time period, I became one of the debtors, and Bolino one of those who controlled the debts. When I was being hounded, threatened, and beaten by some of the loan sharks, I asked Bolino why he let some of the things happen to me when he could have intervened as a friend.

"You see, Joe," he said, "when you made Joe Junior your best man, he was on top of the wheel and you rode with him. Now the wheel turns. Now we're on top of the wheel, and he's at the bottom."

What he meant was that I had chosen to take my ride with Colombo while he was in the driver's seat, but with him dead, those who rode his coattails were at the bottom, while those who stayed with the Persicos, as Bolino did, were sitting at the top, steering that wheel and calling the shots. The king was dead, and so were his jesters, in a manner of speaking.

In 1969, my wife and I had just been married a year and the two-family house we were living in was located at 1460 Eighty-third Street, Brooklyn, just a short distance from Colombo's own home when he asked me for the use of our place for a night. It was a three-bedroom apartment with a living room and a kitchen-dinette—a nice apartment, but nothing elaborate.

As luck would have it, my wife was planning to go to bingo at St. Bernadette's with some friends anyhow, so I didn't have to say too much about what was going on. I just asked her to do the things Colombo wanted her to do. She got the cookies from a popular Italian bakery nearby, and then she made the pot of demitasse espresso I asked her to make before she left.

Once she was gone, I moved our kitchen table, which was octagonal in shape, away from the wall and more toward the center of our kitchen-dinette, and around the table I placed five chairs, as I'd been instructed to. No one chair was to be placed at the head of the table. Just five chairs distanced equally from each other around the table. In front of each chair, I placed a demitasse cup, and in the center of the table I placed a large silver tray filled with the cookies.

On the kitchen stove was the pot of espresso, and in the living room near the door I set up a sixth chair, as Colombo had told me to, for his bodyguard and captain, Rocco Miraglia. Then I went to the ground floor, walked out to the stoop, and sat at the top to watch and wait.

It was about 7:00 P.M., just getting dark, when the first car arrived with Colombo and his driver, Miraglia. Colombo stepped from the car, smiled, walked up to me, shook my hand and asked, "Where's the apartment?"

I motioned to the second floor of the two-family apartment house I lived in. "It's upstairs," I said. "Let me show you. I got everything fixed up like you wanted me to." I led him up the stairs to the apartment as Miraglia drove off in the car.

"Looks good, Joe," he said. "Now go downstairs and sit on the stoop and help anyone who needs to know where to come."

So I did. By the time I got back to the stoop, Miraglia had returned on foot after parking around the block.

Twenty minutes later, the second car arrived. Driving was Jimmy Failla, Gambino's capo in charge of the garbage industry and a familiar face I saw often either at the office, when Gambino was visiting, or at a social club near the office where he often met with soldiers from his family. Gambino stepped from the car, nodded, politely said hello, and walked up the stairs while Failla drove off.

In the next fifteen or twenty minutes, three more cars pulled up, each dropping off a boss. The third car was driven by Nicky Bianco, a capo with the New England crime family of Raymond Patriarca. He dropped off an older man I didn't recognize, but who walked up to me. I told him where the apartment was, and he went up to it. Bianco then drove off. Right behind him was Joe Notch. He was driving for Frank (Funzi) Tieri, who I knew was the boss of the Genovese family and to whom my father had introduced me years earlier at the office. Funzi stopped in front of me after getting out of the car, and like Gambino, he shook my hand and said hello before going to the meeting. The last car was driven by somebody I had never seen before. The passenger was a big, heavyset man who must have weighed three hundred pounds or more. I didn't recognize him either, but I did notice that he wasn't a dapper dresser like Tieri or Colombo or even Gambino. He puffed a bit as he walked toward me.

"Where?" he said gruffly.

"Upstairs," I said, watching as he slowly climbed the stairs.

I knew something important was going on, but I didn't have the slightest idea what. I did know enough to do one thing: keep my mouth shut and ask no questions.

The meeting lasted about two hours, and all that time I sat out on the stoop, acting as sort of a lookout while all their drivers, except Miraglia, who was upstairs bodyguarding the group, circled the area in their cars or parked on nearby streets and waited. There were no other lookouts, nothing out of the ordinary to cause the slightest interest by a nosy neighbor. They had the routine down pat, and nobody in the area was the wiser.

Suddenly, the cars stopped circling, and one by one, at three- or four-minute intervals, they pulled up to the stoop to pick up their individual passengers. It was as if they knew exactly when to be there to pick up their bosses. As they pulled up, their passenger, whether it was Gambino or Tieri or one of the other two men, came out of the apartment house, down the steps, and walked passed me to their cars without saying a word. Then they drove off.

The last to leave was Colombo. Miraglia preceded him, walked around the block and got the car and then drove up and stopped at the curb near the stoop as Colombo came out of the house. He stopped for a moment as he reached where I was sitting. "Thank you very much," he said, and drove off without another word.

I looked around and stood there for a minute, alone, scratching my head, and then I picked up my folding chair and returned to the apartment. The demitasse pot of coffee was empty, but there were still a lot of cookies left. I cleaned up, cleared the table, moved all the furniture back into the kitchen, where it belonged. By the time everything was cleaned and put away, it was 11:00 P.M. and my wife was walking in the door from a night of uneventful bingo.

I didn't realize it then—in fact, it took years before I understood it—but I had hosted a meeting of the Cosa Nostra, the Mafia Commission, an almost legendary group that wiseguys talked about for the most part in whispers or in a sort of street code that only other wiseguys understood.

Colombo, because of the relationship we had developed through working together and being Masons together, had trusted me enough to select me and my home for a meeting of such importance. There was no one else in his family whom he felt secure enough with to entrust with such a meeting. I wasn't made, I wasn't a goodfellow. I didn't have outside interests, but I was known and apparently acceptable to both Gambino and

Tieri. No one else, to my knowledge, has ever hosted a meeting like this in his home and lived long enough to testify about it.

It wasn't until much later, in conversations with Peewee Campagna, Mike Bolino, and others that I learned that the Commission was the ruling council of the Mafia in this country—a sort of board of directors of organized crime. Only it didn't meet in boardrooms like a corporate board of directors such as those of General Motors or AT&T. Its board meetings were held in apartments like mine, in offices of warehouses, in restaurants like La Stella's, places where the bosses felt they could talk privately without the worry of being overheard with electronic bugs or being watched by the cops.

There had been lots of newspaper stories about the Commission, and I had read some of them, but they were based on what was supposed to be conversations in some illegal bugs and the U.S. Senate testimony of Joe Valachi. I just never really believed that stuff until I heard it from someone I trusted, like Peewee.

While I don't think any Commission meeting was ever bugged, there were, in later years, surveillances of meetings by law enforcement. What the bosses talked about sometimes leaked out when they talked about what went on to their soldiers or underbosses in their homes, offices, and even their cars. Peewee was one of those who heard about some of the things that went on from Colombo and from those who replaced him, and when he was trying to make a point or impress me with something, he would occasionally tell some of the stories to me.

The Commission was made up, I found out, of the five bosses of the crime families in New York. At times there were more than the five New York family bosses sitting on the Commission. Sometimes they had out-of-town bosses, guys like Tony Accardo or Sam Giancana from Chicago, Stefano Magaddino from Buffalo, and Angelo Bruno from Philadelphia; and even Santo Trafficante of Tampa and Carlos Marcello of New Orleans would come in for meetings.

They showed up—the out-of-towners—to talk about problems that affected places outside New York, like a decision to execute a boss or dump him, the way they did Bonanno, or investments they all had together, like casinos and unions they controlled and sucked money from through pension and welfare funds, such as the Teamsters. Even with the out-of-towners, the New York families always kept the edge, had the majority vote.

Most of the time, it was the New York bosses who held the meetings. They were sitting and deciding on things like family disputes over territories, trouble within families over leadership, like the Gallos' fight with Profaci. Sometimes they met to cut up profits on kickbacks on highway and building construction or other investments they all worked together on to make money. They also considered and approved new recruits, who were sponsored for membership in different families.

This was a very powerful group of men who decided on survival, on life and death in the Mafia, and for the most part that life or death was decided by the five bosses of New York. They were the supreme court of the Mafia, and when they made their decisions, there was no appeal.

On June 9, 1977, I found out what happened when a wiseguy appealed the decision of a boss and lost. My lesson in Commission politics took place first at a Chinese restaurant called the Hong Pan, where I met Peewee Campagna almost every day.

After Colombo died, there were a number of changes in the family leadership. At first Vinnie Aloi was named the temporary boss. Then he went to jail, and Carmine Persico took over. When Persico was dropped on a hijacking case, Thomas DiBella, an old man Persico could control, took over while Persico's brother Allie Boy (Alphonse Persico) became the *consigliere* or adviser before taking over as the acting boss. There were some people who didn't like that arrangement, and one of those people was Anthony (Abbe) Abbatemarco, an old-time capo with a lot of influence in high places.

Peewee, however, was a survivor. He did what he was told, followed orders, and kept out of trouble. His job was to work the garment center and answer weekly on action to Albanese, a family soldier, and his boss, Abbatemarco.

Peewee sat back and shook his head. "They were stupid . . . very stupid," he said.

"Whaddaya mean?" I asked.

"They were upset over the way Allie Boy was running the family," he explained. "They thought he was too greedy, and they wanted a piece of the pie, so they went over his head . . . they went to the Commission. Abbe had some friends there . . . or so he thought.

"So Abbe presents his story to the Commission, and the Commission questions Allie Boy, who, you gotta remember, sits on the Commission when Junior [Carmine Persico] isn't around.

"The next meeting of the Commission, they have Allie Boy there, and Sally and Abbe and the other Commission members. They've listened to the story, now they hand down the ruling.

"The ruling is that Allie Boy is the acting boss of the family, and if Allie Boy wants to take the whole pie, he can take the whole pie. If he wants to take a piece, he can take a piece, and if he doesn't want to, he doesn't have to. He's the boss. You, Sally, and you, Abbe, you do what you are told. So now you shake hands, you kiss and make up, and you forget the whole thing.

"What happens now, Joe," Peewee continues, "is that Allie Boy is in the position that if these guys do the slightest thing wrong, they go." Then he gives me an example. "If Sally Albanese is at a table with Allie Boy and he's drinking black coffee and he spills a drop, that would be enough of an excuse for Allie Boy to use to get rid of him . . . and that's what happened to Sally. Allie Boy got rid of him."

Peewee didn't say that about Abbatemarco, who, as I said, had friends in high places. Abbatemarco just disappeared. A lot of people thought he had been killed, but he wasn't. He was allowed to disappear—make himself scarce, change his name, move someplace. I know that up to a year ago the FBI knew where he was.

The Commission had given Allie Boy a license to kill by backing his hand . . . and kill he did.

Commission members may not always have agreed with each other or been on the same side on inside political fights, but when it came to showing public respect for each other, it was a given. Respect came with the title, and no one had the right to insult or threaten a boss without paying the price. One of those who paid the costliest price of all was Carmine (Mimi) Scialo.

Mimi was a powerful soldier and the head of gambling and loan-sharking around Coney Island. He was, in fact, called by many the King of Coney Island. When he was sober, he was a piece of bread, the nicest guy you could ever meet. When he drank, he was hell on wheels, a man of incredible violence.

He hated blacks, particularly when he was under the influence, and if he saw them anywhere in his neighborhood when he was in that condition, he would think nothing of beating them up or killing them on the spot.

He also headed up a vicious gang of enforcers for the Colombo family, leg-breakers and killers who were as tough as any in the family, including those of Persico. There was one well-known tale about Mimi and some kids he'd hired to burn down a night-club in the Boston area. The story went—it was told in a New York State Senate crime hearing—that when the kids came to collect the one thousand dollars Mimi promised to pay them, he told them to get lost.

He was, of course, drunk at the time. Under normal conditions, Mimi would never refuse to pay what he owed. Anyhow, these kids were too stupid to know they were playing with fire and walk away from things. Instead, they came to a club where he was at, pulled him out of his chair, and dragged him to the men's room, where they stuffed his head in the toilet bowl and flushed it. Then they ran. They couldn't run far enough. Mimi and his killers found them and ran them over with a truck and beat them almost to death with chains. One lived long enough to tell the story at the hospital, but everyone who heard the story had a loss of memory when it came to trying to convict Mimi of the murder of the two guys.

I heard that story as well as others on the street before it came up at the state-senate hearings. It wasn't unlike Mimi to be that violent when he was drinking. He was just a wild man, crazy when he had booze in him.

He also had a reputation as a cop beater, and he got away with it. On more than one occasion, he beat up cops when he was drunk, actually broke some legs, and the charges against him were dropped. All that just added to his reputation as a vicious killer.

Mimi finally went too far one day in Garguilo's restaurant in Coney Island, a popular Italian eatery where a lot of important people came to *mangia'*. One of those people was Carlo Gambino, who walked in for dinner with some friends. Now this was after Colombo was shot, he was still alive, but unable to run the family.

Mimi was drinking at another table, and he spotted Gambino and started to hassle him in front of his friends. "You fuckin' old man," he shouts, "who the fuck do you think you are?"

He kept harassing Gambino, who, as always, kept his cool and tried to calm Mimi down. Carl was a peacemaker, a negotiator. He didn't like fights or violence unless it was absolutely necessary. It took others to shut Mimi up and get him out of Garguilo's, but it wasn't long before the whispers started in the streets: "Mimi's gone."

The whispers were right. A year or so later, on October 9, 1974, FBI agents found Mimi encased in concrete in the basement of Otto's Social Club on President Street, and the guy who had him done in was a Colombo capo they call "the Moose." But the order to handle the action came to "the Moose" from the Persicos. They probably got their marching orders from other Commission members, who weren't about to let an insult like that pass unanswered.

As for Mimi's murder, it remains unsolved, although the FBI had an informer who told them where to find the body. When they bury people like Mimi, there usually aren't any witnesses around who want to talk about it. It was sort of fitting. There were never any witnesses who lived long enough to testify about any of Mimi's murders, and he was reported to have been involved in nearly a dozen.

A short time after Mimi disappeared, some of his people decided they were going to take their revenge on the people they thought had handled Mimi's murder. The trouble was, they talked about it in a bar and one of the bar's employees dropped a dime, and the Moose's enforcers showed up to wipe out the

so-called avengers. The Persico army was swift in ending talk
of rebellion.

One of the more popular godfathers who sat on the Commission
was Tieri. He was known as Funzi, short for Funziola, but his
real name was Alphonse. He was old, in his sixties when I first
met him, and he moved slowly, but he was always the gentleman
when he talked to you.

Funzi was like Colombo as a dresser—flashy, color-coordinated, thousand-dollar hand-tailored suits and handmade
leather shoes. He also wore a lot of jewelry—expensive gold and
diamond cuff links, big gold pinky rings with huge diamonds
and a different fashion watch for every occasion, like Pierre
Cardin or Omega or Rolex, all of them encased in diamonds.
Although he stood about 5'8" or 5'9", he was bent over like an
old man, so he looked shorter than he actually was. By the time
he was in his late sixties, he had to use a mechanical voice box
to talk with, I guess because he'd lost his vocal cords to cancer
or some other disease.

For all his so-called physical frailties, Funzi could be a menacing person when he wanted to be, and in February 1974, he
scared the hell out of my godfather, my uncle Sal.

Uncle Sal had by then left my father's real estate office and
gone off on his own, investing in real estate and business ventures that looked like winners. One of those investments was in
a new restaurant known as Eddie Arcaro's in the Kings Plaza
Mall. One of his plans was to sell pizza out of Arcaro's and
compete with Sbarro's Italian deli, which also sold a variety of
Italian foods, including pizza.

The first time I realized there might be a problem was when
Funzi stopped me in front of Cantalupo Realty one day in February. "Is your father in?" he asked as he stepped from his car.

"No, sir," I said, "he's away on vacation."

"Will you do me a favor," he said with that mechanical voice
of his. "Will you get in touch with your uncle Sal and bring him
over to Sbarro's on Sixty-fifth Street. I want to see him because
I heard he's gonna put pizza in Eddie Arcaro's, and I don't like
the idea. I don't want pizza in Arcaro's."

I promised Tieri I would find Uncle Sal and bring him quickly over to Sbarro's for the meeting. I did. I called Uncle Sal and brought him to the Sbarro's office at Sixty-fifth Street and Seventeenth Avenue after explaining to him what Funzi had said to me. We got there maybe an hour to an hour and a half after Tieri first talked to me.

We went to their office on the second floor of the multistore-and-apartment building that Colombo, my father, and I had once owned and had sold to Sbarro at Tieri's request for only a ten-thousand-dollar profit.

In the office was Gennaro Sbarro, the founder of the company, and his son, Mario. They asked us in, and the elder Sbarro got straight to the point.

"We hear that you want to put pizza in Eddie Arcaro's," he said. "Our uncle [Tieri] does not want you to put pizza in Eddie Arcaro's. We'd appreciate it if you would not do this."

Sbarro was very polite but very firm about what he was saying. There were no threats, no raised voices, no shouting or pounding of desks. There didn't have to be. He had Tieri.

Uncle Sal is not known for his diplomacy or his smarts. He did, after all, know the same people my father did. People like Gambino and Colombo and a lot of high-ranking members of organized crime whom he grew up with. He exploded. "Not you, not your uncle, nobody's gonna tell me what the fuck to do!" he shouted. "Let's get outta here, Joe. Let's go."

I tried to be polite as I left, shaking hands with the Sbarros and expressing my regrets over the problem.

Uncle Sal stormed from the office, fuming as he went. "Who the fuck does Funzi think he is?' he shouted. "This ain't his territory. If Colombo were around, he wouldn't dare even ask something like that. I don't give a shit what he says, I'm gonna put pizza in the goddamn restaurant."

I tried calming him down, not too successfully, and he left cursing a blue streak about Funzi and Sbarro's and what was wrong with the world.

The next day I met Funzi outside my office again.

"Has your uncle decided what he is gonna do?" he asked.

"I don't know," I said with a shrug. "He hasn't told me."

Funzi turned around and looked straight into my eyes. His brown eyes were flashing, and the skin on his face tightened and was almost white.

"You tell your uncle Sal that if he thinks he's gonna fuckin' put pizza in Eddie Arcaro's, he's better off trying to put pizza in Scarpaci's," he said with his voice box, pointing to Scarpaci's Funeral Home across the street. Then he drove off.

Now I was a little nervous about the whole thing, so I called Uncle Sal right away and met him, telling him what Funzi said. The color drained from Uncle Sal's face, but he didn't say anything. A short time later, he sold out his interest, about 25 percent, in Arcaro's. Such is the fear the godfathers could generate with a hand motion, a name, a hidden message with a clear meaning. They never actually had to say, "I'm going to have you killed."

As far as I know, Arcaro's never did put pizza in, and Sbarro's grew from a small neighborhood chain to a popular nationwide complex. Its headquarters moved from the Sixty-fifth Street building to a modern multimillion-dollar headquarters in Commack, New York. In 1985, it became a public corporation, and its stock was sold on Wall Street. And Funzi? Later, I had to testify about him and all this in a federal racketeering case in which he was convicted and sentenced to ten years in jail. He died before he had to go to prison, and they buried him out of Scarpaci's, the same location he suggested Uncle Sal might end up in if he sold pizza in Arcaro's.

7

CIVIL RIGHTS— MAFIA STYLE

Patrolman Barry Stein shifted nervously in the hallway of the office before he spotted me working on a file at my desk.

"Where's J.C.?" Stein half-yelled across the office as I got up to greet him.

"He's not here," I said. "I don't know where he's at."

"Well, somebody's gotta come with me to Eighteenth Avenue," Stein said. "The social club is crawling with feds, and they're making a lot of noise about beatings and blood in the place."

Big shot Joe Cantalupo. Didn't know enough to keep my nose out of it. My curiosity was up, and I volunteered to go with Stein, whom I knew from the neighborhood. Stein was assigned to the Sixty-second Precinct, and every now and then stopped by to say hello to Colombo or someone else he knew at the office.

The social club was really just a converted storefront at 8648 Eighteenth Avenue, Brooklyn, where local hoods would gather, play cards, or plot their latest jobs. It was run for Colombo people by Fat Caesar Vitale, a half-assed wiseguy who, when he wasn't playing at being a hood, operated a furniture store.

Now you can find social clubs in Italian neighborhoods from the Bronx to Kansas City. They are, more often than not, gathering places for older men to sip their espresso, play cards, and boast about life in the old country. But in Manhattan's Little Italy and in Brooklyn, the social clubs were and still are a way for the mob to do its dirty work.

Places like the Ravennite Social Club on Mulberry Street in Manhattan's Little Italy or the Bergen Hunt and Fish Social Club in South Ozone Park in Queens have almost become legends in the papers because of their members. That's where people like Aniello Dellacroce, or "Charlie Wagons" Fatico, or John Gotti learned their trade and rose to positions of power. Vitale's club wasn't like that—it didn't have character or stories that buzzed in the papers—until late December 1969. That's when a local bartender named James Tumolo was beaten up in the club because he was late in paying off a loan-shark debt. He was killed a short time later in a bar fight.

By itself, that wouldn't have meant diddly squat, but somehow a story got around that the club was used as a mob torture chamber, a place where a family soldier named Salvatore D'Ambrosio was killed by Carmine Persico. "Sally D.," as he was called, apparently took a while to die, and his screams attracted the attention of a nosy female neighbor.

Calls were made, and before long the FBI, which had been looking for Sally D., raided the club. What they found were bloodstained walls, a blood-soaked shirt with Sally D.'s initials, and a fingerprint of Tumolo's.

At the time Stein showed up, I don't know what they'd found, and I had never been to the club. I didn't even know that Stein had told the FBI he was going to our real estate office to get "J.C.," Joe Colombo, to get things straightened out. He got a J.C., all right, only it was Joe Cantalupo, not Colombo.

When I arrive at the social club, agent Tallia is standing outside with another agent. He motions to me. "Come here, Joe," he says. "I want to show you something."

With that, Tallia leads me into the social club, which is nothing but one room with chairs and some tables and a bathroom, and we walk to the bathroom.

"You see this?" he says, pointing to the bloodied walls of the bathroom and an evidence bag with a bloodstained shirt. "We think Sally D., who's missing, got murdered here."

"Oh, really?" I said with a smirk. "What makes you think that?"

"This shirt," he said pointing to the bag. "It's got Sally D.'s initials on it, and it's soaked with blood."

"Let's see it," I said, reaching for it.

"No . . . no," he said. "That's evidence."

"Forget about it," I answered, and walked away as he took the bagged shirt and put it in his car.

Nothing more was said, and I left, but two hours later, FBI agents were at the real estate office, swarming all over the place, and they suddenly became nasty as hell. Two of them grabbed me, pulled my arms behind my back, and handcuffed me so tightly that my wrists were black and blue and hurt for a week afterward. All this without a word of explanation.

The next thing I know, I'm being hustled out into a car, driven downtown, fingerprinted, and then paraded before a waiting press that was about to have a field day writing stories about the social club "torture room," the bloodstained walls, and the screams of Sally D. as he was being killed. All I could do was keep my mouth shut and ride out the storm.

At first Tallia and his buddies accused me of trying to take the shirt from the crime scene. Then the press was told I was being investigated because I had come to the social club to "take care of things" for Colombo when the FBI raided it. I had to appear before a special federal grand jury investigating the disappearance of D'Ambrosio and one of his friends, Fred (No Nose) DeLucia.

I didn't know anything about the killing. I didn't know what kind of trouble Sally D. was in or with whom—I didn't even know for sure he'd been whacked. All I knew was what Tallia had said and what the papers were now saying.

From January 18 to January 20, Stein, Joe Notch, Colombo, me . . . everyone was paraded before the jury. At the same time, my father was making his own headlines, testifying about the good character of Colombo before a state legislative crime hearing, complaining about the FBI staking out our real estate office and harassing everyone because of Colombo.

"In my opinion," my father told the committee, "Colombo is a perfect gentlemen." Then he zeroed in on the FBI. "The FBI parks their car directly in front of my office. I have been harassed for many years because of Colombo. I had a good reputation as a businessman and now I have lost that. The Italians in my neighborhood have got me down as the head of the Mafia."

It was a three-ring circus, and the media was making life miserable. Then, without warning, the feds flipped the case to Brooklyn District Attorney Eugene Gold, and on February 25, 1970, Stein and I were indicted for perjury and tried.

A year and a half and more than three thousand dollars later, a jury took just fifteen minutes to acquit me when it heard Tallia admit on the stand that I had asked "to see" the shirt, "not take the shirt."

I was smiling as I came out of the courtroom with my attorney until I saw Tallia standing in the hallway.

"So now you're a stand-up guy, is that it, Joe?" he asked. "They're all gonna talk about you 'cause you didn't fall, right? When are you gonna learn, Joe? You ain't in the paratroopers now . . . you're in the big boys' playpen."

"I've got nothing to say to you, Tallia," I answered. "Go frame somebody else—if you can."

It was the first heavy-handed squeeze play by Tallia since we had met. Up to this point, it had been all talk between us. He had tried to convince me to stay clear of Colombo and his friends—an impossible thing to do if I wanted to work for my father. Besides, I liked Colombo, I liked his style. Now, Tallia was starting to play hardball with me, and I didn't care for it too much. It had been expensive both in time and money, and nobody—not even Colombo or my father—was around to help. It was like the time I got hassled by the law in a Suffolk County jail as a kid, and later in North Carolina while I was in the 82nd Airborne.

On a scale of zero to ten, my indictment was probably a zero in terms of important events, but it was, like my father's public testimony, the beginning of a new kind of trouble—of what was to become open and public warfare between Colombo and the FBI.

March was a red-letter month. Gambino was indicted by a federal grand jury in Manhattan for conspiracy in a $5 million armored robbery. It looked like a trumped-up case to me. I couldn't imagine Carl getting involved in cheap street crap like that, but he kept me busy notarizing statements from his doctors and lawyers about his health being too poor to appear in court. Colombo was indicted twice, first for tax evasion by a federal grand jury and then for perjury when state officials said he lied in trying to get a state real estate broker's license. These events produced indictments of a half-dozen other important organized crime figures, and headline stories about what bosses talked about when they were secretly and illegally taped by the FBI in New Jersey.

All this angered Colombo more and more, but on April 30, the FBI and the Eastern District Federal Strike Force pushed him over the brink by arresting his son, Joseph Colombo, Jr. The charge was melting down $500,000 worth of U.S. coins illegally for their silver content. They really hit a raw nerve with that charge.

Colombo had gone out of his way to keep his kids out of trouble. He spoiled them rotten, gave them money, jewels, clothes, businesses—you name it, they had it. He really wanted them to stay out of the mob and out of trouble. He had even warned his own shylocks and family members not to lend them money or get them involved in any activities that even had the smell of illegality.

Despite what their father said and what he gave them, Anthony and Joey Junior, in particular, were always walking on the edge because they were always broke. They spent like drunken sailors on the high life, wine and women. They also loved gambling—horses, sports betting, cards, craps, the casinos. They knew better. Who else should know better? You can't win at gambling. They knew it. I knew it. Anyone in the mob knows it, yet for some crazy reason some of the worst gamblers in the world are in the mob. Joey and Anthony were among them. They'd bet on the next raindrop just for the thrill.

As a result, they always needed money. When the price of silver went up and the government decided to put copper in its coins, Joey came up with a scheme to melt down old U.S. coins for their silver and sell them to silver dealers.

Joe Junior had access to a lot of the coins from mob vending machines and businesses in Brooklyn and upstate. Rocky Miraglia and Joe Notch were working with him on the scheme. He supplied the money, a lot of the coins. With a coin dealer's help, they were going to sell off their hoards at huge profits. Only the price of silver dropped. Joey lost money. Miraglia and Joe Notch not only got mob people to cover Joey's losses, but they applied some muscle on the dealers to cover some of the losses. One of them talked. The result was the indictment.

Colombo just couldn't believe it. He was convinced it was part of a conspiracy by the FBI and the strike force to get him, and now they were making it personal, going after his family. He couldn't understand it any more than any father could understand why his son holds up a liquor store or mugs an old lady. He never wanted his children to be part of the crime world, but they were.

"It's bullshit!" he screamed. "Why would my son want to do that? If he wants money, I give him one hundred thousand dollars . . . whatever he wants! Why would my son want to do that?"

He pounded the desk in the office and yelled at the top of his lungs. "Those fuckin' feebs! They ain't satisfied with going after me, they gotta go after my kids. They're trying to get at me through my kids. They're fuckin' rotten."

While everyone in the office watched him blow off steam, Colombo kept ranting about his son Joey. "Those bastards, they got that poor kid locked up till tomorrow!" he shouted. "For what? He ain't done nothing. This is discrimination, that's what it is. It's because the kid's named Colombo, because his name ends in a vowel. The Mafia, the Mafia . . . bullshit the Mafia. They're just trying to screw me. They just want to screw Italians," he continued. "You don't see them do this to Jews or the Irish or the Polacks. Just fuckin' Italians. Well, they can't do that. I'm not gonna let them get away with it."

That was the beginning the Italian-American Civil Rights League. There in the office of my father, with Colombo screaming and raising hell, the league was roughly formed. Colombo called me over and told me to get sticks and cardboard and crayons and paint.

"I want you to make up signs!" he yelled. "I want them to say, 'The FBI Frames Italian-Americans . . . Italians Unite.' Yeah that's good . . . 'Italians Unite.' And have some say, 'The FBI is prejudiced against Italians.' I like that. Make up signs, Joey, lots of signs. We're going to go out and picket those motherfuckers. They're not gonna push me and my kids around anymore."

Hours later, after I'd managed to scrape up some wooden posts and signboards and write them out in crayon and paint, Colombo, his wife, JoJo, Anthony, some of his crew who had come to the office to sympathize, and some neighborhood families and their kids marched out, drove into Manhattan, and began picketing the FBI at its headquarters on Sixty-ninth Street. While they picketed, Joe Junior, Miraglia, and Joe Notch sat locked up in the Federal House of Detention waiting to be arraigned in court the next morning.

That overnight detention probably saved Joe Notch's life. I am almost certain that Colombo would have killed Joe Notch if he could have gotten his hands on him first. He almost killed Joe Notch one time earlier, when he had used his association with Colombo to get him credit at a Las Vegas casino where he ran up a bill of over ten thousand dollars.

Colombo found out about the debt when he got a call from a friend of his at the casino.

"Is Smitty there?" the caller asked.

Smitty was the code name that friends of Colombo used when they called our office looking for him.

"Who's asking for him?" I said.

"Tell him John the Wop from Vegas," he answered.

I went to Colombo's office and told him who was on the phone. He picked up the receiver, and I could hear his Vegas friend ask if he would vouch for Joe Notch's credit.

Colombo went bananas. Joe Notch had lost ten thousand dollars at a casino that Colombo visited regularly with friends. The casino people reasoned that since Joe Notch had been with him on some of these visits as his driver and gofer, his credit was good. Colombo guaranteed Joe Notch would pay, and then called Joe Notch in from the street where he was keeping an eye out for Bureau agents.

Colombo completely lost his cool, grabbing the towering Joe Notch by the jacket, shaking him as if he were a tree, and slapping him across the mouth.

"I'm gonna kill you, you stupid bastard!" he yelled, choking him at the neck. "I swear to Christ you'll be a dead man if you ever run up credit in Vegas again. You hear me?" Joe Notch was nodding and shaking from head to foot. I don't know if he was shaking because Colombo was grabbing him and shaking or because he was just plain scared. It was probably a little of both. Colombo, whose face was red with anger, shouted some more. "Now you get that money, you son of a bitch . . . and you get it tonight if you wanna see daylight."

Joe Notch raised the money somehow, and Colombo kept him around. I never could figure out why. It was a mistake. He wasn't loyal like Miraglia. Joe Notch was one of those who got Joey Junior gambling heavily. He'd have screwed Colombo in a minute if he thought he could do it safely.

Joe Notch had no conscience. He didn't care who he hurt when it came to gambling, even his own kid. He once won $110,000 in the numbers racket. Then he came to my father for help in getting his son into LaSalle Military Academy. The tuition was five thousand dollars, and he gave my father the money. The next month he'd lost all he had and came to my father to get the five thousand dollars back. His kid was thrown out of the academy because Joe Notch couldn't pay the tuition.

When Colombo died and the mob family was split up, Joe Notch went to work for Rambar, the chicken company owned by Pete Castellana, who was a soldier in the Gambino crime family. He worked for Rambar by day, and at night he dealt cards in a Mulberry Street game for Jimmy the Blond Corrao, whose son is now the underboss, the second of the Gambino family under Gotti. Anyhow, Joe Notch liked to drink a lot as well as gamble, and one night he gets a little smashed and asks this girl who had been with Jimmy the Blond if she would drive him home. She agrees, and then Joe Notch tries to come on to her, suggesting they spend the night together and that she can do this to him and he can do that to her. She tells him to drop dead and drops him off at his home. The girl turns out to be Jimmy the Blond's daughter. The next thing I heard was Joe Notch was in Victor Memorial Hospital. When Jimmy the Blond heard what he'd done, he sent his people out looking for Joe Notch, and when they got through with him, he had to spend a week in the hospital recuperating. You don't do things like that to the daughters or even the girlfriends of wiseguys. Joe Notch just didn't care.

The night of picketing was just the beginning. A couple of nights later, Colombo held a meeting at Vinnie Buffa's Pisa Caterers across the street. He called in a lot of chips for that meeting; a lot of friends, and politicians like Meade Esposito, who was the Democratic boss of Brooklyn, judges, businessmen, and people with influence were called in. Colombo was popular with a lot of people, both in and out of the mob. He'd done a lot of favors, contributed a lot of bucks to a lot of political campaigns, and they all owed him.

"We're gonna organize," Joe announced. "We're gonna set up an organization—an Italian civil-rights organization—and we're gonna break the FBI's chops. I want it real legal, like the Jewish and black groups, you know, B'Nai B'Rith, or the NAACP. We're gonna make Brooklyn the Selma, Alabama, of the Italians. Right?"

Everyone cheered, and that's exactly what he did. He put Nate Marcone up as the front man to head the organization, but it was Colombo who was calling the shots. He picked Marcone because he was a legitimate businessman, a caterer, not a gangster or politician or lawyer. Then he named people who would do as they were told to be captains in the Italian-American Civil Rights League, and I was one of them. So were a lot of members of his mob.

Our job was not unlike the job of capos in his family. We were to organize our friends into groups of ten or more and get them to join. They, in turn, were to get their friends who were Italian to join the league. We were to organize Italians all over Brooklyn and Long Island and get them to join the organization. Membership would cost ten bucks a year, and we'd have chapters in Coney Island, Bensonhurst, all over. The idea was to organize and get more people out on the picket lines to make the FBI's image lousy—to show they were picking on Italians, linking us to the Mafia, arresting people just because their names ended in vowels.

The truth of it is, it was all hype. The real motive was to give Colombo political muscle he never had. I know he never expected it to work the way it did. It just took off like a spaceship for Mars. It was simply incredible. Thousands joined from all over the country—big names, small names, entertainers, politicians, judges, legislators—it was unbelievable.

Within six weeks, we had five chapters in Brooklyn alone, and a rented headquarters office at the Park Sheraton Hotel in Manhattan. And the money . . . it was coming in by the bucketful.

Not only did Italians who thought they were being maligned send in millions of dollars to support the cause for Italian civil rights, they joined the Sixty-ninth Street picket lines with Colombo, who was out there night after night, every night. They waved their red, white, and green Italian flags and wore buttons with Italian colors and slogans like "Italian Power," "Italians Are Beautiful," and "We Want Equal Rights." They gave Bronx cheers and shouted at agents when they left FBI headquarters or when they brought in people for arrests. When Colombo was busted on a bum jewelry case in Nassau County, Italians from all over rallied to give him moral as well as financial support. And when a civil suit was filed to stop the picketing by so-called neighbors of the FBI, Italian supporters jammed a state supreme court courtroom in Manhattan to protest the action.

In the courtroom, Colombo kept his people in line, and *The New York Times* quoted League attorney Barry Slotnick as telling the judge, "The defendants in this courtroom have all taken a day off to maintain the last semblance of dignity they have— their right of free speech."

The *Times* quoted Judge Starke as saying he was impressed "with their reasonable conduct" in the courtroom and that he would postpone making a decision on whether or not to limit the hours of the picketing until after he personally visited the picket line and observed their conduct.

What a crock. They couldn't have put on a better performance if they had been on Broadway. Marcone told the *Times* that Colombo, his son Anthony, Joe DeCicco, and myself had organized the League. Of course, he didn't say where or why, and no one noticed that Joe DeCicco was "Joe Butter," a Gambino family soldier.

"What we do is law-abiding," he said. "We get the people in buses, cabs, and private cars and bring them in. We picket for our rights, and we do it within the law." Colombo said they picketed from 4:00 P.M. to 11:00 P.M., and that they were picketing because the FBI was picking on his family to get at him.

"If I do something, then I deserve to pay the penalty," Colombo told the *Times*. "But the FBI shouldn't harass my children and relatives because of what I do."

Colombo had done in the court and on the picket line what no other crime boss since Al Capone had done, he had gone public—he was using the media to fight the FBI and the U.S. Department of Justice. The trouble was, he wasn't smart enough to figure out that all this picketing, all this publicity, was just making him a bigger target than ever for the FBI.

A month after the courtroom appearance, Colombo and the league organized the biggest rally for Italians in the history of New York. It was a mob fiesta, and everybody joined in the celebration, including politicians who would normally have never been caught dead with Colombo or his hoods or even someone like me. It was a command performance.

8

WHEN CAESAR DIES

They came from Detroit and Rochester, from Newark and Staten Island, from Long Island and Queens, but mostly they came from Brooklyn. Thousands of them—50,000, 60,000, 70,000 of them—swarmed around Columbus Circle on Joe Colombo's self-proclaimed Italian Unity Day.

They closed the waterfront from Brooklyn to New Jersey. Bakeries, restaurants, delicatessens, shops, and stores of every kind closed in Bensonhurst, Bay Ridge, Coney Island, all to celebrate June 29, 1970, Italian Unity Day.

Was it voluntary? Was it spontaneous? For the most part, I think most Italian-Americans were caught up in the excitement that Colombo was generating, but there was a lot of orchestrating and, where necessary, pressure.

Colombo and the Italian-American Civil Rights League had sent out more than eighty thousand placards throughout Brooklyn to stores in advance of Unity Day advising consumers that the store, the bar, whatever the business, would be closed that day. The store owners were told to display the placards and follow the rules—close up for the day.

A majority of the store owners were willing. They wanted to keep their customers happy; they didn't want to antagonize people. If they were smart, they could use their support of

Unity Day to get more customers. But not all the businessmen
saw it that way. Not all of them were thrilled at the thought of
losing money for a day, so they resisted, and some got visits from
friends of Colombo. Others got more violent reminders, like
broken windows or the suggestion that what was clean and open
on Unity Day might be dirty and need sweeping out the following day if they didn't join in our fiesta. A few visits like that and
the word spread like wildfire, there were all kinds of rumors of
what might happen to those who didn't "cooperate." It was
more rumor than substance, but it was effective. Brooklyn was
closed up tight.

I remember Fat Caesar Vitale telling the New York *Daily
News* that league members had heard of "close on Monday or
sweep up on Tuesday" pressure on businessmen and denying
any truth to the rumors. "We have checked out every report,
and I mean checked out the reports of threats. They are not
true," he told the *Daily News*. What Vitale didn't say was that
he sent people out on Colombo's orders to keep stores in line.

Vitale was only twenty-four, but he was close to Joe Junior
and Anthony, who were around his age, and Colombo's brother-
in-law, Joe La Rosa, who was in his forties. Colombo made
Vitale the league's secretary-treasurer, while Anthony was the
vice-president. Vitale owned the social club where Sally D'Ambrosio had been whacked. He ran a well-known furniture company, but his biggest asset was his connection with entertainers
like Jimmy Roselli and Frank Sinatra. He had friends who had
access to them, and he was able to handle the entertainment
people for the league, get them to appear and perform at rallies
and at fund-raisers like the one at the Felt Forum later that year.

Obviously, Vitale was no saint. He wasn't just window dress-
ing either. He was part of the mob woodwork, an up-and-com-
ing, business-oriented street guy with lots of smarts and plenty
of ambition. He wasn't a made guy, but he had potential. He did
the right things for Colombo, Colombo's kids, and later the
Persicos.

Vitale's career in the mob ended violently in Florida in 1982.
He was running a furniture business in Oakland Park as he did
in Brooklyn, and he was using his entertainment connections to

book acts for a restaurant and music theater he managed. At the same time, he was working for a branch of Carmine Persico's family that was involved in narcotics. In February 1982, the cops found him after he had been shot a dozen times and had his throat cut. His wife was killed, riddled with bullets, and his house ransacked. The killers, I was told, were looking for a million-dollar stash he had hidden under a staircase. I don't know if the killers found it, but I was told police believed he was killed because of a narcotics deal that went sour with a Cuban and Colombian drug dealer while he represented the Persico group's interest.

Vitale was typical of the fringe guys Colombo put in the league's management. Around guys like him were heavier hitters to make sure that things moved and shook the way he wanted—Miraglia, Iannaci, DeCicco, Colombo's son Anthony, as well as people like me. The league was a great cover for the wiseguys and the associates as well.

While I was close to Colombo and his kids and I had what you'd call position in the league, I wasn't all that effective at times because I was too busy playing around . . . cheating on my wife. Sometimes it got me in a whole lot of trouble.

During the early days of the league's formation, I began running around with a good-looking Italian gal, I'll call her Connie. It isn't her real name, but naming her won't serve any purpose except to embarrass her.

I met Connie through a real estate salesgirl I knew. We started dating and then shacking up in an apartment I had with a doctor friend of mine. One night I was on the picket line with Colombo, the next night I was jumping in the sack with Connie. There was nothing more than sex between us, but one night Colombo called me aside when I reported to the picket line and talked to me, like father to son.

"You're screwing around with this girl Connie?" he asked.

I was embarrassed, but I nodded my head. "Yeah, Joe. My wife don't know about," I said, almost whispering.

"That ain't the problem, Joey," Colombo said. "The problem is she belongs to a goodfellow. She belongs to Frankie Butch."

"Yeah, so?" I asked, like a dummy.

"Joey, you can't do this thing," he said. "You can't screw around with a goodfellow's girl. It's against the rules. You can get hurt . . . bad."

I almost shit. I didn't know it, but Connie was the girlfriend of a member of the Gambino family, and word had gotten back to Colombo that unless he put a stop to what I was doing, he'd have to do something to me, or Frankie Butch would. So he sat me down, father to son, and told me what the rules were: that the girls and wives of wiseguys, goodfellows, were off-limits. Those that broke those rules could get beaten or worse, they could wind up the way his father did, although he didn't tell me about his father.

"Okay, Joe," I said. "You told me. That's it. I won't see her no more." And I didn't. I saw her, but I never fooled around with her anymore, and she knew why.

You would have thought I had learned my lesson from that, but I didn't. The next thing I know, I get involved with another gal, a really gorgeous thing who I'm going to call Rosie. I met her in the office when she came looking for an apartment. Funny thing, she couldn't go anywhere without her sister—I'll call her Anne, who was big and fat—because her husband didn't trust her and he didn't trust men. He had good reason.

Rosie's husband, Tony, was a goodfellow, a member of the Gambino family. Once again I didn't know it; I didn't know he was a wiseguy. I knew she was married, but so was I and we were both adults; we knew what we were doing.

Whenever she went out, Tony, her husband, would ask her where she was going.

"I'm going out shopping with Anne," she'd say. "I'll be okay. Don't worry about me. I'll be with Anne."

She'd bring Anne with her to my bachelor's apartment, and Anne would sit out in the living room on the couch and we'd be in the bedroom doing our thing. Rosie would leave the door open and she'd moan and groan while we were having sex, but Anne stayed in the living room.

Rosie was really something. She drove me crazy with her sexual appetite and her attention. When I was sick, she'd send me flowers, everywhere flowers. Flowers in the office, flowers at home, and she'd always sign the card "Charlie." How the hell do you explain to your wife getting a dozen red roses at home from someone named Charlie every time you're sick? I did it with great difficulty.

"Who is this Charlie?" my wife would ask. "Why is he sending you roses?"

I had to think fast and make it sound good. "Charlie's the salesman over Caplan Buick where I buy my cars," I said. "He's a nice guy, but he always worries about my health."

There was a Charlie at Caplan Buick, and I had bought cars there, but I suspect my wife didn't buy the tale. Whether she did or not, she didn't press it.

It didn't take long before Colombo sat me down over Rosie.

"Joey," he said, "haven't I told you not to fool around with a goodfellow's woman?"

"Yeah, Joe, I know," I answered. "I've been doing like you said. I've steered clear of Connie."

"Not her, stupid," he said. "You been jumping Rosie. She's the wife of Big Tony from the Gambinos."

I must have turned ten different shades of white. I could feel the color drain from my face as I stood there. "Honest to God, Joe," I said, "I never knew. So help me, I never knew. I won't see her again." And I didn't. After that, I was a regular at the picket line and at the Columbus Circle rally.

It would be a serious mistake to get the idea that Colombo organized the rally all on his own. He had a lot of clout, a lot of power, but not that kind of power. He did it with the permission of other bosses, at the very least with the permission and support of Carl Gambino. Without Gambino, he could not have closed the waterfront, nor would the longshoremen or the teamsters and warehousemen have walked off their jobs. It was Gambino who gave the green light to Anthony Scotto, who was then a vice-president of the International Longshoreman's Union and the boss of ILA Local 1814, to close down the waterfront and back Colombo. I never figured out why Gambino did it, but I know he regretted it.

June 29, 1970, was a sea of green, white, and red Italian flags and colors. It was beautiful. Wall-to-wall people jamming Columbus Circle, marching to Sixty-ninth Street and Third Avenue to the FBI headquarters, demanding their rights, demanding that the feds stop harassing Italians. And in the crowd, if you look back at the pictures, is a Who's Who of Colombo's mob and wiseguys from other mobs. Greg Scarpa, DeCicco, Colombo and his two sons, Miraglia, Iannaci, Nicky Bianco . . . pick a Colombo mob name, and if he wasn't in jail, he was there, egging the crowd on, soaking up the attention and the cheers of the marchers.

Colombo was like I'd never seen him before. He was caught up in this thing. He greeted the politicians as they came up to the speaker's platform behind the statue of Christopher Columbus—politicians like Democratic congressmen Mario Biaggi and Adam Clayton Powell; the city's deputy mayor, Richard Aurelio, who tried to stand in for Mayor John Lindsay and got booed because Lindsay didn't have the guts to show himself; and the former city controller, Mario Procaccino, who had lost to Lindsay in a mayoral campaign but got cheers when he spoke to the crowd.

The loudest cheers were reserved for Colombo, who was like a Caesar up there. "This day belongs to you, the people," he told the crowd. "You are organized, united, and nobody can take you apart anymore." The crowd went wild, pointing their right index fingers to the sky and chanting, "One . . . one . . . one."

The march to the FBI's headquarters ended three months of picketing, but something had happened in the meantime to Colombo. He liked the public attention. He liked being on TV shows like Dick Cavett's. He liked the attention the media gave him, particularly the television reporters. When people like Walter Cronkite interviewed him, I think he really began to believe his own shit—he really thought he could be somebody other than what he was.

He teamed up with a radical Jewish leader named Meir Kahane, whose street-fighting Jewish Defense League members caused more than a few problems for legitimate Jewish organizations. Kahane later moved to Israel, to run for office over there, and gave up his American citizenship. But Colombo and our league and Kahane and his league demonstrating together, recruiting together, mouthing off to the media together, just caused more and more problems.

The league brought money and, most important, power. Colombo was named Man of the Year by the *Triboro Post*. The league had the fund-raiser at the Felt Forum with Sinatra, Sammy Davis, Jr., Vic Damone, Jerry Vail, and Connie Francis. They raised nearly a million bucks for a hospital the league was supposed to build but never did in Brooklyn. Colombo and his kids were out there showing their muscle with the league, squeezing advertisers of the TV series *The FBI*, until they forced them and even the Department of Justice to stop using the words "Mafia" and "La Cosa Nostra." They forced other advertisers to stop making commercials that ridiculed or made light of the Italian language. They forced Al Ruddy, the producer of *The Godfather*, to delete the same words that *The FBI* had deleted from their script and, in the process, hire some of Colombo's people to play in street scenes and in some select roles of the *Godfather* story itself. In return, Colombo, with the help of Gambino and Tieri, got Manhattan's Little Italy to roll over, let their shops and streets and people be used for movie shots. And they got the unions to play ball and not hassle the producers.

All this made Colombo think, really believe, that he was invulnerable . . . an untouchable. Instead, he was a lightning rod attracting jolts of trouble. He didn't stop the Bureau or even some local law-enforcement people from going after him. He just prodded them to squeeze tighter.

A month after the big rally, then Nassau district attorney William Cahn and a grand jury indicted Colombo and twenty-three others on charges of criminal contempt, shylocking, and gambling. Colombo did exact one concession from the Nassau DA. Cahn never used the words "Mafia" or "La Cosa Nostra" in referring to Colombo. He told a television reporter Colombo was an important organized crime figure who ran a crime family, but he wouldn't use "Mafia" no matter how hard the reporter pressed him.

All this while hundreds of demonstrators, myself included,

paraded outside the Mineola, Long Island, courthouse with placards I had helped make up charging Cahn with being anti-
Italian and being a tool of the FBI. Anthony, the league's
vice-president, and Joe Junior kept the demonstrators in line so
there wouldn't be any trouble.

On December 1, 1970, the federal coin-melting case against
Joe Junior ended in a mistrial in Brooklyn Federal Court when
some jurors admitted they'd read stories in Long Island and
New York newspapers identifying Joe as the son of a crime boss.

A little over two weeks later, the FBI went Colombo-hunting.
They didn't call it that, but that's what it was. The Bureau had
a warrant for the arrest of Miraglia for perjury, for lying to a
federal grand jury about Joe Junior's deal to melt down silver
coins. They could have nailed Miraglia anytime, because they
always knew where he was. He and Colombo were always being
watched by Tallia and other agents. The Bureau, however, likes
to make a statement when people like Colombo give them a hard
time, so they waited for the right moment, they waited until
Miraglia parked his gold Buick station wagon in the official
parking space of some New York State Supreme Court judge at
60 Centre Street. Then they closed in. Of course, Colombo was
in the car, and beside him was a briefcase. It was his briefcase
with the entire membership list of the league, including the
name of Gambino and some other top mob people. The agents
grabbed Miraglia as he sat next to Colombo and they seized the
briefcase, using the excuse that they believed it was Miraglia's.

Colombo screamed like a stuck pig. He made so much noise,
in fact, that a city police team came by and handed Miraglia a
parking ticket for parking illegally. Then the agents took Miraglia and Colombo's briefcase off to the Brooklyn Federal
Courthouse, leaving Colombo sitting in the car, fuming. He got
the briefcase and its contents back eventually, but not without
the feds leaking out some of its contents and forcing him to
appear before a federal grand jury to explain who "Carl" was
and why there was an entry for thirty thousand dollars next to
his name, and who Frankie the Beast and John the Wop and a
whole lot of other people were and what the figures next to their
names were. The people he named, like Gambino, were called

before the jury and made to squirm. It was embarrassing for Colombo, for Gambino, and for the league. Another wiseguy on the list, acting boss Tommy Eboli of the Genovese family, was shaken down at Kennedy Airport by customs when he came back from a trip to Europe. He was really pissed. The Bureau was making people understand more and more that the league was really just a front for the mob, and that a lot of people were being used and didn't realize it.

Colombo was in that parking lot that day because he was being tried in state supreme court for lying on the 1967 sworn affidavit he filed to try to get the real estate broker's license. Less than a week after the briefcase incident, he was convicted by the state jury for lying on the affidavit.

Colombo didn't let up. He kept criticizing the FBI in the media, and in February 1971, it looked like his pressure was paying off.

On February 23, the case against Joe Junior fell apart. The government's number-one witness, coin dealer Richard Salamone, recanted his original testimony that Joe Junior had given him twenty thousand dollars to invest in the coin-meltdown scheme. He said the money came from Iannaci and that he had repaid Iannaci.

When the federal judge said he didn't intend to let the case even go to the jury because of the turnaround in Salamone's testimony, Colombo took more shots at the FBI and at Tallia in particular.

"That's the face of crime in this country," he told a *New York Times* reporter as he pointed to Ray Tallia. "We don't fear them and we never will." Then he added it was "the FBI's frame-up" that led him and other league members to protest the arrest of his son by picketing the FBI's headquarters.

The federal jury acquitted Joe Junior, but a month later Colombo was jailed in Nassau County by DA Cahn, this time for getting paid to act as a mediator in a dispute between thieves in a $750,000 jewelry heist.

While Cahn made the arrest, the FBI and the federal strike force that had gone after Joe Junior were behind the indictment. Cahn said they'd worked on the case for three years with men from his office. It wasn't much of a case, but it kept Colombo in the Nassau lockup overnight while his lawyers hustled to find a judge to free him on bail. A week later, on March 11, Colombo was sentenced to two and a half years for the real estate perjury charge. He didn't lose a minute letting the press know how he was screwed.

"They have one set of rules for the average man and a special set for Joe Colombo," he told a *New York Times* reporter. "I hope to God," he added, "they let me out on bail while this case is appealed and leave me alone to do all the good things I want to do."

The good things he said he had planned were the construction of a hospital, a narcotics-rehabilitation facility for addicts, and a home for the elderly he and league members wanted to build. That was really hype for the media and the politicians. The millions he and his people were collecting was going south. There wasn't going to be a hospital, or a home, or a rehab center—that was just talk that kept the money rolling in.

Meanwhile, things were really getting out of hand. Colombo wasn't paying attention to business. People were losing money. Associates, soldiers, capos—worse, other bosses—were starting to feel the heat. The more Colombo mouthed off, the more he was publicized in the press, the more the Bureau turned up the heat.

On March 22, in Huntington, Long Island, Colombo was honored as Man of the Year by the league at a $125-a-plate dinner that raised nearly $200,000. He loved it, so did the family and all his friends. More headlines.

A day later, the TV show *The FBI* drops the words "Mafia" and "La Cosa Nostra" from its scripts. At the same time, four league members, one of them Marcone, were busted by police on Staten Island for assaulting a cop while they picketed the Staten Island *Advance.* They were picketing because the paper had identified some mob people living on Staten Island. The articles and the picketing were bad for business, bad for some of Gambino's more important capos who were singled out— people like Jimmy Failla and Paul Castellano.

Squeeze some more, said the Bureau and the Justice Department higher-ups, so on April 3, they arrested Colombo again with twenty-one others, including his girlfriend, for operating a gambling ring. More bad publicity . . . more lost business . . . more pressure on everyone . . . more attention on Colombo and the league . . . more grumbling in the mob.

The worst of the grumbling came from the Gallos, the same group that had rebelled against and fought Profaci. In March, Crazy Joe Gallo was released from Sing Sing State Prison after serving more than nine years there. His gang members had a big party for him, and I was told Colombo sent over some welcome-home money that Gallo told him where to shove. By May, Crazy Joe was challenging Colombo's authority in south Brooklyn, particularly around President Street, Carroll Street, and Atlantic Street.

It was in that area that Gallo and his people started going to shopkeepers, ripping out league signs from their windows, and warning them to stay open on June 29, the day Colombo had planned a second Unity Day rally of the league.

"Colombo's just using the dues from poor Italians to pay for his lousy fight with the FBI," Gallo told some merchants. He told the shopkeepers to "stay open" Unity Day. Those that didn't, he suggested, would have trouble . . . serious trouble.

When Colombo found out what was happening, he sent his sons back into the area to tell the merchants to put the signs back in the windows and stay closed on Unity Day. They guaranteed that the shopkeepers would be safe. A lot of merchants weren't convinced. They were between a rock and a hard place. Defy Colombo, lose business and get in trouble . . . defy Gallo, get burned down or worse. In the middle of all this comes a fight. Some of Gallo's muscle went after Miraglia and Colombo in front of the real estate office, and I wound up beaten to hell by one of Gallo's golf club–swinging thugs.

The long and short of it was, Colombo was losing control because too much of his time was spent on pushing the league and fighting publicly with the FBI and the Justice Department. Toward the end of May—I can't really place the date except I know it was just before the fight with the Gallo muscle—

Colombo turned away from the man he needed the most—the man who had made him what and who he was.

I was standing next to a telephone pole in front of Cantalupo Realty with my father and Colombo. They had just come back from Gambino's house, where the old man had talked to Colombo like a son. It was at that point that I realized Colombo's ego was out of control.

"Joey . . . do me a favor," my father was saying. "Take Carl's advice. Step down from the league. The old man asked you to step down from the league. Jesus, Joey, do it."

Colombo shook his head, staring at something on the ground. My father continued, "Joey . . . put a politician in . . . an entertainer . . . a movie star, and step back. Step away. Get out of the spotlight. You know what Carl said. You can do everything you're doing now, but do it from behind the scenes."

Colombo shook his head vigorously. "No!" he said angrily. "This is *my* thing. I don't care what he says, what he thinks. This is *my thing*, and I'm gonna run it."

It had become an obsession with him. He couldn't let go. He loved the fame, the publicity. He was like a little Caesar, and he was ready to be crowned on Unity Day.

My phone rang at home as I put the finishing touches on what I was going to wear to the Unity Day rally.

"Joey, what are you doing?" asked Doc John, the doctor who shared the bachelor's apartment with me.

"I'm getting ready to go to the rally," I answered.

"Don't go, Joey," he said heavily. "Joe just got shot."

I sucked in the air, almost fell into the chair next to the phone, and sat silent for almost a minute before saying anything.

"Jesus, is he dead?" I asked.

"Not yet," he answered. "They took him to Roosevelt Hospital."

I hung up. A half hour later, I was part of the teeming madhouse at the hospital. It was like a scene out of *The Godfather*. Wiseguys on the doors. Wiseguys in the corridors. Wherever I looked, there were wiseguys—big shots, loan sharks, hitters, whoever—milling about. And there were cops, all kinds of cops, in uniform and plainclothes, asking questions, keeping watch, or just standing there like lumps.

JoJo—Lucille Colombo—and her sister-in-law, Loretta, the kids . . . they were all there in the waiting room. Joe Junior, Anthony, Vinnie Colombo . . . all the boys were in a daze. Colombo's youngest kids, Christopher, ten, and Catherine, five, were kept safely at home. Nobody said much. Some weeping, some praying, people like me paying their respects. Colombo was in surgery. He'd been there for nearly an hour, and he would remain in surgery for five hours and then live like a vegetable for nearly seven more years.

Anthony was taking it the hardest. He was not with his father when he was shot. He'd left him to go back to the Park Sheraton Hotel to change clothes when his father was shot. "I shoulda been there . . . with him," he said, his voice breaking. "Maybe . . . if I was there . . . this wouldn't . . ." He covered his face as his eyes welled up, and walked down the corridor away from those of us who had been talking to him, trying to console him.

He got his act together quickly and talked to some newsmen who were badgering people for statements. "This was my father's pride and joy," he said of the league as he talked to the newsmen. "It was all that he lived for this past year. I'd be a helluva son if I didn't make sure it continues." That same night, he said league plans to open a 230-acre upstate summer camp for kids three days later would be carried out. It was crazy, bizarre, as if he was building a monument to his father even though he knew it was all like a card shark's sleight of hand—now you see it, now you don't. They had the land and they did announce the opening of the camp, but nothing happened after that that I heard of.

Anthony was right on one thing. He'd put his finger on the cause of his father's shooting without realizing it. Colombo had spent the last year living for the league and the publicity he could generate with it. If Colombo had been paying attention to business, mob business, he would probably still be alive today.

In the corridor outside the waiting room, the wiseguys were already plotting their revenge. Miraglia, Joe Notch, Vinnie

Aloi, bodyguards . . . "How we gonna get revenge?" one said. "We gotta get Gallo for this," another answered. "With time . . . with time," a cooler head advised. Colombo was still on the table—surgeons were still picking pieces of his skull out of his brain—and the wiseguys were plotting a war while the women cried. Joe Junior and Anthony were numb, and they were afraid because they didn't know who was going to be next—whether it would be one of them or one of the capos they were supposed to trust. Right out of *The Godfather.* So help me.

Caesar had been struck down, and everyone was certain that Joe Gallo was responsible. A black man named Jerome Johnson had shot Colombo for no apparent reason.

It had to be Gallo, they reasoned. He'd defied Colombo. He had recruited black militants into his gang and befriended blacks in prison. Johnson was a black. He had a prison record. But they never got to talk to Johnson. He was killed by one of Colombo's bodyguards, a kid they called Chubby. They made Chubby a wiseguy later because he did the right thing. It had to be Gallo, they all said. There was no one else.

The rally went on without Colombo, but the turnout was small—fewer than fifteen thousand people, according to police. The politicians and some clergymen and some league people praised Caesar, but it was halfhearted. Scotto stayed away. The longshoremen had stayed at work, so did the whole waterfront. Many of the Brooklyn shopkeepers kept their stores open. Wiseguys who had backed Colombo on Unity Day in 1970 stayed away from Columbus Circle in 1971 as though they were certain they would catch the plague if they showed up. Only a few entertainers who had promised to be there, like singer Connie Francis, showed up.

Colombo's closest friend had shut him down. Carl Gambino had sent a message that Colombo was not Caesar. He was just another wiseguy who lost his head.

The television and the newspapers and the magazines were alive with speculation about Colombo's death. Most said Gallo was behind it. A few said it might be black revolutionaries. An even smaller number guessed that Gambino had something to do with it. I didn't know, I wasn't in a position to know, and I didn't want to get caught in whatever fighting was to come. I remembered one thing. Colombo was worried, concerned that someone was trying to get him. He had started carrying a gun around in his briefcase. He used to come into the office, pull it from his briefcase, and drop it into the secret compartment in his office. Whenever he'd leave, he'd leave with the gun, in the briefcase. He'd never done that before. It wasn't natural for a boss to carry a gun like that. You have to be afraid, worried about your life. He had that gun in his briefcase at the rally when they shot him.

It was a week later that Doc John saw me.

"Look, Joey," he said, "your friends Anthony and Joe Junior . . . they are getting out of hand. If they don't keep their places, don't stay where they belong, they are going to get hurt. Tell them, Joey. Warn them."

Doc John had a lot of friends. He was really wired with the right people in the families, and he heard things. He wanted to be helpful, but what he told me was in confidence. I was supposed to let the Colombo kids know without getting him involved.

So I went to see Joe Junior with my uncle Sal, and we took a drive in my car. Then I pulled over to the side of the road between Bay Seventh and Bay Eighth. I pulled over to try to explain what I had heard, to try to warn him and Anthony.

"Listen, Joe, I don't know what you're doing or what you're planning," I said, "but you better maintain a low profile, because I got the word you'll get hurt if you and Anthony don't stop . . . you'll both get hurt."

I'd hardly finished what I was saying when Joe Junior went off the walls, went absolutely bananas with me.

"Who told you that?" he yelled.

"I can't tell you, Joe," I answered. "It was told to me in confidence . . . friendly advice."

"You tell me," he shouted, "or I'll bury you, your wife, and your kids!"

I couldn't believe what I was hearing. We'd been raised together like brothers by his father. He'd been my best man, I'd been to his wedding . . . to Anthony's. We were family. You don't do things like that to family. You don't threaten family . . . wives, kids. I was giving him advice to help him. It was from a good source, whom I'd promised not to give up.

Doc John had heard from a lot of people that the Colombo kids had been throwing their weight around—making it known they wanted, they intended, to follow in their father's footsteps, to take over where he left off, and they weren't even made guys. They were nobody—just the kids of Colombo, not crew members, not soldiers, not capos. They were playing the wiseguy bit, and people didn't like it.

"You're gonna tell me, you lousy fuck!" he shouted again. "You tell me or you . . . the wife . . . the kids . . . I'll bury you all."

I didn't want to, but I told him, and he got out of the car where we were and went to see Doc John. I didn't even have time to warn the doc. Nothing happened to the doc, but the kids did lower their profile after that. They stopped trying to take over.

The score with Gallo was eventually settled on his birthday, April 6, 1972. He was tracked into Umberto's Clam Bar on Mulberry Street by hoods who worked for Joe Yacovelli, Joe Yac, and Vinnie Aloi, who became a temporary boss. It was a spur-of-the-moment thing. Joe Luparelli, who worked for Joe Yac, was standing on Mulberry Street with Matty the Horse Ianiello, a Genovese family capo, when police said Gallo pulled up and asked Ianiello about the food in Umberto's. They parked and went inside. Matty the Horse sat at the food counter. While Gallo ordered food, Luparelli rounded up hitters, who quickly got guns. The hitters, led by Carmine DiBiase, who they called Sonny Pinto, came in and gunned Gallo down in front of his wife and sister and wounded his bodyguard, Pete the Greek Diapoulos, while Matty the Horse dropped to the floor to avoid the fireworks. Pete the Greek was certain Matty the Horse was part of the plot and tried to kill him, only he'd run out of ammo.

With all the publicity and all the stories, I just never believed Gallo could be that stupid to have killed Colombo and then come strolling into Little Italy and party in mob joints with his family and his friends. He was nutty, but not that nutty. I've always thought Colombo was set up and Gallo was the convenient fall guy. Colombo was out of control, getting political, dreaming dreams. Someone else, someone high in the mob, or maybe someone even in the federal government, set him up. Have I any proof? No . . . just a gut feeling. But then, nobody else has proved anything for sure either.

I didn't see Colombo again until 1975. By then I had been recruited as a paid informer, and the Bureau was anxious for me to see Colombo. They had heard different stories about him— that he was talking, that he was doing well, that he was giving orders, that he was a vegetable. They didn't know, but they were worried about a possible comeback.

At first Colombo was kept at Anthony's home in Brooklyn. They boarded up the garage and kept him in a room there, because they were afraid of another attempt to kill him. At the same time, they were busy fixing up Colombo's home upstate with all the equipment that would be needed to rehabilitate him, to help him. It took more than six months to get things fixed up, then the boys moved him, when nobody expected or knew about it.

With all the movement, all the street talk, all the buzz on the wires and the bugs, the feds weren't sure about Colombo. They always had a lingering fear that he'd return and reorganize things and cause a whole lot of trouble again. It bothered the Bureau. When things bother the Bureau, they bother other people. They had to know, so they pushed me, pressed me, to arrange to see for myself how he was.

I arranged to go to Colombo's Blooming Grove, New York, home with my father and a friend of the family who had some papers to deliver. I'd been there many times before. The house was a big, beautiful brick ranch set up on five acres of land. A long winding driveway ended at the garage underneath the house. Inside there was a huge den that they had converted into an exercise room with a whirlpool bath, and an overhead sling that they used to put him in the bath.

Upstairs we had to go through double doors to a tremendous living room, maybe 30' × 40'. I remember it had a huge gun rack

on the right side filled with rifles and shotguns, and there was
this tremendous fireplace . . . absolutely huge, at least fifteen feet
wide. There was a big kitchen and dinette that was about 30′
× 40′, and a big dining room plus four bedrooms and I can't
remember how many bathrooms. Outside was a big horse barn
complete with an apartment upstairs, as well as a big swimming
pool and patio and fences around the entire five acres of land.

Colombo was in a special bedroom that had been fixed up for
him with a hospital bed. He was lying there like a lump with
plugs in his head where he'd been shot. I remember thinking,
Why the hell didn't he die when they shot him? Why should he
have to lie there like this . . . like a piece of nothing?

JoJo, his wife, was with us. She still looked great—still a
beautiful blond lady. Still loyal and still hoping for a miracle.
I remember thinking, What a wonderful woman. What hell
she's been through, and still she's cheerful.

JoJo pushed a button on the side of the bed, and Colombo's
limp form rose to almost a sitting position as the mattress rose.
He was dressed in fancy pajamas. His hair was slicked back and
carefully cut the way it always was, and his hands . . . his nails
were manicured. He had the same barber I did, and twice a week
the barber would come to the house in Blooming Grove, cut
Colombo's hair, and manicure his nails just as he did when
Colombo was running everything back in Brooklyn.

JoJo started to spoon-feed him, and the food sort of dribbled
down his mouth. She wiped it clean and turned to my father.

"You got to say things to him that may shake him," JoJo said.
"The doctors say remembering something . . . it may make him
snap out of it."

I looked at her and at the youngest kids, Christopher and
Catherine, and I couldn't say a word. I was dumbstruck . . .
numb. My father wasn't.

"Hey, Porky," my father said, "when the hell you gonna get
the hell out of this bed?" Nothing . . . not a glimmer. "Come on
Porky, snap out of it, you stupid bastard."

The eyes darkened just a shade, and drool came from his
mouth, but he didn't move . . . not a trace. He was a vegetable
. . . just a vegetable.

We left an hour later. I felt sick to my stomach. When I got back to Brooklyn, I made arrangements to meet with my Bureau contact and told him about Colombo. He smiled a little, then patted me on the back. "You did good, Joe," he said. "We had to know."

I felt like shit. Three years later, on May 23, 1978, when they waked Colombo out of his own funeral home, out of Prospero's Funeral Home on Eighty-sixth Street, Brooklyn, I made sure I was out of town. I just knew that if I went to the wake with my father, the Bureau would make me do something I didn't want to do, like carry a body mike inside or plant a bug or something. I couldn't do that, not to Colombo, not after seeing him in Blooming Grove.

9

THE INFORMER

The mob held its wake for Joe Colombo long before his body was brought to the Prospero Funeral Home in Bensonhurst. He and his sons just never knew it. While Colombo lay like a vegetable in Blooming Grove, New York, and his wife, JoJo, spoon-fed him as if he was a baby, the men he trusted the most would come to the real estate office, verbally cut out his heart, and make excuses for jumping from the sinking ship.

"Whaddaya think of about your big-shot friend now?" cracked Rocky Miraglia. "All those bucks he made us give him to invest . . . for the Yellow Submarine . . . for the newspaper stock. It all went south in his pocket."

"Yeah," chimed in Nicky Bianco. "That son of a bitch. He wasn't such a nice guy, was he? He was no fuckin' good."

I kept my mouth shut and looked at them blankly, but my mind was churning. What bastards, I thought. When Colombo was around, here in the office, you were kissing his ring, kissing his ass, for a flicker of recognition from him. Now that he's dying, you want to cover your ass . . . tell the world you weren't really that close.

When Colombo was in the office, giving the orders, wheeling and dealing, they all jumped at his idea for putting their money into what he called the Yellow Submarine—investing in a company that was going to build this special deep-diving yellow submarine and go out into the Atlantic Ocean, dive to the bottom to pull the treasures of jewels and gold and whatever from the rotting, sunken Italian liner *Andrea Doria,* and then float it to the top. The so-called submarine-recovery idea was floated by two guys from Brooklyn, and Colombo not only bought it, but he made his whole mob invest in it. Everyone had to put up money, from a couple of hundred to a couple of thousand, depending on how high up you were, to buy shares of stock in this outfit at a dollar a share. The trouble was, when he was shot, nobody had any shares of stock to prove they had an investment. Colombo had kept all the money and all the stock, if, in fact, he ever put any into the scheme, which flopped anyhow.

The newspaper scheme was pretty much the same shakedown. He had members of his mob put up money to buy up stock of a New York daily newspaper that had gone belly-up. Colombo was going to revive it and make it work for him and the Italian-American Civil Rights League. The trouble is, all that money went south into his pocket when he was shot. Nobody could come up with a dime that they had invested with him on his orders.

So some of the rank and file—some of the guys who had been closest to him and were his most vocal supporters when he was in the room next to them—were now bad-mouthing him, looking for a place that was safe, a place they could jump to and survive. He was their hero, their god, when he kept them in gold, put food on their tables, and made sure everybody in the "family" ate, made sure everybody got a piece of the pie. Now, the only thing that mattered was survival, distancing themselves from Colombo, his kids, and his years of rule.

I think it was Miraglia's defection that stunned me the most. Rocky was more than just Colombo's bodyguard and driver. He had cherished Colombo. He had loved him, protected him as though he were his brother. He was more than protective, he was a fanatic about Colombo's safety—overprotective. He was an animal, crazy, physical, vicious to those he saw as a threat to Joe. If he shot you in the head once, he would have stood over you and shot you six more times in the head to be sure you couldn't harm Colombo. On the day Colombo was shot, Rocky couldn't stand in the way, couldn't take the bullet meant for Colombo. Suddenly, he didn't have Colombo to protect—and worse, he didn't have anyone to protect him and help him put food on the table for his wife and the nearly dozen kids they had. His alternative was to jump the fence, to find a safe place to land, and that place was with the Gambino family.

Long before Colombo was cold and in his box, Miraglia called in whatever chips he'd acquired while he worked for Colombo to get approval to move to the Gambino family. So did Joe Notch, who went to work for Gambino-family soldier Petey Castellana in a chicken company while dealing card games for Jimmy the Blond on Mulberry Street.

And Bianco . . . he had run off to Rhode Island to rejoin his old mob, the Patriarca crime family of New England, where he had gotten his start. While Colombo was alive and actively the boss, Bianco held a position of stature in the family because he was the man who had been selected to come down from New England to mediate the war between the Gallo brothers and their mob and old Joe Profaci. He had quickly latched on to Colombo and was with him almost every day in the office, a dapper, well-dressed guy with a clickety-clack mind that was fine-tuned to the channel for survival. The only ones who kept their mouths shut, who didn't spend their time bad-mouthing Colombo, who held their ground and didn't panic, were the money men and the power brokers, guys like Peewee Campagna, Frankie the Beast Falanga, Michael Bolino, Vinnie Aloi, Greg Scarpa, or Carmine and Alphonse Persico, who stayed around to build their own dynasty.

Even Carl Gambino didn't waste any time picking at the bones.

When it was apparent Colombo wasn't going to recover from the assassination attempt and return as boss, Gambino sent a message to my father that he wanted to see him at his home. The visit wasn't social. It was to remind my father that Colombo owed Gambino one third of the principal on the $100,000 loan that had been made to the Brooklyn trucker—the same trucker I had collected interest from weekly and delivered to Colombo at our office.

While my father never put a dime of the money up for the loan, he shared in the interest that had been split up between the three men, more than $156,000. Since he shared in the benefits, Gambino reasoned, my father should share in the losses, and since Colombo could no longer pay his end of the principal of the loan, it was my father's responsibility to pay it because he had arranged for the loan. My father didn't like it one bit, but there wasn't a thing he could do about it. He certainly wasn't about to debate it with Gambino and lose favor with him. He bitched a lot about having to come up with thirty-three thousand dollars for Gambino, but he paid it. That wasn't the only bone-scraping that Gambino did.

There was the funeral home, Prospero's. It was well known that Colombo owned 50 percent. My father had publicly testified to Colombo's investment and part ownership in the funeral home at state hearings, and Colombo himself admitted to it. What wasn't publicly known was that Gambino owned half of whatever investment Colombo had, including Prospero's. Restaurants, catering halls, trucking firms, loan-shark money, real estate, nursing and funeral homes . . . whatever Colombo owned, Gambino owned half because he'd put up the original money that had financed Colombo's operations as a crime-family boss.

Long before Colombo was even being measured for his casket, Gambino went to people handling that investment and demanded his 25 percent interest in the funeral parlor. Some of them were shocked. They were unaware of the Gambino interests, but they didn't even think of complaining. Who would they complain to? So Gambino got his 25 percent in cash, but how it was paid I never learned.

Later, the man who thought he owned his own funeral home until he let Colombo buy in, Nicholas Prospero, was killed as he shoveled snow in front of his home on West Twelfth Street in Brooklyn in January 1981. Police said he was shot four times by one of four men who stopped him just after his wife had gone into the house to get some salt to melt the ice on the sidewalk.

No one has ever explained why he was killed, and I never found out the reason. The murder was never solved.

It was a very unstable time. Family members, people from the Gallo group and in the Colombo crew, were getting shot and killed everywhere I turned.

From the time Colombo was hit in 1971 to the fall of 1972, there had been at least six killings, including two bystanders in a restaurant called the Neapolitan Noodle. Mimi Scialo had disappeared. I knew why, but it didn't comfort me or anyone else. Two of his close associates, John Coiro and Tommy Barbusca, were gunned down in their car outside the Seventeen Seventeen Club, a social club at 1717 Eighty-sixth Street, not too far from the office.

Miraglia and company reasoned it was no time to be running around without a rabbi—without a godfather to stand up for you. The uncertainty of family rule was having its effect. It was also making me think more and more about my future. As I thought, there were the ever-present FBI agents . . . prodding, always prodding.

"You don't belong with these people," Tallia would say, again and again. "Better get out while the getting is good. Think about it." And I did, more and more.

Vinnie Aloi had taken over temporarily as the acting boss, but he hated the job. Everywhere he went, Bureau agents like Tallia were close behind, hounding him, tailing him, watching his every move. Things got so bad that Vinnie used to go to movie theaters in the afternoon and come out at night, hoping the feds would no longer be on his tail. He was, of course, wrong.

In November 1970, long before Colombo was shot, Aloi was indicted with the then–acting boss of the Lucchese crime family, Carmine Tramunti, and one of his most influential capos, John (Johnny Dio) Dioguardi, in a stock conspiracy. The guy who put them in the box was a stock swindler named Michael Hellerman, who dreamed up the scheme and then nailed everyone he brought into it by testifying against them.

Despite the indictment, the trouble with the feds, and the heat they were putting on him, Aloi had the prestige and the respect of the family. He had been very close to Colombo, but he still managed to be close to the Persicos and all the other factions. He didn't make many enemies. I used to see him regularly at Colombo's upstate estate with all the capos, all the money-makers from different groups of the family. He was always friendly. He was liked by a lot of people, but he was a soft leader.

Aloi didn't want to be a boss, not for a moment. It was a job that was pushed on him by factions within the family until they could figure out what was going to happen to Colombo. When Colombo was shot, Aloi had to meet with people in the family in an apartment in Nyack, New York, to plot how they'd get Joe Gallo for setting up Colombo's shooting. That cost him too. In January 1973, the Manhattan District Attorney's Office indicted him for perjury, for lying about the meeting, saying he was never there. The district attorney's ace in the hole was a flaky character called Joe Luparelli who was a witness and participant in the Joe Gallo hit at Umberto's Clam Bar. I never heard of the guy until I read about him.

I did know Aloi, though. He and I were friends because of his relationship with Colombo and my father. He had attended my wedding with his wife and had sat at the head table with Gambino and with Joe Colombo and their families. So he was favored by the bosses, particularly Gambino. He was bright. He ran a florist shop and a profitable trucking business in the garment center and he was the power for Colombo and the family in the garment center.

Aloi had learned early that the FBI would target him if he took over the leadership, but because of his father, Sebastian (Buster) Aloi, and his position of respect in the family, he was the natural choice. At his father's urging, and that of Gambino and others in the Colombo family, he took the job . . . temporarily. It quickly cost him. By December 1973, he'd been convicted on both the perjury case and the federal stock conspiracy, and was looking at sixteen years or more in prison on federal and state charges.

Boss or no boss, when the Bureau arrested me for bank fraud in 1972, Aloi wasted no time, after my father made some calls, in getting an attorney to handle my case. The charge was simple. I had signed my wife's name on an auto-loan application to

Caplan Buick. No big deal. I wasn't hustling money, just using my wife's name instead of mine. The Bureau, however, never forgets. The feebs don't like to be beaten, and I'd won the perjury case. The name Cantalupo stuck in their throats. When it popped up on bank applications they were checking, it rang bells, just like the name Mike Bolino and the names of a dozen other characters who had applied for loans. I hadn't gotten a dime . . . just applied!

It was a bad case, but that didn't stop the Bureau or the Eastern District Strike Force from using it to make their headlines, and, zappo, I was busted along with a dozen others, including Bolino. The feds figured they had another bank-fraud case where Colombo people were using money for shylocking. They knew I wasn't, but that didn't matter. It was a way of breaking shoes, and that's what the Bureau wanted to do. Break shoes— remind me that they were still there to haunt me. Eventually, the case was dismissed, but it was a catalyst for things to come.

No matter where I went, who I talked to, no one defended Colombo except my father. To the day Colombo died, my father was always in his corner. He used to tell me, "Remember, Joe . . . without Colombo, we wouldn't have what we have." But he was virtually alone. No one of importance in the family supported him, and they sure as hell didn't care for the kids.

I began to think like the rest of them. There was no one going to protect me or take me with them. With Colombo, I could skate through some deals. I didn't personally have to beat up people. I might have to watch, but I wasn't the muscle. I sometimes just looked like the muscle. It satisfied Colombo, but not these other people.

Colombo was my rabbi. Without him, I was nobody . . . I had nothing. There was no chance for anything without him. With him, I had opportunity for future things. I knew, with him, if I got in trouble or wanted to do things, I had him. Under him, I might have even become a made guy. Now, he was gone. His sons were off doing their own thing. They didn't give a damn about me. Joe Junior had threatened me, my wife, and my kids. Aloi was about to go to jail. There were all kinds of killings—

people taking care of old scores, housecleaning in the family.

All this ate at me, that and the indictment and the fear that was churning my guts, making me lie awake sleepless night after night; I was out there naked and alone in a vicious and violent underworld, and someday someone would decide that Joe Cantalupo was fair game. I couldn't live with that, and I couldn't be a wiseguy, I couldn't kill just for money or threaten wives and kids whose husbands and fathers were in hock to the loan sharks. I wasn't an angel, but I hadn't dipped that low yet. Not that I hadn't tried.

I had become a part-time bookmaker with a young guy named James Zippo Gredda. He was a bookmaker and numbers-racket operator for Michael Bolino, who had introduced me to him. At the time, I was pushing football point-spread slips for Bolino, selling them to Chinese workers at the Hong Pan restaurant, other restaurants, and places where a lot of my friends and customers hung out. Bolino was giving me 20 percent of the action I sold, and I was taking home an extra $200–$300 a week, most of which I bet myself on football games. Gredda worked for Bolino on other gambling deals.

I should have known there was something wrong about Gredda when he talked to me about branching off on our own. Here he was, handling numbers and bookmaking for the Colombo family, and he wanted to handle some action on his own. That should have been a signal of trouble to me, but it wasn't.

So we started a small bookmaking business together. We used my apartment. He had people call me up, and I would take the bets. It was a money-maker. Not big, but a money-maker— splitting up maybe five thousand dollars a week in profits. That's how life with Gredda got started, but it's not how it ended.

Meanwhile, occasionally I was still going with some of Colombo's old loan sharks on their collection routes. It was on those collection sweeps that I realized I wasn't cut out to be a mob wiseguy, a tough loan shark. Oh, I could threaten to break the windows of some kid's limousine—the only source of income he had in the world—to make him pay his weekly vig, but

I'd get sick to my stomach when I saw some people get terrible beatings or see wives and kids begging for food because the shylock took their old man's last nickel.

I could still hear a woman crying, see her pleading with Joe Notch as he beat her husband for being late with the weekly vig. Now, her husband, Matty, was in jail. He still owed a bundle to Joe Notch, who each week would go to her apartment and try to force her into sex with him as part of the vig payments. I'd stand and watch and cringe as the woman, an attractive brunette, cried and begged with Joe Notch to leave her and her husband alone.

"Want me to forget this week?" he demanded. "Get on your knees and take care of this," he'd say, grabbing his crotch. She'd always refuse his demands for oral sex, but she lived in terror, week after week, as he tried something new every visit.

There were others like that, women, children, scared out of their minds by guys like Joe Notch and other loan sharks, some who did what was demanded of them, some who were beaten, some who were even raped. I couldn't have handled that. I knew that if that was what it took to be a wiseguy, I couldn't handle it.

"Call me, Joey," Tallia had said. "Why don't we get together . . . have lunch?"

Week in, week out, for years I'd heard those words or words similar to that. Tallia just never let up. Always nudging, always prodding, pushing, just a little . . . making me think, making me worry.

"Who ya got now, Joey?" he said after Colombo was hit. "Who's gonna take care of ya now?" And every week I'd see him, in front of the office, near the pork store, at a telephone booth, in a store. He was like a shadow I couldn't shake.

My brain had always warned me against falling into his trap. I knew that would be all I'd have to do—just one time—because that's the way they set you up. I'd say, "Okay, Ray, let's have lunch," and the next day, after the lunch, he'd stop me or call me and say, "You know what, Joe? You know who we saw outside the restaurant after we had lunch?" Gimmicks, games, ways they play on your mind and then trap you like a mouse and play with you in their little laboratory.

I was ripe that September morning in 1973 when I made the choice, when I decided I couldn't be a wiseguy, but maybe I could be an underworld spy, a big wheeler-dealer with federal protection; maybe I could use all my connections with all the mob people to my advantage and make money for myself . . . and nobody would ever be the wiser. It was like a light bulb that flashed on in my mind all of a sudden; something inside of me said do it, change your life.

I walked to a phone booth and dialed the number that Tallia had given me to his office. "FBI," the girl answered.

"Let me speak to Ray Tallia," I said.

"Who's calling?" she asked.

"Tell him Joe Moser," I answered.

"Tallia," a male voice interrupted.

"Listen, Ray," I said. "You don't know me by name, but you know me by sight. Why don't we have a meeting? I want to talk to you about something."

"Okay," said Tallia. "Where you want to meet?"

"Someplace safe," I said, "where wiseguys don't sit."

"You know where the FBI headquarters is?" he asked.

"Yeah," I said.

"Around the corner there's this Chinese restaurant," he said. "Guarantee it's safe. I'll meet you there at one [P.M.]."

"Done," I said.

For the next hour or more, I fidgeted, I twisted, I turned. I saw people coming out of shops, I drove around blocks twice to make sure I wasn't being followed, and when I got to Sixty-ninth Street, I parked my car far from the Bureau headquarters. I walked up one block and down another, in one place and out another, always making certain that there was no one on my tail. I was soaked with cold sweat when I finally entered the Chinese eatery and spotted Tallia.

"I knew it was you," he said with a smile. "I worked on you for so long, I just knew it had to be you." He motioned for me to sit down. Next to him was another agent I recognized, Jimmy

Cullen. I looked nervously around. There was no one else I recognized there.

"It's secure, Joey," Tallia said, "just like I promised."

We had lunch and we talked, and as we talked I wondered why the hell I was there with them, talking to them. I must be crazy.

"I don't know why I'm here," I said suddenly. "I can't figure out why I called you."

"Sure you can, Joey," Tallia said. "You're not one of them. You're too smart. You don't want to wind up like Colombo or some of his people."

I shook my head. "I don't know," I said shakily. I was really scared at that point.

"We can do a lot together, Joey," Tallia said. "You can make a whole lot of money, and no one will ever know . . . and you'll always have protection when you need it."

"Look, I don't want to be somebody's patsy, a witness or something like that," I said.

"Guaranteed, Joey, it'll never happen," he said. "You just give us information—intelligence on things that are happening—on people and places in the neighborhood, things you hear, things you see, and we take care of you. From now on, you're a code number . . . and when we talk, you'll be Joe Moser."

"What happens if somebody gets wise?" I asked. "What do you do for me and for my family then?"

"We take care of you, Joey," Tallia said soothingly. "The Bureau never deserts its people. We take care of you. We'll move you . . . the family . . . everything . . . to a safe place . . . give you a new start if it ever comes to that. But it won't. Guarantee it won't."

"Whaddaya want me to do?" I said with a sigh.

"For now, all I want is information," he said. "I want to know when you see Sal Profaci or Johnny Magliocco or some of the other people who visit the office or the Pisa Caterers. I want to know about their businesses—Profaci's olive-oil business and other companies and his investments, about Magliocco and his investments and activities with Peerless Importers. Tell me about Charlie Moose, or Greg Scarpa, or Jimmy Failla, or Campagna, or the Colombo kids, or what you see at the 19th Hole with Chris Furnari. Keep your eyes and ears open. If the information you come up with is worthwhile, we'll pay you. You'll do well and you'll be safe."

We didn't cut a deal then, just talked and I said I'd get back to him, but I could see he was clearly excited, and I had the feeling that I could do a lot of things, provide a lot of information, without ever endangering myself. The office, after all, was still a nerve center for organized-crime people, and most of them talked freely in front of me or took me with them as they shook down shylock victims and made their collections.

"No promises, Ray," I said. "I'll get back to you."

Just before I made the final decision to inform for the Bureau, for Tallia, the federal charges against me were dropped. Tallia told me what was going to happen, and when he did, I talked to him about one of the federal judges that I knew.

The judge, who is still on bench, interested the Bureau. They wanted to make a case against him, but they needed approval from Washington, from the Department of Justice. They never got it—at least that was what they said, but I've always wondered. The Bureau is great for getting an edge on some people in the right places and then squeezing them when they need them. That was J. Edgar Hoover's style.

This judge was a lover. He was from Brooklyn, and he liked the dollies—especially those that some of the boys could provide. I had information that he was going to exclusive parties, and I gave it to Tallia. They took pictures of the judge going in and out of the place I told them about with a broad. The judge also used to hang out at the Hong Pan restaurant, a Chinese restaurant where Chris Furnari and a lot of the wiseguys used to hang their hats and do their business. Did he do things with the mob? There were always suspicions, talk, but I never came up with anything that could prove he was on the take. The mob sure had enough to compromise him with, but that's all I know. The Bureau kept tabs on him, though, for all the years I worked for them. For all I know, they still do.

If there was any doubt in my mind about going to the Bureau, it was erased when this case was dropped. Aloi's friendly attorney tried to hustle me for ten thousand dollars.

"I can get you off without your ever having to go to trial," the attorney said, "but it'll cost you a few bucks . . . ten thousand dollars."

The clear implication was that he had an in with the judge, that he was buying a dismissal of the case. What he didn't know was that I knew that the Bureau was going to drop the charges against me. How he found out about it, I can only guess. The courthouse grapevine is very fast.

"Screw you," I said. "I'm not giving you a fuckin' penny."

"Well, you got to be in criminal court next week," he said, "and I don't do charity work."

I appeared, and sure enough, someone from the prosecution walks up to the bench and whispers in Judge Mark Constantino's ear, and he ordered the case dismissed because the government had dropped the charges.

I wouldn't pay the attorney what he wanted, but it wasn't long before my father got a message from Danbury Federal Prison, where Aloi was serving his time. He said pay the lawyer or else. We paid him the advance five-thousand-dollar fee, nothing else.

Tallia and the Bureau had good reason to deliver the dismissal the way they did. I'd given them the chance to make headlines in December 1973, and they took it.

Before Colombo was shot, my father had transferred a building to him that we owned at 1432 Eighty-sixth Street. In the front, we had the pork store, where Colombo often went to hold meetings. In the back was a social club, and upstairs were a couple of apartments that were rentals. Colombo's kids had turned the social club into a gambling setup complete with a bar and crap tables. It had become a hangout for Colombo-family regulars, many of them Colombo movers in the Italian-American Civil Rights League. The club interested Tallia and his people, who had been watching the activity there for months, but they didn't know what the club was used for other than meetings.

"We need to know more about the place," he said. "We have to know what the security is and how to get past the front door without losing all the work inside."

"Tell you what, Ray," I said. "I give you the layout, and this." With that, I held up a key to the front door, a key that I had kept from when my father owned the building. The lock, I knew, hadn't been changed.

"What they do inside," I said matter-of-factly, "is run high-stakes games—crap, poker—and they take bets. It's heavy action in there."

Then I described the security. There was only one entrance, and it was guarded by Fat Philly, the same Fat Philly who had ripped me off on the jewelry deal with Colombo. Backing him up was Caesar Vitale.

"You gotta knock on the door," I explained to Tallia, "and they check you out through this peephole. If they don't know you or you don't have someone to vouch for you, you don't get in." I thought about it for a moment. "And if they know you got a key . . . I'm dead meat."

"Don't worry, Joey," Tallia said, "we'll figure something out. You've been a big help."

I guess I was. On December 1, 1973, the FBI hit the social club. They didn't bust down doors, or surround the place, or anything dramatic like that—they just put the key I gave them into the lock, and before Fat Philly or Caesar or anyone realized it, they were inside grabbing people, money, gambling records, what have you. In all they got over sixty-five hundred dollars in cash. They arrested seventeen people, including Anthony and Joe Colombo, Jr., Colombo's brother-in-law, Joe La Rosa, Vitale, Fat Philly, and Joe Butter DeCicco, who had just been released from Danbury Federal Prison after serving time for making a false statement on a bank loan.

The Colombo kids, those in the club, and everyone in the mob never had a clue that I was involved. They were convinced the Bureau had a new sophisticated gadget—a special gun—that the feebs could put into a door lock and open it with. I don't know how Tallia and his men got that story going, but the streets were alive with the tale. Everyone was changing locks, beefing up security at their social clubs and gambling hangouts all over the city. No one ever suspected that I had provided the agents with the key to the front door. That was really the first score the Bureau made with information I provided, and they kept their word; I was in deep cover, at least for the time being, and I had been paid eighteen hundred dollars for the information I'd provided between September and December 1973.

10

DANCE, PINOCCHIO, DANCE

J ames Zippo Gredda was a loser. He was short—about
5'5"—and stocky—about 160 pounds—and he was a loser.
He was in hock to everyone, and I didn't have a clue. My good
friend Michael Bolino didn't give me a clue . . . no one did. In
fact, I thought he was swimming in money.

Zippo worked for Andy Mush. Andy Mush's real name was
Andrew Russo, and he was a cousin of Carmine Persico. Later
he became a captain in the family, but at the time, Russo ran
some of the family's bookmaking rings in Brooklyn. He had his
hand in the garbage rackets on Long Island, and he was into
trucking, construction, gambling, and loan-sharking. When the
Hollywood bunch came to town to make *The Godfather*, Russo
became friendly with Jimmy Caan, who turned up at his son's
wedding and at his trial when I testified against him. I met him
through Bolino and Zippo. I regularly arranged through the
real estate office to rent Andy Mush apartments in two-family
houses so they could run their numbers and bookmaking operations every month from safe new locations.

In reality, there was nothing safe about the locations. Every
time I rented them a new location at above the monthly rental
rate, I would provide information on their operations and locations to Tallia so the Bureau could keep tabs on them. They

were never raided because the Bureau was getting valuable intelligence on their operation through surveillance, through watching who came and went and who they used as couriers and where they picked up their action. In the end, it wasn't the FBI that nailed Andy Mush, but an undercover Internal Revenue Service intelligence agent named Richie Annichiarco who he tried to bribe.

Zippo was one of Russo's lower-level flunkies, who, I thought, operated with his blessing. After all, Bolino had introduced us; Zippo was handling gambling action for Russo's bookies. I was renting rotating apartments to them at different locations each month, and Zippo brought me the rental money from Russo. I figured he had to be safe. Bad figuring, bad assumptions.

From the time we hooked up together, Zippo and I made money. Every week we were splitting up to five thousand dollars in profits from our bookmaking enterprise, which I ran out of my home. We were handling football bets, basketball, and a lot of horse bets from the Chinamen working at the Hong Pan and other Oriental restaurants in the area. The Chinese workers I knew loved to bet, loved to look for a quick score, I guess because they had so little. What the hell, I liked quick scores myself.

We weren't cutting into anyone else's action, since the regular bookies weren't paying that much attention to the Chinamen, and the Chinamen didn't know too much about who to go to. Since I was in the Hong Pan every day, they went to me. When the bets got too heavy on one horse or one team, Gredda would lay off some of that action with one of Russo's or someone else's bigger bookmaking centers.

As a rule, we'd keep the good stuff, the near-sure things in betting, and lay off the bad action. We were working both ends and piling up the bucks, and no one was complaining.

Super Bowl of 1974 was our biggest profit-sharing venture. We made more than fifteen thousand dollars profit on that game alone. My weekly cash flow was getting bigger all the time. Every week I took in one thousand dollars or more from the real estate office. I was handling the sales and rentals of houses of a lot of the family members: loan shark Greg Scarpa in Brooklyn,

Carmine Persico when he sold his house in Hempstead, Long Island, and moved to Brooklyn—Russo's bookmaking locations. The list was long and varied—people from a lot of families used our office.

I was also pulling in another five hundred to a thousand on selling point-spread tickets for Bolino. I'd take the football point-spread sheets out on Tuesday and spread them around with bettors I knew, then I'd pick them up on Friday with the money, and Bolino would give me 20 percent of whatever I brought in. That added up, since I was bringing in anywhere from two thousand dollars to five thousand dollars a week in bets. Then I had the bookie money that Gredda and I were hauling in at my house.

Things were so successful, I even began moving some shylock money out on the streets for myself. The owner of the Hong Pan, for example, Wah On Lee, borrowed $4,000, and he was paying me $120 a week in interest. There were a half-dozen others, all solid loans that I didn't have to apply muscle to collect weekly vig on.

With all the money coming in, I was forever short on cash. I loved to gamble and I loved to party, and because of that, I was always getting involved with women through the office. There were times I was jumping into the sack with one during the day and another in the evening. I had learned one lesson, though, from my days with Colombo. I managed to steer clear of the women of family guys. With no Colombo around to advise and protect me from the violent anger of the different families' good-fellows, I was doubly cautious.

With all the screwing around, my wife never knew. I usually had a convincing explanation or story, and I always took care of her needs, physically as well as financially. By 1972, we had our first son, and in 1975, we had our second. I'm not going to use their names here, because they don't know what I did, and they now live their own life with their mother. Right now they just know we had to get away from the bad guys and change our names because I was a federal witness before my marriage broke up.

Gambling caused me almost as many problems; in fact, it almost cost me my life before I became an informer.

Playing cards was almost an addiction with me at times. It wasn't so much the money, it was the excitement—the challenge of the game—and the game I loved the most was pinochle. I learned it as a kid, sitting on my grandfather's lap in Valley Stream while he and my father and two of my uncles played. He'd let me throw a card in when he had to make a play, but for the most part he taught me the tricks of pinochle, the memorization of suits and how to play your trump cards and get the most out of them. Grandpa hated to lose, and he loved the excitement of outwitting his opponents . . . outthinking them. When he died, I took his place for a while in the games at home, then I branched out and began playing for the money as well as the excitement and the challenge.

While most of the games that I played in were high-stakes games where thousands of dollars were involved, the game that made me certain that my young life was about to come to a sudden end was a social game at Michael Bolino's home. When I say social, I mean we were only playing for five dollars a game with some minor sideline bets. The wives were elsewhere in the house, and I was partners with Tom Gaggi, while Bolino was partners with Shorty Spero.

In 1974, Shorty was a hitter, very close to Bolino and the Persicos. He looked like a boxer—who'd been in one fight too many—pug ugly and not too bright. He was about 5'7" or 5'8", but in that small body was a raging tornado . . . a man of extreme violence and just a little crazy.

Shorty was not yet a made member, a goodfellow, of the Colombo family. That would come later, when Bolino and Anthony Colombo were made in a ceremony with a lot of others at Tomasso's restaurant in Brooklyn. He was bitter about having to wait to be made, particularly because he had handled a lot of dangerous jobs for the family and he felt he deserved a reward.

Anyhow, we were playing pinochle, and I spotted Michael

giving him signals on the trump suit he wanted Shorty to play to. Shorty gave signals back, and I opened my big mouth.

"Shorty, you can't do that!" I protested. "That's cheating."

"Whaddaya mean, I can't do that?" he snapped. "I can do anything I want!"

Because my grandfather had always cautioned me against cheating in games, I never thought twice about calling Shorty on what I thought was wrong. "No, Shorty. Giving signals is cheating," I insisted.

Shorty's eyes flashed, his face flushed, and he slowly took his gun, a .45-caliber automatic, out of his pocket and put it against my head.

"Don't you ever call me a fuckin' cheater again, Joe," he said, "or I'll blow your fuckin' brains out."

Feeling that cold steel against my temple, realizing that there was a lunatic squeezing the trigger and threatening my life, I had what I would call a normal reaction: I wet my pants. I called my wife and left Bolino's house. That was the way Shorty lived. He had a quick temper. That's why he died. He told the world he was going to kill those who'd killed his brother. They just killed him first.

I never kept much money in investments. Banks were places you got money from, not put money into. In fact, the only real assets I had were my shylock loans, which were bringing in a weekly 2 percent interest clear profit like clockwork. Trouble was, there wasn't that much money out there invested in shylock loans—maybe $30,000–$40,000, and that money wasn't all my own.

Because I had good connections, something Gredda didn't have, I had gone to loan sharks I knew, people like Bolino, Petey Leather, Johnny Russo, and others, and borrowed money from them at two points. I even tried to get a loan shark's rate from the loan shark's loan shark . . . Greg Scarpa.

When Greg came into the Hong Pan, I introduced him to Gredda, who pipes up that he's in the shylock business himself. Scarpa answers, "Well, I'm a loan shark's loan shark."

"Greg," I asked, "what does that mean . . . a loan shark's loan shark?"

"It means," he said, "that I give out half-point money because it's guaranteed."

"Yeah, well, can't I get ten thousand dollars of it?" I said with a smile.

He grinned as he looked at the two of us. "Fuck you, Joey," he said as he walked away. Later, he gave me a couple of loans that totaled about four thousand dollars, but I had to pay him three points a week, not a half-point.

Scarpa would loan money like that out to fellow loan sharks, or members of his crew or businessmen who had family sanction and whose debts were guaranteed, not to two schmucks like us. Instead of borrowing from someone like Scarpa at a half-point a week, I had to borrow from other loan sharks at a point to two points a week—and those were good rates, those were rates you got only with connections. They were rates I could make the two points a week clear profit on easily.

Gredda didn't have those connections, and he'd come to me and ask me, "Joey, can you get me two thousand dollars for this client . . . four thousand dollars for that client," and I'd get it for him and he'd pay me the vig that I was paying the loan shark and a piece of his action as well—or so I thought.

So I would get five thousand dollars and pay the loan shark two hundred dollars a week, while I was loaning it out at four points a week, or, four hundred dollars. I was making a neat two hundred dollars a week profit on every five-thousand-dollar loan that I was lending out, and the money wasn't even my own. Instead of letting the money double like a good loan shark would by keeping the profits out on the street making more money, I kept spending.

That lack of security—of cash to fall back on—left me wide open for trouble, and trouble came in the form of the death of a loan shark Gredda had introduced me to by the name of Alfred Gallo, no relation to the Gallo brothers.

Gallo was Gredda's main man, his main source of money. He was a loan shark, and strangely enough he was a nice guy. He was miserable at home, but away from work he was a nice guy, and he loved to party. So I accommodated him. I wined and dined him, provided him with broads . . . I even threw a big bash for him at a really swank bachelor's apartment I had in the same apartment house where my father lived, in Sea Cliff Towers in Staten Island.

Gallo wasn't a made guy. He was an associate of an old-time mafioso they called Jimmy the Bat Cordello. The first time I borrowed ten thousand dollars from Gallo at the Hong Pan, Jimmy the Bat came with Gallo when he brought me the money. Martin Odorisio, an attorney, was with him.

I later found out Odorisio was his partner. I had to pay Gallo two points—two hundred dollars a week—for the loan. Odorisio's job was to keep the books straight for Jimmy the Bat.

Eventually, I had twenty-seven thousand dollars in loans with Gallo, and my uncle Sal had another three thousand dollars that I was responsible for. My weekly vig to him alone was $540, but I was bringing in $1,080 a week, so I wasn't worried. Then he dies suddenly, and I'm called to a meeting with Odorisio, who explains that when Gallo died, he left him the books and records that showed I still owed him thirty thousand dollars. Since Odorisio and Jimmy the Bat were part of the loan operation, I now had to pay Odorisio to make good on what Gallo owed them.

It was about this time that Gredda came up with a scheme to make a big score quickly, but to do it, he needed thirty thousand dollars.

"Joey, I got a way to make a pile of dough . . . fast," he said.

"Jimmy, you always got ways of making money, only I never see it," I said angrily. "I'm tired of laying out bread for you and not seeing the returns you promise."

"Joey, we did good on the Super Bowl, didn't we?" he asked. I nodded my head. "We been making good bread every week on the book, right?" I nodded. "So the shylock business is down a little on my side. It's gonna get better—I promise on the eyes of my mother."

I shook my head warily, tired of Gredda's double-talk yet

unconvinced that he couldn't come up with another pot of gold.

"Coke . . . I can get my hands on some pure coke," he said. "You don't have to do nothing. Just get the twenty-five thousand dollars, and I'll triple our money, maybe even more."

"What the hell is coke?" I asked. At the time, cocaine was not a big thing, not well known, at least in the circles I traveled in, and I'd never seen the stuff, let alone tried it.

"It's hot stuff . . . great stuff," he said. "I can unload a key [kilo—2.2 pounds] in a week. I got the contacts to move it."

"You talking narcotics . . . like heroin?" I asked. "I don't want no part of that shit. Jesus, they bury you around here for playing with that crap."

There was a rule in the Colombo family—not one that everybody lived by, but one that a lot of people died by—that you don't deal in junk. If you did, you suffered the consequences. Sometimes it was murder, sometimes—as in the case of Odorisio—the loss of your assets.

Odorisio was caught by police on Long Island with a planeload of marijuana. While the Suffolk District Attorney sent him to the pokey, the mob put him in virtual bankruptcy. They took over all his shylock books, and in my case, they wrote off a twelve-thousand-dollar loan. I had worked a twenty-seven-thousand-dollar loan down to twelve thousand dollars, and because he played with drugs I didn't owe him a dime. Bolino came to me one day after his bust and said, "Joey . . . forget about the loan. You don't have to pay Marty no more, he got caught with a load of grass."

The key was that those rules went for some and not for others. When they caught Persico's son-in-law dealing in drugs in Florida and threw him in jail, he didn't lose a dime of what he had because what he had were assets of Persico's. The same for Little Allie Boy Persico, Carmine's son. The mob didn't penalize him for dealing in drugs because they couldn't—he was the boss's son. Odorisio didn't have those hooks. He was just an attorney, just a bookkeeper for Jimmy the Bat and a partner, not a made guy. By violating the so-called rules, he lost his part of the shylock book, and those with family connections didn't have to pay their debts. There's nothing that says that mob justice is justice—it's just designed to keep the strong stronger and richer.

As for Gredda, he was certain that the rules didn't apply. This wasn't heroin, this was coke. It was flimsy, but I listened.

"Not this, Joey . . . not this," Gredda said confidently. "No one gets hurt with this. I'll handle everything. You just get the money."

So I did. I borrowed another twenty-five thousand dollars from the loan sharks for the cocaine, but I didn't tell Tallia what was going on. I got fifteen thousand dollars from Gallo, which brought my bill with him up to the twenty-seven-thousand-dollar mark. And I got ten thousand dollars from Nick the Baker. The rest came from other loan sharks.

Nick the Baker wasn't a street loan shark, he just liked good investments. When I told him I was going to triple my money on a deal with coke, he wanted to be my partner. So I made him a partner, and while we waited to get the coke and unload it, I agreed to give him a point a week on his ten grand.

A few days later, Gredda shows up with the coke—a full key—and we head for my bachelor's apartment on Staten Island, the same place we held parties for Gallo, in a building owned by my friend Al Wasserman, who gave me money for my first suit as a salesman.

"We need some milk sugar," Gredda says.

"What's milk sugar?" I asked. "What's that do?"

"We can cut the purity," he answers. "Double the amount of coke we have to sell."

Now in those days, because of heroin traffic, the only way you could get quantities of milk sugar was through a pharmacist or an illegal supplier. I had something almost as good; I had a girlfriend who knew a druggist, and she got me the milk sugar Gredda needed. To learn the trade, I watched him cut it and mix it and bag it. Then we stored it in the apartment.

It was obvious neither of us knew what the hell we were doing. Instead of storing it in a refrigerator and keeping it cold, I stuffed it behind the radiator, figuring it wouldn't be found by some broad who I brought to the apartment to party with. Then I waited for Gredda to do something. I waited and waited, and nothing happened.

I waited some more—we sold a gram here, a gram there, we gave out samples all over the place—and nothing happened.

In the drug business, you have to have contacts, distributors to sell the junk and get rid of it right away, turn it over and make more money. Gredda had no one and I damned sure didn't, and suddenly the coke turns into a brick, a solid brick of shit.

No customers, no sales, I'm out twenty-five thousand dollars, and Gredda gives me the excuse that the coke just went bad because of the heat; it was too close to the radiators and it went bad and turned into a rocklike brick. We had to flush it down the toilet; we had to flush more than ninety thousand dollars worth of junk—two pounds two ounces of coke and a pound of milk sugar—down the toilet.

I'm off the walls, ready to kill this Gredda, but I can't do anything. I'm out twenty-five thousand dollars. One of the first things I did was tell Nick the Baker. I thought he was going to have apoplexy.

"My money . . . what about my money?" he yells.

"Can't do anything now, Nick," I explained. "If I get another score, I'll make sure you get yours. Meanwhile, you knew there were risks—so all you got is hope. There's nothing more I can do. You can't get blood from a stone."

Three months later, Nick the Baker went blind, and he blamed me for it. It was his diabetes—and maybe the stress of losing the ten thousand dollars as well—but he went blind. In later trials, the defense attorneys questioning me as a government witness would always ask me in front of juries, did I take money from a blind man? Nick the Baker wasn't blind when I got the money; he just went blind after the deal went sour. My father later said he paid Nick back because he felt a family obligation. I never believed that, but I never knew for sure.

Gredda, meanwhile, is in a lot of trouble because he is deeply in hock, although I don't know it, to a whole lot of loan sharks himself. In fact, I learned later that he had taken fifteen thousand dollars of the money I gave him to pay off some of the loan sharks who were promising to crush his skull if he didn't come up with some of their money.

Out of desperation, Gredda comes to me and promises to

come up with a way for us to get our money back. He gets a new supply of coke—about twelve ounces—from a guy they called Vinnie Moon, a relative of John Mooney Cutrone, a Gallo mob enforcer who got killed in the backlash of the Colombo shooting.

Now I'm pissed and I want my pound of flesh, so I tell him I'll handle the distribution; I tell him I have a customer, but I need a sample of what he's getting to convince my potential clients it's good stuff. My potential client is, of course, Ray Tallia. I figure I'll kill two birds with one stone—I'll nail Gredda for screwing me, and I'll get some money from the Bureau for giving them a coke case.

The cocaine sample I brought to Tallia tested high quality— about 70 percent pure—and when the results came back, Tallia told me he wanted me to sit down with an agent who was a specialist in this type of work, an agent they called the Cowboy. He really fit his nickname, down to his carved leather boots, his ten-gallon hat, his phony Texas drawl, and his flashy red Eldorado convertible. This guy was out of a dime novel.

"We gotta set up a buy, boy," he drawls. "You and me and this fella of yours. We gonna put the boots to him."

I shook my head and kinda winked at Tallia, but I agreed to set things up.

The buy location was an apartment house of a friend of Gredda, and the price for seven ounces he was selling was going to be ten thousand dollars. When I got to the apartment, Gredda had the coke in a bag on the table ready for the buyers.

I went downstairs to the lobby to wait for the Cowboy, and as I did, I noticed a Corvette parked next to a fire hydrant under a light with a guy and a girl in there apparently making out. At that moment, the Cowboy pulls up with another agent—a DEA agent—with him. I didn't expect that, but it wasn't the first or the last thing that happened that night that I didn't expect.

I led them upstairs to the apartment and introduced them to Gredda. The agent with Gredda proceeds to take a sample of the junk and run a test on it, and when he finds it's good, he and the Cowboy suddenly get up, go to the door, and announce they are going downstairs to get the money from the car trunk. As they leave, they take the coke with them. Surprise, surprise! Just a night of surprises.

Quickly, I follow them down to see what the hell is going on and to keep an eye on the coke. Sure enough, they go to get their money, and when we get back to the apartment, there's another surprise in store. Gredda has flown the coop. He took the back stairs down, avoiding the elevator, and slipped out of the building . . . apparently in a panic.

Now, what the hell do we do? Without warning, the Cowboy and the agent grab me, hustle me downstairs to a car, and drive off to the Belt Parkway, to a parking lot near the water at a place that was then E. J. Korvettes, a big discount department store in Brooklyn.

The parking lot looked as if they had a fire sale on at 11:00 P.M. The place was swarming with DEA agents, including the Corvette I saw with the couple that were making out. Almost immediately, the head man starts abusing me. Suddenly, I'm the bad guy, the fly in the ointment.

"You lousy fuckin' junkie!" he hollers, "I'm gonna put the screws to you."

"What the hell's the matter with you?" I yelled. "I'm supposed to be with you! I ain't wearing the black hat."

"Fuck you, you greaseball!" he shouts. "Where's that fuckin' partner of yours? Where's he hiding?"

"How the hell do I know?" I yelled back. "You guys screwed this thing up . . . not me. He got scared and ran off. What do I know?"

"I tell you what I'm gonna do," the agent continued. "I'm gonna keep the junk and the money and I'm gonna turn you loose on the street and put the word out that you fucked this deal up . . . that you work for the feds."

"Jesus Christ!" I cried out. "What kind of people are you?"

Meanwhile, the Cowboy had called Tallia to the scene, and he grabbed the DEA supervisor and began talking animatedly to him out of earshot.

Ten minutes later, the supervisor returned to where I was standing with the loudmouthed DEA agent and the Cowboy, and told his agent to cool it.

"Give him the coke," he said, "and let him go home."

"Are you crazy?" protested the agent.

"*Do it!*" the supervisor said angrily. Then, turning to me: "The Cowboy will take you home. We'll set up a new meet."

I got home at midnight, shaking like a leaf. I was too scared to be angry, but I had nowhere to turn except to Tallia, who had already spoken for me.

At 2:00 A.M., the phone rang. It was Gredda.

"You okay, Joey?" he asked.

"You son of a bitch!" I shouted. "Where the hell did you go?"

"I got scared, Joey," he said, almost with a whimper. "I thought it was a setup when they went downstairs, and I got scared . . . so I ran."

"And left me there to take the rap!" I shouted back. "You schmuck, they just went to get the money. They put me on the griddle 'cause they thought I'd set them up when you took off."

"I'm sorry, Joe . . . I'm sorry," he said.

"We got another deal," I said, recalling what the Cowboy had told me before I left him. "We gotta meet the Cowboy in Staten Island the day after tomorrow. I'll drive. You make the exchange. I ain't going alone."

That's what we did. We drove to Staten Island to the parking lot of a restaurant, where I pulled my car up next to the Cowboy's Eldorado. He pressed a button and rolled down his window, and Gredda did the same. The Cowboy, who was with the agent who tested the junk on the first deal, passed Gredda the money, and Gredda apologized for panicking and passed him the coke. Everything was recorded because the Cowboy was wired for sound.

The whole exchange was covered by other agents, who watched and photographed the whole deal. Then we drove off, but as we did, in my mind I said, No more . . . I'm not doing this crap anymore.

The phone at my office rang, and the secretary buzzed me. "A Mr. Moser wants to talk to you," she said.

Moser . . . that was my FBI code name. I used it to call Tallia and other agents later. They used it to let me know they wanted to reach me. The name was out of my past. It belonged to a high school quarterback who called plays that always resulted in a pounding for me when I ran as a halfback. I decided to adopt the name as a reminder I was inflicting a little pain on the mob that was making my life as miserable as Moser did.

I picked up the receiver. "Meet me at the Chinese place, four o'clock," Tallia said, then hung up.

"Sure, Mr. Moser," I said, speaking into a blank phone. "I'll be glad to show you the apartment." I got my hat and coat and told my secretary I'd be gone for a few hours.

"I got to show a client a couple of apartments," I said as I left.

I went to our central meeting location, the Chinese restaurant a block from the FBI headquarters in Manhattan. Tallia was there; so was Jimmy Cullen.

I was upset when I arrived. The experience with the DEA had left a bad taste in my mouth. I didn't want to get involved in any more deals with the FBI. Being an FBI fly on the wall had only brought in eighteen hundred dollars in 1973, from September to December, and in 1974 they only gave me a little over thirty-five hundred dollars for the whole year. It wasn't worth the risk, and I didn't need the abuse.

"I want out, Ray," I said. "This last thing was terrible. I could have gotten killed. They treated me like I was some dog."

"Can't do it, Joey," he answered.

"What do you mean, I can't?" I said, feeling a cold chill rise through my body. "That wasn't our deal. You told me when I wanted out, that was it . . . I was out."

"Things have changed, Joey," he said, shrugging his shoulders. "You got to work for Jim Cullen here. I'm leaving. I'm being sent somewhere else, to work on something else for the Bureau. You gotta work for Jimmy."

"And if I don't?" I asked.

"Then I can't help you," he said. "Jimmy can't help you. The DEA wants to prosecute this case. If you're working for us, they can't go public; but if you're not, we can't put it on a shelf . . . we can't stop it from going public. If it does, they gotta call you as a witness, a coconspirator. They have to say you been working for us at the trial."

"Oh, Christ," I said. "What you're doing . . . that's not right. That's not our deal."

"It's out of my hands, Joey," Ray said. "Its the only game in town, and you aren't a spectator anymore."

It was either play or pay . . . with my life.

It wasn't too long after the meeting that Gallo died, and when he did the squeeze was on from both sides.

Before he left, Tallia helped me out of a jam with the Internal Revenue Service, advanced me some money, about two thousand dollars, to pay off some tax bills that suddenly came due. That helped keep some of the "good guys" off my back . . . at least for a while.

With all the shylock money I owed, a good part of it because of money I borrowed for the coke deal and for Gredda to lend money out to his clients with, I had nothing to pay tax boys with. So I asked for and got help from Tallia—sort of a parting gift. Only it was no gift. It was money I had to work off by doing things that Cullen and the Bureau wanted me to do. The squeeze was on.

With the Bureau, there's no such thing as a freebie. They always want more, more, more, no matter how much you give them, no matter how little they give you.

I'd given them the Colombo boys' gambling house, the drug case, I'd given them intelligence about Sal Profaci and his move to New Jersey. I'd told them about young Magliocco and his uncles and how they ran the liquor-distributor business and a linen service to catering halls. I'd even given them inside information on a restaurant meeting between Anthony Abbatemarco and Tommy DiBella, a meeting I'd heard about from Bolino.

The meeting was attended by Sally Albanese and Charlie "Moose" Panarella. At the meeting, in June 1974, DiBella had made arrangements for Abbatemarco to take over the family if he went to jail. Now that was before Abbatemarco got superseded by Allie Boy Persico and he and Albanese decided to challenge Persico's authority as a boss—a challenge they not only lost but that cost Albanese his life.

But the Bureau wanted more, and they were willing to put my life at risk to make me play by their rules. Either I continued to do what they wanted me to, or they would surface me—make my role as an informant public knowledge in the mob by making me testify against Gredda. They had me between a rock and a hard place.

When Gallo died, Jimmy the Bat took over his clients, and I paid him for a while. He was an old man, not too well, thin like Gambino, almost frail, and he spoke in broken English, always respectful, always the mafioso, the man of respect who expected respect. He walked very slowly, using a cane to help him hobble along. He couldn't have weighed 120 pounds soaking wet, and he only stood about 5'5".

I remember making a point of being on time with payments to him. He didn't make you fear him, just respect him. Then he died, and I found that the shy book had been passed to Odorisio and Cockeyed Allie. Every week, I had to go down to Third Avenue, near President Street, and hand Cockeyed Allie his money, nearly gagging from the smell of the smoke and alcohol and overworn sweaty clothing.

Cockeyed Allie was the opposite of Jimmy the Bat, a huge man with huge hands and a breath that always smelled of alcohol instead of garlic, and a low, gravelly voice that sort of growled out of a voice box that had been implanted in his throat after doctors had removed his larynx. Every now and then he'd pause, as he was cursing me or someone else out, so he could suck in some air through his box. It slowed his speech, but not his mind or his ability to make you realize that he had the power to snuff out your life any time he wanted to.

Finally, the demands of Cockeyed Allie and a half-dozen other shylocks were becoming too much, and I was having serious problems meeting the payments, which were now topping two thousand dollars a week. I needed help, and I went to Gredda for relief, to collect some of the money he'd borrowed from me so I could pay off some of the shys I owed.

"Jimmy, the guys that took over Gallo's books, they want their money back," I said. "I need the money I got for you for your clients and your share of the coke."

"I ain't got no fuckin' money, Joey," he said, throwing up his hands.

"Whaddaya mean, you ain't got no fuckin money?" I

screamed. "What'd ya do with all the bread I got you? Collect it from your clients."

"I ain't got no clients, Joey," he said sheepishly. "I was paying off what I owed with what you got for me."

That left me holding the bag with a lot of debt. I was caught in a vise, squeezed by both the good guys and the bad guys. I couldn't worry about Gredda. I had to worry about myself . . . and how I could survive. I had dug a hole for myself, and I didn't know how to get out.

As for Gredda, he disappeared shortly after that and has never been seen since. Still on the shelf, waiting to be brought to trial, is the drug case against him, which, if he ever surfaces, will require my appearance in court.

11

THE TIGHTENING VISE

I stood outside the Prospero Funeral Home on Eighty-sixth Street in Bensonhurst and shuddered briefly as I shook off a sudden chill that swept through my body. It must have been 90 degrees on the streets of Brooklyn, yet I felt cold, as though I'd been in an icebox and my blood had frozen and there was nothing inside to keep me warm, to keep me alive. How long, I remember wondering, would it be before they would be carrying me out of this place in a box?

I looked up and down the street. Nothing unusual. It was quiet . . . almost too quiet. The elevated rail of the subway that once provided the noisy and shadow-filled scenery for the movie *The French Connection* was strangely silent. No clickety-clack of train wheels, no roar of rocking, dirty subway cars, no screeching brakes. Just an eerie silence. I wondered where Jimmy Cullen and his agents were hiding. If they were in their cars, I couldn't spot them. They had to be somewhere . . . but where? In a parking field? Somewhere under the el? Where?

Beads of cold perspiration formed on my brow. I took out my handkerchief and wiped it dry. My brain was churning, and the palms of my hands were cold and clammy. The two Valiums I'd taken a short time before weren't helping. *Stop thinking, stop worrying about where they are. Do what you have to do. Be calm.*

I looked at the sign on the front lawn—a familiar sign in front of the familiar two-story brick building. PROSPERO'S FUNERAL HOME. Out of the corner of my eye, just before I approached the steps, I saw a car ease to a stop down the block. It must be Cullen, I thought.

Slowly, I walked in the front door. Nick Prospero was there waiting for me.

"Ah, Joey, you're here," he said softly. "Carl is upstairs in my office. He will see you in a few minutes." With a pat on the shoulder, he pointed to a funeral-parlor viewing room. "Wait in there. I'll call you when he is ready to see you."

It was a bright, warm summer afternoon, and I was at the funeral home to meet Carlo Gambino. The meeting had been arranged by Prospero at my request. I was desperate. I needed relief from the loan sharks; I needed support from my father, who wouldn't give it to me; and I was calling in one of those godfather favor chips Colombo told me to hold in reserve. I was seeking Gambino's advice and possible help.

It is not often that godfathers of the stature of Gambino will take time to meet with someone like me. But I had been his notary, and I had been injured and my car destroyed while in his service. To a man like Gambino, it was a debt, and godfathers of his stature always repay debts, if not in kind, at least as an adviser. It was part of his tradition, a tradition that is now dying out in the new generation of the Mafia.

Cullen passed me an envelope with a wad of hundred-dollar bills inside. I opened it under the table in the restaurant booth, fingered the bills briefly, and stuffed everything in my pocket.

"There's one thousand dollars there," he said, "but you're going to have to come up with some better information if you want anymore."

"I thought that DiBella meeting was pretty important," I said, "and I've given you everything I hear about Profaci and Magliocco."

"We gotta make some more cases, Joey," Cullen said. "Gredda's one thing, but we need more cases—or you got to testify!"

"Jesus . . . there you go with those threats again," I said. "Haven't I got enough problems? The shys are beating at my door day and night, I can't keep up with them. Gredda's really put me in a box."

"That's your problem, Joey," Cullen said. "You got to deal with it. Not me."

"Look, maybe I got something that'll interest you . . . something that's worth your while," I said. I was reaching for straws, anything that would keep the feds at bay. I needed time. I had to buy time on both sides of the fence.

"What, Joe?" Cullen asked. "What have you got that's new?"

"I got a meeting with Carlo Gambino." I answered. "A private meeting at Prospero's."

Cullen pursed his lips as if he were going to whistle, but didn't. "How about bugging it—carrying a wire?" he asked.

"Are you *nuts?*" I half-shouted. "Jesus . . . you people really want me dead, don't you?"

"Sssh . . . sssh, calm down, Joey, calm down," he said. "What's the meeting about?"

Half a dozen people in the restaurant where we had met looked up from the tables and into the darkened corner booth where we were sitting. I felt stupid exploding like that. Attracting attention was the last thing I wanted to do.

"I'm looking to get his help with the shylocks," I said. "I got a favor coming, and I'm looking to get help from him because of that. Shit . . . you guys won't help. Maybe he will."

"Tell you what, Joe," Cullen said. "We'll cover you. We'll cover the meeting, and after it's over, you tell us what happened."

"No wires?" I asked, half-pleading.

"No wires, Joe," he answered. "Just information, intelligence, and we'll see what he does after the meeting."

Jimmy Brown Failla pulled up in front of Prospero's. He jumped from the driver's side, and strode briskly to the sidewalk to open the door on the passenger side, reaching down to help Gambino stand up. As Gambino safely entered Prospero's, Failla drove off.

Within minutes, I was behind him, walking toward the front door of Prospero's to meet with him. Now, I was waiting in a funeral viewing room on the first floor. The place was giving me the creeps. I could smell death. It was probably the sickly-sweet embalming-fluid smells from the basement, but to me it was like smelling death.

Suddenly, Nick appeared at the room entrance. "He'll see you now," he said. "He's upstairs, in my office."

I walked into the hallway to a wide staircase and slowly climbed the stairs. As I reached the second-floor landing, I passed the casket room on my left and some viewing rooms on the right before I reached Prospero's office at the end of the hallway. Just before I reached the door, I remember being jolted by the noise and rumble of a passing train on the el outside. That sound, I remember thinking, would wake the dead.

I opened the door, and there sat Gambino, hunched back in Prospero's huge leather executive chair, looking up at me from behind that big crooked nose of his. He stood up to greet me and shake my hand, and as he did, I bent down to embrace him, kissing him on the cheek out of respect. As I stepped back, he motioned to me to sit, and spoke softly to me as I paid my respects and thanked him for seeing me.

"So, Joseph . . . what's the matter?" he asked. "Why have you called on me, and how may I help you?"

As respectfully and diplomatically as I could, I told him about the Gallo loans, about Jimmy Bat and Cockeyed Allie, Johnny Russo, and all the other shylocks who were coming into the real estate office every day, hounding me for money.

"I owe everybody, Carl," I said. "I asked my father to help, to give me some breathing room. His answer, you should pardon the expression, is for me to go fuck myself. He wants me out of the office. All I need is a little time. I will pay everybody, with all the interest. All I need is a little time. I'm in this jam because of this guy Gredda, otherwise I never owe anything to anybody. I've never been behind to the shylocks. I always paid my debts.

"I need somebody to tell them, and my father, to leave me alone, give me a little time until I straighten myself out. That's all I'm coming to you about. I just need a little time."

There wasn't a trace of emotion on his face as he sat there, but he listened. He listened intently to every word I had to say, and occasionally his head would nod up and down or side to side when he understood or when he didn't like what I said. I felt better just having him listen. I mean, that was more than my own father would do. Here's a man in the position he's in—the biggest boss of all the crime families—and he's sitting here in a funeral parlor listening to a jerk like me spill out my problems to him. Finally, he was through listening, and he spoke.

"Joseph, listen," he said. "I have children, all right? They work. They have problems. If something happens to my children or they get in trouble, I take care of them. *Capisc'*?"

I nodded.

"It's your father's responsibility to take care of your problem," he added. "I hope you understand, and that I have helped."

The meeting was at an end. I got up. "I understand, Carl," I said, "and I thank you very much for your time and your advice."

He had done nothing about the shylocks, nor would he. I don't think, deep down, that I believed he would. My hope was that he would talk to my father. He didn't, but he did give me a message for my father, that it was up to him to face up to his family responsibilities and do the right thing. He should help a son who was in trouble.

When I got back to my office, I went to see my father. "So what did the old man say?" my father asked.

"He said it's your responsibility to help me out because I'm your son," I said.

"Fuck him," my father said, "and fuck you. You got yourself into this shit, now you get yourself out—only you do it somewhere else. I want you outta here. I don't want you here with all your shylock friends coming around. It's bad for business."

I was stunned, really stunned. I couldn't speak. My eyes were brimming with tears, and it was all I could do not to break down and cry.

"Clean out your desk, Joey," he added, "and leave the key to the office with me."

I was drained. I was out of work, deeply in hock to the shylocks, and under pressure by the FBI to produce. The only thing I had to deal with was my street smarts, my contacts, and a real estate office that I would set up for myself in July 1975 to pay my bills.

The FBI debriefed me on the meeting and told me the feebs had followed Gambino as he left the funeral parlor. They never said where he went or who he met, but it was the last time I saw Gambino alive. He died a year later.

I later heard from Prospero about the meeting.

"I got in trouble over that meeting, Joe," Prospero said. "The old man, he said, 'Why do you call me with this shit? I have better things to do.' Now he's mad at me for arranging the meeting, Joe. He says he shouldn't be bothered by someone else's family problems."

The phone in my apartment was ringing as I unlocked the door. I dashed to grab the phone before the last ring, leaving my keys dangling in the lock.

"I got a great business opportunity for you, Joey," the caller said. "Come over to the office so we can talk about it. This is something that won't wait for long."

The caller was a business friend of long standing. He had heard about a real estate business that was going to be put up for sale, and he had thought about my predicament.

"It's ideal for you," he said. "The perfect spot. Luca Dana's Fortway Realty. It's just perfect for you, and he don't want an arm and a leg."

Luca Dana was an old-time, well-respected real estate broker who operated a small but profitable business at Seventy-fifth Street and Thirteenth Avenue. He operated from a leased two-story building that was in the very center of the old-style Brooklyn real estate firms.

Almost directly across from Luca Dana's Realty was Arthur Galasso's Realty and shylock Greg Scarpa's social club. Down the same block was Jerry Marinelli Realty and Aldo B. Girasoli Realtors, where Bolino worked. From a business point of view, my friend was right. It was perfect . . . and it was available.

Luca Dana wanted to retire, take life easy, and for about twenty thousand dollars he was willing to sell his business name and his following. In those days, a respected following like that was a sure ticket to success with a little hard work. But at that time, in the bind I was in, twenty thousand dollars might as well have been $20 million.

My friend offered to put up ten thousand dollars to help. "You'll have to raise the rest yourself, Joey," he said. "That's the best I can do."

I thanked him for telling me about the location and for the offer of help, and told him I'd get back to him in a few days. Then I made arrangements to see Tallia, who still hadn't left the Sixty-ninth Street FBI headquarters for his new assignment.

"Ray," I said, "I need help to get this business . . . ten thousand dollars. It'll be perfect for the Bureau and for me to do what the Bureau wants."

Tallia sat there, toying with his drink, listening as I laid out an idea I'd spent the whole night lying awake thinking about.

"I told Bolino my father was throwing me out of the office," I continued. "I asked him to tell all the goodfellows—Allie Boy, Scarpa, everyone—to bring their business to me, mortgages, rentals, sales, whatever, and I'll get them good breaks. The Bureau could get an inside track on what's going on."

Tallia smiled. He liked it. He wanted to build on it. "We can set up the greatest sting the mob has ever been hit by," he said. "I love it, Joey, I love it."

Tallia wanted the Bureau to put up the ten thousand dollars and additional money to remodel the building as well as take care of the rent to prevent people from nosing around. His idea was to install hidden cameras and microphones throughout the building to record everything that went on. It would have been a gold mine of information—better than all the bugs they used at the Mafia Commission trial years later, better than the famous Jaguar bugs that for months monitored some of the conversations of Lucchese family boss Antonio "Ducks" Corallo and his soldier Salvatore Avellino.

The real estate sting scheme could have been more productive than the bugs they placed in the kitchen of boss Paul Castellano or inside of the social clubs of John Gotti and Anthony Salerno. It would have produced more because the Bureau would have had inside men to photograph and monitor the conversations constantly, like they did with the ABSCAM transactions of congressmen, only they could have done it for years. Even more, it would have given the FBI access to the financial transactions, the investments, of mob bosses and their closest aides, because the office would have become not just a center for Persico and his people, but for the Genovese, the Gambino, the Lucchese, and the Bonanno people who wanted to invest in land and buildings or arrange bank loans and mortgages. It could have provided more evidence against the leaders of organized crime than all of the other bugs combined!

Tallia was excited, really excited, when he left the restaurant meeting with me. "I'll take it to some people in Washington," he said, "and I'll get back to you within the week."

He kept his promise. Several days later, he called and we met again.

"They turned it down, Joey," he said. "No financing."

"But why, Ray?" I asked. "This could give them—"

"I know, Joe, I know," he said, cutting me off. "Great minds aren't exactly functioning on this case. The answer is no . . . *nada*. Just do what you been doing."

"Great, and where do I do it from?" I asked. "How?"

"I'm afraid, Joey," Tallia said with a sigh, "that's a problem you have to deal with. I'm outta here. That's orders."

So what could have been the greatest sting in Bureau history was deep-sixed by some Washington bureaucrat who had never seen a Brooklyn street, who wouldn't know a mobster unless he saw mug shot, and who didn't give a shit about tracking the mob's finances. He was probably too busy lining up publicity shots and sucking up two-martini lunches on Pennsylvania Avenue.

The Bureau left me no choice. I had to turn to Bolino in hopes of finding some help in setting up my own office.

I was home, plotting new ways to make a fast buck with some new friends I was developing, when Bolino called me.

"Joey, I think I got a solution to your problem," he began.

"Whaddaya mean, a solution?" I asked.

"Look, you go to Cockeyed Allie and he'll take care of all of the wolves, and for that he'll want ten, maybe twenty percent of whatever business you set up."

"You sure?" I asked.

"You can go to the bank with it," he said.

"Okay . . . set up a meeting," I said.

The next morning I arranged to meet with Cullen near the Bureau headquarters and told him about the meeting that Bolino was arranging.

"Let's bug it," Cullen said.

"No way," I said, alarmed by his suggestion. Whatever I suggested, whatever intelligence-gathering plan I came up with lately, he wanted to bug it.

"Hey, Joey," he said. "No big deal. We wire you up so they never find it, and we monitor everything they say, when they say it. We'll be right outside. You get in trouble, we're in there to help."

"No way, Cullen!" I said excitedly. "I'm not sticking my head out there for him to chop off. He finds a body mike, I'm dead—dead, dead, dead. Forget it!"

"Okay, Joey . . . calm down," Cullen said. "You just call us. We'll keep an eye on everything outside, then we talk about what happens later." He patted me on the shoulder lightly as he stood up to leave. "But, Joey, sooner or later you gotta do this for us. You gotta do this, or we're going to have to take the Gredda case off the shelf and bring it to court."

Several days later, the call came from Bolino, and I arranged to pick him up to bring him to the meeting with Cockeyed Allie. The location agreed on was a small neighborhood Italian restaurant on Fifth Avenue and Eighty-fourth Street. I let Cullen know before I picked up Bolino. He and his agents were in place, parked in the area by the time we arrived.

Cockeyed Allie was already there, sitting at a table with Marty Odorisio. Cockeyed Allie stood up, and those huge, ham-like hands of his stretched out to shake mine and then pound me on the back with real authority. If I had been wearing a body mike anywhere, that pounding would have either broken it or shaken it loose.

"How are ya, Joey?" he growled through his voice box. "Sit down and find something you like to eat."

As I looked over the menu and ordered some pasta e l'entichie (pasta with lentils) for an appetizer and as a main dish veal marsala, Cockeyed Allie asked me who I owed and what I owed. I had the list in my pocket, and I went over it with him, one by one. Among the debts, of course, was the twenty-seven thousand dollars I owed him from the Alfred Gallo loan he had taken over. There was also money I owed Scarpa and Johnny Russo, a Genovese family soldier. I figured if he picked up all the obligations, including his, it was worth 20 percent of my business.

He looked over the list, and then back at me. By then I was shoving some of the pasta into my mouth. "Okay . . . we'll take care of this," he said. "If I take care of this, I want forty percent of your business, and I want your answer by the time I finish dinner."

I nearly choked on the pasta. I nearly choked on everything I ate, and I couldn't eat a helluva lot. Nothing tasted right after that; my throat was tightening, and my crotch felt wet from the sweat that was pouring from my body.

I finished my demitasse and Italian pastry. Then I looked up at Cockeyed Allie. "Can't do it, Allie," I said. "I can't go forty percent. I ain't giving you forty percent of my business. That's just too much."

"What'd ya say?" he growled through his voice box, sucking air in and out. "You little shit. You're gonna regret that." He slammed his huge hand down on the table, making all the silverware and the glasses bounce in the air, tumbling with a clatter to the table.

"Come on, Michael," I said to Bolino. "Let's go. Let's not waste any more of Allie's time."

Once outside, I breathed a quiet sigh of relief, happy I'd escaped with my life. In the car, I began yelling at Bolino.

"You son of a bitch!" I shouted. "You told me no more than twenty percent . . . he'd want no more than twenty percent of the business, and he was gonna settle up on everything and keep the wolves away. Now, he wants forty percent. What, are you crazy?"

"You got rocks in your head, Joey!" Bolino shouted back. "Forty percent was a good deal."

"No, Michael," I said. "Twenty percent was a good deal. Forty percent sucks."

I dropped Bolino off at his girlfriend's home and left for my apartment. I probably could have cut the deal for 40 percent. I could have covered up anything going in and out—sales, leases, rentals, whatever, and Cockeyed Allie would never have known. But he had Odorisio there with him, and I figured that he was going to put Odorisio in the office with me to monitor transactions. If I had gone for the deal, he'd have bled me dry—the biggest wolf at the door I would have had to worry about would have been Cockeyed Allie, and he was more than I could handle alone.

I told Cullen the next morning what had happened. He shrugged. Neither he nor the Bureau were offering me a way out. In fact, he was about to be transferred to the New Rochelle office, and I was going to have to work cases for him there.

A couple of weeks later, I wound up in a rented office on Eighteenth Avenue and Eighty-sixth Street under the corporate name of J. Cantalupo Realty. It was a spin-off from my father's Cantalupo Realty name. I figured by using the J. In front of the Cantalupo, I could get some of the kickoff from his business. Clients, instead of calling Cantalupo Realty, would call me . . . at J. Cantalupo Realty. For a while, some of them did.

12

THE FLEA-MARKET SCAM

Everybody likes a bargain. Week after week, every week, department stores, supermarkets, electronics shops, and car dealers fill newspapers with advertisements on so-called bargains. Most of the bargains, however, really aren't what they are hyped up to be. Even the sharpest consumer, the one who hunts down the lowest advertised price on a product, is paying a premium on what he buys.

The truth is, someone has to pay the overhead—the rent for the store, the salaries for the employees and the executives, the cost of the advertisements, the utilities, insurance and shipping costs, and the taxes—all that is figured into the overhead and tagged on in one form or another to the price of the bargain-priced product anyone buys. So the bargain isn't really a bargain. Well, sometimes it is, like in a mob flea market, and even then the bargain may be a foreign copy, a counterfeit, or stolen swag from the waterfront or a hijacked truck.

In July 1975, I didn't know the first thing about flea markets. I heard about them in passing conversations, but I'd never been to one, and I didn't have a clue about how they operated. All that changed when I got a call from two friends of mine who ran a business on Coney Island Avenue. They had an idea, a plan to set up Brooklyn's first flea market, and they reached out for my help in finding a location and financing it. They never invested, but I did.

Flea markets operate on the principal of low overhead, quick sales, and staying one step ahead of the tax collector—particularly the ones that organized crime runs. One person, a group of people, or a corporation rent a large location, generally a vacant parking field, an empty warehouse, an arena, even a racetrack, for the least amount of money possible. They then subdivide that location into hundreds of smaller businesses—booths where independent vendors sell their wares. Usually, there is nothing elaborate about the booths, nothing secure, and vendors have to pack up at night only to return the next day and set up again.

The vendors pay low rent for their booths, far lower than they would have to if they had to rent a store of their own. They avoid high insurance costs for theft and fire, they pay minimum wages for employees, generally keeping employment in their own family, and they usually buy and sell products without warranties or guarantees. As a result, they can sell name products at well under what a regular retail store can and still make a nice profit.

Sometimes the products they sell are the real thing. More often than not, they are cheap copies or counterfeits of popular name-brand products. And if the product booths are run by the mob, you can bet your bottom buck that what they are selling was heisted somewhere from someone probably less than a week from the day it is offered for sale.

The flea market, I found out, was a great place for the mob to unload its smuggled cigarettes, hijacked coats, stolen jewelry, and operate untaxed vending machines from pinballs to cigarette machines. Today, they run video games, Joker Pokers, and even illegal slots.

A lot of the vendors in flea markets are mom-and-pop operators working extra hours to make a few bucks to put bread on the table. The worst thing they might do is avoid paying Uncle Sam or New York State income and sales taxes, although that's becoming harder and harder every day for legitimate people to do. There was and still is an enormous underground income that flows untaxed in the economy through flea markets from one end of the country to the other. Millions of dollars' worth of untaxed goods are sold daily through these open-air shops, and still more millions of stolen goods are peddled through these markets by mob-associated vendors with their own booths.

For a mob guy, it's like having a golden goose. All you do is feed the goose to get him to lay the golden egg. On Long Island, Carmine "Tutti" Franzese and his cousin Michael Franzese ran a flea market two or three days a week from a huge parking field on Long Island.

They rented the space through a front for a top fee of two thousand or three thousand a month. At the same time, they rented out space to more than five hundred concessionaires for a minimum of ten dollars a week and maybe as high as fifty dollars, depending on the space. Each month they were paying out tops three thousand dollars a month for rental and collecting no less than five thousand dollars to six thousand dollars a week in vendor fees. At the same time, they ran a parking concession that collected twenty-five to fifty cents a car, and during a given two-day prime weekend, they were pocketing another two thousand dollars to three thousand dollars in parking fees. Among the vendors they had three or four of their own booths unloading products from smuggled cigarettes and heisted toys to stolen cameras, jewelry, and clothing. Those operations brought in thousands of dollars more a week. For a minimum investment and an even smaller exposure in terms of law enforcement, the Franzeses, who were both members of the Colombo crime family, were clearing twenty thousand dollars or more a week—all in cash—none of it subject to tax by local, state, or federal agents, who didn't have the time or resources available to watch, investigate, and prosecute their operations.

So when my friends came to me with the idea of setting up a flea market in Brooklyn, I jumped at the idea as a way of getting myself out of hock and back on top in the business of making money.

When I left my father's office to set up my own office, I realized I needed some help and protection to do business and keep the loan sharks at bay. In terms of mob alignment, I was considered "with" the Persicos; that is, I was associated with the Colombo family, but not a member by any stretch of the imagination. The man I reported to and shared my profits with to get this "family protection" was Bolino.

I needed more. Bolino could help me deal with loan sharks in the Colombo family, but I was also in hock, about seventeen thousand dollars worth, to a very violent loan shark in the Genovese family, John Russo. I needed a way to deal with him, so I sought out Louis LaRocca.

LaRocca was a big man, a big tough guy who use to come regularly to my father's office to talk to Joe Colombo. He must have stood 6'2", and weighed in at 240 to 250 pounds. He could be mean and rough when he wanted to be, but his value to me was his influence with Funzi Tieri.

LaRocca lived in Staten Island, and he was a soldier, a goodfellow with Funzi Tieri. It was apparent to me that he had clout with Tieri. When he came to see Colombo, it was to iron out any problems between the Genovese and Colombo families. He was the liaison between Funzi and Colombo, particularly when it came to gambling territorial problems. That gave him rank, stature, something I needed in his family.

Just after I left my father's office, I sat down with Russo and LaRocca and asked Russo for some breathing room. Russo never said he'd give me the breathing room, but he and LaRocca suggested that my office would be a good front for LaRocca's operations in gambling and loan-sharking as well as for meetings in much the same way as my father made his office available to Colombo. I agreed, and my uncle Jimmy and I then physically revamped the office space I had rented to operate in the same manner my father's had. We built a room with a see-through mirror for LaRocca. I had the same type of gate between the entrance and the office salesmen, and there were two or three salesmen and my secretary at desks in front of my desk, which was at the center, where I could see everything going on.

With LaRocca was a Jewish friend of his, Sol Janowitz, who ran apartment houses in the area. Janowitz used to come into the office and hang around. He had connections that LaRocca found useful, among them then–state assemblyman Harvey Strelzin, who was chairman of the State Assembly Consumer Affairs Committee and a lawyer. Strelzin, like Janowitz, owned an apartment house, and he was also in the garbage business. Both Janowitz and Strelzin were later to figure in my flea-market operation.

One of my first real estate transactions when LaRocca came to my office was to sell one of Janowitz's mortgages through my father to someone else. I got a ten-thousand-dollar commission on the deal, and LaRocca took a one-third cut for steering the Janowitz mortgage deal to me.

While all this was going on, Cullen was once again made aware of what was going on and what I would be doing and with who. The first words out of his mouth were, "Let's bug it." Almost as quickly, I refused. All I'd need would be one slip, one mistake, and I'd be dead. I wasn't willing to take a chance like that, not there or then. The Bureau, however, would know who came and went, just as they had at Cantalupo Realty, with one exception. They'd have an inside intelligence source—me—and as time went on, they would wire me up for specific meetings with Bolino, LaRocca, Russo, and others while I managed the market.

When the idea for setting up a flea market was first passed to me, I proposed it initially to Bolino and then to Anthony and Joe Colombo, Jr. All three turned me down. They were unanimous in their reason for saying no.

"It won't work in Brooklyn," explained Bolino. "It's for the suburbs . . . not this area."

That was an excuse, not the real reason for not going into it with me. None of them gave me an honest why to their no, but I think it was because they figured I'd fleece the flea-market accounts to pay off my own loan-shark debts. They were probably right.

I also mentioned the flea-market idea to LaRocca and Russo, and I convinced them to take a ride with me out to Farmingdale to see how the Franzese flea market operated. They were impressed.

Impressed or not, LaRocca went on trip to Florida, so I pressed my case in another meeting with Russo. Janowitz was at the meeting. I explained the whole concept of the flea market and how we could all make a lot of money out of it. But to open up a location, I told Russo, I needed money and partners with authority—someone like Funzi. Impressed by the figures and the scheme, Russo arranged a meeting with Tieri to raise money for the deal. By then I had worked up figures to show that with twenty-five thousand dollars to start, I could set up a business that would return a minimum profit of twenty thousand dollars a month tax free, plus whatever they wanted to unload at their own booths.

What I planned to do was rent a location and break it up into sixty booths, each of them rented for thirty dollars a day or eighteen hundred dollars a day for three days. That was a total of fifty-four hundred dollars for a Friday, Saturday, Sunday operation. At the same time, food concessions run by the market would bring in a minimum of one thousand dollars a week, and a pinball arcade would add another five thousand dollars a month. All told, I figured we'd bring in a minimum of $30,600 a month and our expenses, including monthly rental of $5,000, advertising, electricity, and salaries would total $10,600. For his twenty-five-thousand-dollar investment, I told Tieri, he would get 50 percent of all the profits and the company. Funzi jumped at the deal, said he'd put up the money, and told me to go ahead and find a location. There was one hitch. I had to wait for LaRocca to return before doing anything.

Three days later, LaRocca was back, and I went over the whole deal again with him. Janowitz was again sitting in. At first I thought LaRocca would be upset at my going to the Old Man while he was away, but he wasn't. He arranged for a sitdown a couple of days later in my office that included Funzi, Russo, Janowitz, himself, and myself.

At the meeting, I told Funzi not to worry about the tax man on the twenty-five thousand dollars. "I got a way of covering it for you," I said. "I can put it in a bank account and make it look like it was a commission on a real estate deal. No one can ever trace the money back to you."

That pleased Tieri. The one thing he didn't want was the IRS snooping around asking questions about the financing of the corporation. LaRocca was also pleased—particularly when I told him I was going to give him 20 percent of my 50 percent. And I promised 10 percent to Janowitz for arranging the legal matters, for setting up the corporation and getting the permits and any other legal obstacles cleared through Strezlin. In fact, in the end Strezlin worked as our lawyer on the deal and handed Janowitz and me the ten shares to the company, the Brooklyn Village Square, Inc. Strezlin, when he later had to testify in a case against Tieri, denied he ever knew that Tieri or the mob were hidden owners.

My next step was to find a location, and the one I thought showed the most potential was a building at Eighteenth Avenue and Eighty-fifth Street. The building was a boarded up A&P supermarket. The rental was being handled, I learned, by a lawyer who was a friend of my family. So I called him up and told him what I had in mind.

"I'm sorry, Joe," he said, "but I have a triple-A tenant who wants the location. I don't think we want a flea market there, even for a while."

I told Funzi what had happened, and he decided the two of us should see the lawyer. When we arrived, the lawyer was in conference, but that didn't bother Funzi. He just brushed off the secretary and walked right in. When the lawyer saw him, he excused himself from the conference and walked out of the room to talk with Funzi.

"I hear there is a little problem over here with this building, right?" asked Funzi. "I'd like for you to take care of it."

The lawyer was pale, very nervous, as he looked first at Tieri, then at me.

"Funzi, I'll do my best," he said, "but I have a problem with this triple-A tenant. I just can't tell him to—"

"Do your best," growls Funzi from his voice box.

"Of course," answers the lawyer, who steps up to kiss Funzi on the cheek as he starts to leave. "I will do my best."

Now, I felt like a hotshot. I'd just had a godfather intervene for me and tell a very influential lawyer that he'd better get in line and do the right thing. This flea market couldn't miss.

When I got to my office the next day, my phone was ringing off the hook. It was the lawyer.

"Who the fuck do you think you are, Joey?" the lawyer yelled. "What gives you the right to try and shake me down?"

"I wasn't trying to shake you down," I answered. "I was just trying to show you how important this deal is."

"Its a shakedown, pure and simple!" he yelled back.

"Hey, you said, you told the Old Man you'd do your best," I said angrily.

"Well, I'm not gonna put up with this horseshit!" he shouted. "My triple-A tenant signed the lease, so screw you. Good-bye."

He slammed the phone down.

I was tempted to tell Funzi what he said, but I didn't. If I had, I might have started a feud between mobs, because the lawyer had some friends in both the Colombo and Gambino families.

Instead, quite by luck, I stumbled across what I thought was as good, if not better a location, another abandoned A&P supermarket, with ten thousand square feet of space and a large parking lot. It needed some work inside, but so did the other place. The price was right too, five thousand dollars a month.

Now, I needed the money, and Russo began to deliver it—five thousand dollars here, ten thousand dollars there—only by the time all the loot was delivered, it was twenty-four thousand dollars. He had deducted one thousand dollars in back interest on the twenty thousand dollars I owed him from prior loans.

Under the corporation structure set up by Strezlin, I was the president and Janowitz was the secretary/vice-president, and the cash I received from Tieri through Russo was deposited in the Brooklyn Village Square account at European-American Bank, where we had set up our corporate account.

The money was deposited at different intervals in different amounts as if I were receiving commissions at different times and putting that money into the company. That way, no one could track the money back to Tieri, who, I guess, was pulling money out of one of his many gambling operations that pulled in hundreds of thousands weekly. If the IRS took a look at corporate accounts and records, there was nothing on paper to show they had an interest, and I held all the shares of stock in the office. Janowitz was in charge of keeping the books.

With the location in hand, we should have been off and running, pulling in cash by the wagonload. Instead, we got bogged down in remodeling, electrifying, advertising . . . all sorts of gimmicks that drained away cash.

Instead of playing it smart, cutting overhead, just throwing sawdust down on the floor and letting vendors set up their stands, LaRocca got contractors in to build about one hundred self-contained stalls that could be locked up overnight. He had electricians put in lighting for the booths, inside and outdoor lighting for vendors who were going to sell their wares from the rear of their cars.

I saw what was coming. LaRocca was bleeding this thing, making thousands off the contractor work that he controlled, and I couldn't do a thing about it. I wasn't represented. I had no one to complain to. I wasn't a goodfellow. I wasn't even with anyone in the flea market. I was dealing with Genovese people, and I was with the Colombos, but the Colombos didn't have an interest—they had nothing to protect. To protect my interests, I needed the Colombos involved.

To cover my ass—to make sure they didn't clean me out and toss me out with nothing but the bills—I took one share, representing 10 percent of my 20 percent, and brought it to Allie Boy Persico. My reasoning was simple. Allie Boy had replaced Vincent Aloi as the acting boss of the Colombo family when Carmine Persico was jailed for parole violation. If he has a piece of the market with Tieri, who is the boss of the Genovese family, nobody in the Genovese family is going to take a chance of throwing me out on my ass and offending Persico by jeopardizing his interests.

That little maneuver later paid off. When the market needed more money to keep it afloat, LaRocca went to Allie Boy at the Diplomat, a mob club hangout of Persico's, and asked if I was with the family. Persico said I was. He then asked if he was interested in saving the flea market, and Persico said he was. He got Persico to put ten thousand dollars more in the market.

Months later, Persico tried to collect the ten thousand dollars from me, saying I was responsible for the money. I talked my way out of that one. I reasoned that I hadn't come to him for the money, LaRocca had. I had given him stock in the company with no strings. I'd put his nephew in the arcade business and split the take with him fifty–fifty. Why should I be responsible for the errors of LaRocca? I was managing the flea market, but it was really LaRocca who was running everything—getting everything screwed up. Persico finally agreed.

In January 1976, because we were so far behind in bills, because we'd run up so many bills advertising and in remodeling, I had to go to Russo to ask Tieri to get more money, another ten thousand dollars. I told him what the problems were, and he understood. He said he'd talk to Tieri. Within a couple of days, he came back and said Tieri agreed to put up the money, but there was a hitch. He said he was going to charge the market one percent per week, one hundred dollars a week vig, for that loan. Every week after that, we recorded on our books, "John $100," to reflect the interest we were paying him. The money we paid him came from our share of the arcade pinball revenues.

With the market losing money so fast and falling deeper and deeper in debt to the mob and its loan sharks, Janowitz left the company in January and turned over his 10 percent share of the market to LaRocca's son Joseph, who was brought in to keep the books.

There were so many things that went wrong, it's hard for me to believe as I look back. I wanted the food concession for myself. Tieri nixed that. He assigned that to friends of his, and they pulled in the one thousand dollars a week in profits we were relying on.

When we held our grand opening in December 1975, it was advertised all over town. That cost a lot of extra money, as did the remodeling bills that LaRocca ran up. Then there was the catering bill for the grand opening. Tieri wanted his favorite Italian food supplier, Sbarro's Italian delicatessen, to cater the food for the grand opening. More money out of the company's till. The pinball arcade was assigned to Little Allie Boy Persico, the son of Carmine. He had about fifteen machines in there and picked up about four thousand dollars a month. Instead of 100 percent, we got 50 percent of what wasn't skimmed off without our knowing about it.

There was really no reason for failure except that we overspent, we went far beyond what we should have in remodeling costs and advertising. Even with those costs and the extra money pumped in by Tieri and Persico, the market could have survived and become a money-maker if the mob hadn't screwed it up themselves.

At one point, we had about one hundred vendors, each of them paying about two hundred dollars a month for inside booths. Outside we had another sixty spaces for vendors selling from their cars and vans, which brought in close to three thousand dollars a month total. That was twenty-three thousand dollars clear, plus the arcade and the food concession. We were picking up a minimum of twenty-eight thousand dollars, but instead of pocketing eighteen thousand dollars, we were two thousand to three thousand in the hole every month.

That could have been straightened out, but the mob turned the market into a regular headquarters for organized crime, and that upset a lot of our Jewish vendors, who didn't want any problems and who quietly began dropping out.

First there were Tieri's mob booths. They were churning out everything from stolen cases of tomato paste and cigarettes, to two-hundred-dollar leather jackets that sold for seventy-to-eighty dollars each. Hot jewelry, hubcaps, radios . . . you name it, the mob sold it. The products changed each week—whatever fell off the back of a truck at the warehouse, they'd say. That made legitimate vendors nervous. They worried about a police raid, about being tarred with the mob brush.

Then there were the mob meetings. Upstairs, downstairs, in the cellar, in the parking lot . . . there were thugs of all the families everywhere. Allie Persico, Apples McIntosh, Russo, Jerry Langella, Charlie Panarella, Tieri . . . if he came from Brooklyn and was a hood, you could find him at the Brooklyn Village Square Flea Market. The meetings were daily. Some for a few minutes, others for a half hour or more, and where they were, the FBI and the cops were floating, watching, recording. It was like a thieves' market right out of tales of Ali Baba. The flea market had, in every sense, become a "family affair."

The vendors saw it all, and slowly, one by one, a few at a time, they began dropping out, and business began falling off.

At one point, things got so bad moneywise, we didn't have

enough money to pay for electricity for air-conditioning the market, so we had to call in an electrician the mob knew to jerry-rig the wiring—help us steal the electricity off Con Ed lines without showing the electrical costs on our bills. Later, that electrician would figure prominently in a witness-security situation that jeopardized the lives of witnesses appearing at two of the most important mob trials in history.

In April 1976, I found out how meek and frightened a threatening big bull of a hood like LaRocca can become when faced with the wrath of a godfather.

It all started when I was driving down Sixty-seventh Street toward the flea market. As I passed the Endicott Sportswear Company, which was between Fourteenth and Fifteenth Avenues, I spotted Russo and Tieri standing outside, and I stopped to say hello.

"How we doing at the market, Joey?" asked Funzi.

"Not too good," I answered. "We're behind another five thousand dollars in the rent."

The Old Man suddenly wheeled around on me. "What?" he growled from his voice box. "You tell that motherfuckin' Louie to go get that five thousand dollars, or I'm gonna cut his balls off."

"Yes, sir," I answered, climbing back into my car and driving off to the flea market.

When I got there, I saw LaRocca and told him I'd seen Funzi.

"Yeah, what did he have to say?" he asked.

"He asked how things were, and I told him we were behind another five thousand dollars in our rent," I said.

"Then what did he say?" he asked.

"You're not gonna like this, Louie," I answered.

"Just tell me," he snapped.

"He said for you to get the five thousand dollars or he was gonna cut your balls off," I said.

Louie turned absolutely white. He stood there for maybe a minute and began trembling. Then, without another word, he left. He came back a short time later. With him, he had the five thousand dollars. We paid the rent that day.

It was only a matter of time before the market went under,

but before it did, it had become a two-family investment. Tieri had thirty-five thousand dollars in it with Russo; LaRocca had put in sixteen thousand dollars and Allie Boy Persico had put up ten thousand dollars. I'd even put up $2,500 of my own, and for a while I was held responsible for half of Tieri's losses, $17,500. That was worked down to twenty-five hundred for me and the same amount for LaRocca, but I never paid it.

13

CRIME WORLD

When your playpen is the underworld's backyard, you have to pay for your share of the fun and games. There are no free rides. Sooner or later, everybody gets their hands dirty and pays. It took years for my number to come up, but by 1975 I was in hock up to my throat for my flings in that playpen, and it was time for me to jump in the mud with the other dirtbags.

It would be easy for me to blame my entrance into the sleazy world of street crime on my mounting loan-shark debts, and, in truth, the shylocks made me panic more than once—forced me to make decisions to take the easy way to make a quick buck to pay off a past-due loan and avoid a beating. But the threat of loan sharks wasn't the only reason for me to take a personal leap into the crime world I had managed to remain above while rubbing elbows with the bosses who lived off that sleaze.

I confess I liked the excitement of crime, the danger it brought, the ease with which we made money, and the power I felt from running small gangs of thugs who did what I wanted them to do right under the noses of the FBI agents who were making me jump through their hoops. It was as if I were a goodfellow without all the consequences. I didn't have to take orders from a capo or a boss to do a job. I didn't have to beat up frightened old men or rape shylock victims' wives to collect a debt. I didn't have to kill someone because someone else ordered it. In a sense, I was my own boss—as long as I kept the wolves from my door by paying off my shylock loans and providing the FBI with the information they wanted. I was walking a tightrope over a fire, and for some weird reason I loved it, at least some of the time.

Strangely enough, the bosses of organized crime are in a way like the superstars of the entertainment world—they attract their own class of groupies, from kids who try to act tough, steal, or run errands for their heroes to young hoodlums who have made crime a way of life and are willing to kill to make it their stepping-stone to the big time.

Instead of screaming, fainting, and clawing at the clothes of the stars they worship, the groupies of the Mafia spend most of their lives cooking up schemes to make money, to impress the people who rule their world, to be noticed and used so that they have a chance to move up and be somebody important enough to sooner or later kill or be killed. It's crazy, but it's true.

To reach those bosses, the Mafia groupies try their damndest to please people who know those bosses, who hang out with them, work for them, or appear to be close to them. I was one of those who appeared to be close to the bosses. I dressed well, I lived well, I was seen at important functions, at mob social clubs, and in the company of the most important of the bosses. It was, as a result, natural for younger Mafia groupies who wanted to get somewhere, to be somebody, to impress me by coming up with money-making schemes. Most of the schemes were as hare-brained as the people who dreamed them up, but I managed to find a hard core of about seven or eight young toughs who went beyond the groupie image, who had some smarts as burglars and thieves and just needed a little direction.

Sometimes they worked together, sometimes they split into separate crews to do different jobs. A lot of the time they did things on their own, without direction, and more often than not they stole from each other as well as those they worked for, myself included.

It took a little time, but I became a sometimes leader for all of them at one point or another, depending on the jobs we were working, and they became my crew. For almost three years, they played a very important role in my survival, helping me raise the money I needed to pay the loan-shark bills and the people I answered to for survival in the mob world, people like Michael Bolino. At the same time, they made money and a reputation for themselves. Most of this was done without telling the FBI a word. In fact, it's likely the FBI wouldn't have gotten a lot of its information I fed them if I hadn't become a player in the world of everyday crime. It's also probable that they wouldn't have solved a lot of crimes and made the sizable property recoveries they did in some cases if I hadn't handed it to them on a silver platter.

My first introduction to street crime was actually through my uncle Jimmy Cantalupo in 1969. It was Christmas Eve when he called me in a half-drunken stupor to meet him at Big Daddy's restaurant on Coney Island Avenue, where he worked as a general maintenance supervisor.

The Big Daddy restaurant was one of a chain run by Robert Knapp. I knew Uncle Jimmy had physically helped build the restaurant in Brooklyn, as well as one in the Bahamas, as a contractor. Physically, he couldn't do work like that anymore, so he worked for the restaurant as their maintenance supervisor.

Uncle Jimmy was furious when I got there.

"What's going on? I asked, noticing that the restaurant where he worked was closed.

"Those bastards didn't give me a Christmas bonus!" he shouted. "I'm gonna take a bonus, and I want you to help. You get half of whatever we find."

At his insistence, we burglarized the place, but all we got for our troubles that night was a case of corn and some french fries . . . and a safe with no money. A side benefit, one that I didn't acknowledge even to myself at the time, was the excitement, the thrill of taking the chance at being caught. As it turned out, it was only the first of three jobs I did on Big Daddy's for Uncle Jimmy. The next was more profitable, and it came at a time in 1975 when I needed money desperately to keep some of the loan sharks at bay.

I was still working at my father's real estate office when Uncle Jimmy paid me a visit. He remained bitter about the way he was being treated at Big Daddy's, and he wanted to do a number on the boss's nephew.

"You need money, right, Joe?" he asked.

"You got it, Uncle Jim," I said. "I need a lotta bucks . . . and I need them fast."

"I got a way so you get the store receipts—easy as pie," he said. "You keep whatever you get. All I want is to see that little bastard crawl."

"I'm listening," I answered.

"On Sundays," he continued, "Knapp's nephew is in the store. On Saturday nights, he counts all the money, and on Sunday mornings he walks across the street with a zippered bag and puts it in the bank box—you know, the night-deposit drop that you need a key for. He does it every Sunday, like clockwork."

I was playing softball on Sundays then, so I first watched how this guy made his deposits, then I sketched out a half-assed plan and called on two of the young guys in my crew to handle it for me.

We had two cars. I parked across the street on Coney Island Avenue. One crew member, who looked like a kid, was playing handball against the bank wall. The other guy was in his car parked around the corner. When I saw Knapp's nephew come out of Big Daddy's carrying the satchel of money, I honked my horn twice. As he walked past my handball player, the player came up behind him and grabbed the bag from him, knocking him to the ground accidently as he did. Without a word, my player ran to the car waiting around the corner. Then they took off west on the Belt Parkway, getting off on Bay Eighth Street. I followed behind them to be certain they weren't tailed.

We all met at my father's real estate office, which was closed on Sundays. I opened it, and we went to the basement to count out our take. It came to just exactly five thousand dollars. I gave the getaway driver one thousand dollars, and the handball player and I split the remaining four thousand dollars. Although he didn't ask for any, I later gave my uncle Jimmy a few hundred out of my share.

Without another word, everyone left to meet again at the softball field to play the game we were scheduled to play. I remember feeling a sense of elation as I sat behind the wheel of my car and left for the game. It was the first robbery I'd ever been involved in. No one was really hurt. The guy who had been robbed probably had a lump on his head from his fall, but there were no problems, and I'd picked up a quick two thousand dollars for doing virtually nothing—just planning the heist, watching, and counting the split. It was an easy way to pick up some bucks.

It wasn't too long after when Uncle Jimmy and I hit Big Daddy's again. This time there was no rough stuff. Uncle Jimmy just used his key, walked in late at night, and riffled the restaurant's office, carrying out its safe to a waiting station wagon.

We took the safe to my grandmother's home in Valley Stream, where the two of us carried it into her garage. There I punched it open with a chisel and a sledgehammer, knocking off the dial and the handle and opening up the safe's belly, a technique I'd learned from a tenant we had who lived in an apartment upstairs next to my father's office.

The tenant was a guy named Johnny Buyer. He's dead now, but at the time he had a shop in the Fulton Fish Market, where he was a fishmonger. On the side, he was an expert safecracker. I went to him to open the first safe Uncle Jimmy and I stole out of Big Daddy's. He didn't ask for a dime. He was just glad to help, especially when I told him Joe Notch and all the other hotshots from the Colombo crew didn't know how to open a safe. He laughed like hell, then he took me aside and showed me step-by-step just how to peel a safe.

It was heavy work, but it could have its rewards in those days. The second safe at Big Daddy's netted me about seven thousand dollars, which I used to pay off part of a loan-shark bill. Uncle Jimmy buried the safe.

When the people at Big Daddy's raised hell about the office alarms not working and the safe being stolen, Uncle Jimmy blamed the night supervisor for not properly setting the alarms before he left. They never once suspected that he had anything to do with the theft.

Uncle Jimmy wasn't the only one who had information that

led to burglaries and safe jobs in that period. One of the best tipsters was a neighborhood lady, a married woman I used to have matinees with. Her husband wasn't in the mob, and she was concerned about the trouble I was in with all the loan-shark debts and the danger she was certain they placed me in. So when we weren't under the covers balling, she kept her eyes and ears peeled for opportunities that might be money-makers for me.

One of the ideas came in the form of an apartment in a house less than a block from where I lived. In the apartment lived a hotshot relative of hers who kept a safe he had hidden in an upstairs room filled with money and jewels—or so she was told.

Using the information she gave me, which included a list of his more important clients, I began watching this guy, and finally, when I thought I had his routine down pat, I called in two guys from Yonkers who sometimes did jobs for me. One was a Latin kid, an illegal immigrant named Miguel, the other was a cat burglar I knew as Mikey.

At the same time, I gave my uncle Sal one hundred dollars to go to Ferrara's pastry shop in New York's Little Italy to buy me a big basket of Italian goodies. My plan was to have my Yonkers hustlers take the basket of goodies to this guy's apartment after he left and give them to his wife to gain entrance to the apartment. Attached to the basket of goodies, which Ferrara's was famous for making up as gifts during the holidays, was a card made out to the relative. The card also identified one of his best clients as the giver of the holiday basket.

It worked like a charm. She asked them to bring the basket into her dining room, and, once inside, as she took out two dollars to tip them, they ordered her to take them upstairs to the safe her husband had.

The woman was scared to death, but she did what she was told, protesting all the while that she didn't know the combination to the safe, that only her husband knew. That figured. A lot of husbands don't tell their wife things like that because they don't want them to get their hands on their money.

Miguel and Mikey were told no violence. I didn't want anyone hurt. So they gagged her and tied her up, and then they pulled the safe from the closet, where it was hidden, covered it with a sheet, and carried it downstairs and to a waiting car in broad daylight—at 9:30 A.M., while I watched the whole scene from a safe distance in a parked car. They then took off with me following to the Golden Gate Motel, where we'd agreed to meet. There, we transferred the safe to the trunk of my car and drove, once again, to my grandmother's, where I put the safe in the barn.

We all went inside to see my grandmother and have some coffee. While they were at the table, I excused myself to go to the barn. At first Mikey wanted to go with me, but I told him no. "No one sees how I do this," I explained. "It's something I keep to myself."

I told them I'd be back in fifteen minutes, and I was, with a bagful of more than seven thousand dollars cash, and jewelry that was worth a few thousand more. There were also a couple of IOUs that the safe owner had that were for ten thousand dollars. I figured I couldn't collect on them and he was probably squeezing the guy who he held the IOUs on, so I just ripped them up.

We split up the money between the three of us, and I gave my grandmother five hundred dollars for letting me use her barn. That weekend I came back and dug a hole in the yard, where I buried the damned safe. She never knew what I did. More important, neither did the FBI until I became a witness.

There was one thing I learned quickly about operating with a crew. Never trust those in your crew. More likely than not, they will take the information you give them to do a job and pocket a good piece of the proceeds without ever telling you they found what they pocketed—like the crew of characters I used to rifle apartments in the Staten Island apartment house where my father lived.

The apartment house was owned by my old friend Wasserman, who had a master key to every apartment. He also had a list of all the tenants in the building and their private phone numbers.

I managed to get the whole package, including a copy of the master key, through one crew member, a character who worked for Wasserman and who had a relative who was a made member, a goodfellow of the Gambino crime family. Then I called in Mikey and Miguel to round out my crew of thieves.

The plan was relatively simple. We zeroed in on a day when I knew most of the tenants were out working, then we called the private phone numbers of thirty of the tenants. One by one, as they failed to answer, I sent the team of thieves into the apartments to steal what we could. Now one of the targets was the apartment of one woman who had a small safe with a two- or three-carat diamond ring and some cash, as well as other jewels.

They hit her apartment all right, but they claimed they never found the ring, although I was told later she reported it stolen. In fact, we came up very, very short of what I thought we should have come up with for the afternoon's work and all the careful planning. I was looking for at least $15,000, and maybe as much as $40,000 in cash and jewels, but all they netted was about $4,000–$5,000 worth of stuff.

What happened? I learned later that guys like Miguel and Mikey thought nothing of swallowing the diamond ring and other valuable gems, and then later shitting them out when they were alone—taking the gems from their bowel movements and cleaning them off before peddling them to the nearest fence. That way, they didn't have to share the profits with their partners, including me. I knew what they'd done—that's why I didn't have the slightest trace of guilt later dealing them to the FBI. Screw me, screw you!

Sources of information came from the damndest places and people you'd least expect. I'd met Miguel, for example, through a Yonkers man who became a friend of mine during my honeymoon. He introduced me to people at the Rye Hilton Hotel, who in turn introduced me to Miguel and Mikey.

Mikey was a cat burglar, a really good second-story man who could lift just about anything from just about anybody. Miguel was a crazy little Latin who would do anything for a buck and would follow Mikey through the fires of hell. Between them, they made a pretty good pair of thieves.

Miguel had a girlfriend, a sort of nurse's aide who took care of wealthy old folks in their homes in the Westchester County area. My two hustler friends would use her information about people she served and their living quarters to loot homes where she said the people kept expensive jewelry or artifacts or paintings.

One night I got a call from Mikey at home.

"Joe, I gotta see you real fast," he said excitedly.

"Why? What's the problem?" I asked.

"We got these paintings—ten, twelve paintings—and we don't know how to unload them," Mikey said. "I figured you'd know how. You'd get us the best price."

What comes around goes around.

So I met them and I looked at the paintings. Hell, I didn't know a damned thing about paintings, but any dummy would know that these had some value. As it turned out, they were worth over $110,000 dollars and they'd been stolen from the home of an old man, an invalid who had been under the care of Miguel's girlfriend.

"I don't know how much I can get for you," I told him, "but we gotta store them, and I've got just the place." "Just the place" was the home of another girl I'd been running around with who agreed to let me hide the paintings at her place.

After we stashed them, we separated, and I called Jimmy Cullen, who had been temporarily moved to the New Rochelle office of the FBI, and told him what I had. He and his SAC (supervising agent in charge), Paul Stapleton, decided they wanted to make a case and recover the paintings. They wanted me to negotiate a price with Mikey, and they wanted to tape that negotiation. Cullen was going to play the role of the appraiser.

Before the meeting was arranged, Stapleton arranged to have agents pick up the paintings from my girlfriend's apartment on Eighty-fifth Street in Brooklyn and bring them back to their office upstate.

The meeting was then held in the home of my Yonkers friend, who used to tip me and others to possible scores that he heard about at the bar of the Rye Hilton. Cullen was there with me to vouch for him. He carried a tiny transmitter and a tape recorder, both of them taped to his body.

The transmitter was designed to broadcast to an FBI surveillance car parked near the house that also recorded the conversation on tape as a backup in the event the tape recorder didn't work or was discovered and they had to come in like gangbusters to protect Cullen and me.

Attending the meeting were Miguel, Mikey, myself, and Cullen, as well as the homeowner. Item by item, so it was forever recorded on tape as evidence, Cullen and I went over each and every painting with Mikey and Miguel, pinpointing the description and where they found it in the house. We negotiated back and forth, and the bottom line was that they wanted ten thousand dollars for the paintings.

"Listen," I said. "the paintings are stashed. I'll give you two thousand dollars now, and as soon as we can get a buyer, my friend and I will give you the rest, the other eight thousand dollars. Its gonna take a little time," I continued as I pulled out two thousand dollars in cash that Stapleton had given me to deal with at the meeting, "and you gotta be a little patient."

When they saw the color of the money, they were as happy as pigs in shit, and we left with a solid case of interstate theft for the Bureau. Stapleton ordered the case put on a shelf—kept secret until the time came when he could make it public, when I was out of the area and not in danger, or so he said.

There was still the problem of what to do about the paintings while keeping Miguel and Mikey at bay and not suspicious of my role. Stapleton came up with a near-foolproof scheme. There was a warehouse in New Jersey that the Bureau was about to raid. When they hit it, they found thousands of cartons of smuggled cigarettes . . . and the paintings. Stapleton announced it in the local press.

The following week I called up Mikey and Miguel. They wanted their money.

"Listen, man," I told Mikey, "the FBI seized the paintings in that raid in New Jersey at the warehouse where I had them stashed. I had all kinds of shit there . . . worth hundreds of thousands. I'm busted. I can't pay you for what I don't have. The paintings are gone. We'll try to make it up on the next deal. Meanwhile, at least you guys got two grand out of it. I got zip."

That, of course, wasn't true. I got ten thousand dollars from the insurance company for recovering the paintings for them. I used part of that money, about six thousand dollars, to pay loan-shark bills. The rest I used to get a Lincoln Continental Mark IV from Turis Leasing Company in Brooklyn. I leased the car, and the Bureau paid for the monthly lease fees.

They rigged it for sound, putting tiny microphones inside the car's sun visors. They were rigged to record everything that was said in the car every time I threw a small red switch on the side of my seat. The recorders themselves were hidden in the trunk of the car where no one could find them. That was one of the best investments the Bureau ever made.

Mike Marino was a big, heavyset guy from Flatbush. He originally was a truck driver, until he decided he could make a faster buck cutting up cars, than hassling with them on the expressways, so he set up a chop shop in Worcester, Massachusetts, where he handled hot cars from the boys in Brooklyn. Mike's partner in crime was a character named Joe Provost, who helped run the chop shop until he started a fire, burned it down, and got caught at the scene by police. I met both of them through Uncle Sal, and it was because of them I wound up making a new case for the FBI.

Marino was into a little bit of everything—chop shops, hijackings, moving guns, cigarette smuggling—but he was something of an independent, he wasn't responsible to any family.

A short time after I met him, he and Provost opened a nightclub in Rhode Island, not far from Providence. Almost before they turned the lights on, they were paid a visit by Nicky Bianco, who had moved back to Providence and was operating as a captain with the Raymond Patriarca crime family, where he had first started out.

"He wanted a hundred bucks a week from me," Marino told me later on, "until I told him I had a partner."

"Who did you say was your partner?" I asked.

"You. I told him Joe Cantalupo was my partner," he said with a half-assed smile, "and when I did, he stopped shaking me down. He said if I was with you, then everything was okay."

As far as I was concerned, everything wasn't okay. I wasn't

his partner. I wasn't getting any of his nightclub action, and one day Nicky Bianco would be around to haunt me for helping Marino, and I'd wind up paying the tab. There wasn't a helluva lot I could do until Marino told me about some plastic explosives he'd gotten his hands on that had been stolen from a U.S. Army base in Massachusetts.

"I want two thousand dollars a pound for the stuff," he said. "Can you handle it?"

"Let me see," I said. "Let me see if I can find a buyer."

I could hardly wait to dial the boys at the Bureau and tell them of this latest score. This wasn't a bunch of fur coats nobody could account for—this was twenty pounds or more of C-4 plastic, enough explosives to take out a couple of city blocks. It could take out whole train stations, airport terminals, or public buildings. You could mold it to any shape you wanted, carry it in your pocket, hide it in a suitcase or even on your body, and it would never explode. But with the right detonator . . . baba-boom!

I was right, the Bureau wanted it. They were a little slow in getting the wheels turning—getting approval to spend the money to buy the stuff—but once they got that green light, they wanted action . . . and fast.

After a series of meetings with Marino in November 1976, I arranged for a meeting in the parking lot of a Howard Johnson's on I-95 in Connecticut on December 29. The Bureau had the whole place staked out, and I brought the "buyer," a wired-up agent, to make the buy from Marino.

Originally, they were going to wire me, but they realized that might be inconvenient later on. Besides, I was still too nervous about carrying a bug, so they chose an agent to act as the buyer and used me as the go-between. That way, if they did have to make a bust, they might get away without having to call me as a witness.

The agent they assigned apparently didn't have a helluva lot of experience at wearing a wire. He's playing Mr. Macho with his shirt open halfway to his navel showing his hairy chest—*and* the tape that held the microphone in place.

"Excuse me, George," I said, "I don't want to tell you how to do your job, but I think you better button up that shirt before these guys get here. They see that, and we're both dead meat."

He looked down, saw the tape and the microphone, flushed a little red, and quickly buttoned up the shirt. "Thanks," he said, kind of grudgingly. "Let's get out of the car."

So we went to my Lincoln, which was already bugged, as I said, and I threw the switch just as Mike pulled up.

Mike stood next to the car with my agent friend George and myself, and we haggled a bit in the parking lot, getting the price down to five thousand dollars before Marino agreed to the sale price. Then, while cameras rolled from every angle, and the recorders taped every word, he put the C-4 plastic explosives in my car and then added a separate package containing the detonators while we counted out the money. Before the show was over, Mike and his friend were trying to interest us in the sale of thousands of stolen army rifles.

The Bureau put the case on a shelf for future trial, but it never got to that. Marino and his three friends all copped pleas. For the Bureau, the important thing was to recover the plastic explosives. In the hands of the wrong people, like some terrorists, they could have done a tremendous amount of damage. Last year, just two pounds of stuff like that, C-4 that was supposed to have been made in Czechoslovakia, blew a Pan American 747 jetliner out of the sky over Scotland, killing more than 270 people! The twenty pounds I managed to get confiscated could have done a helluva lot more damage, taken a lot more lives.

Providence, Rhode Island, is something of an Eastern Seaboard center for the manufacture of jewelry. There are silver craftsmen there as well as masters of gold-jewelry design, and there are a lot of small gold refineries that provide the by-products they work with. So it's natural for large quantities of everything from silver bars to gold dust to be transported to and from the refineries to the shops of these craftsmen by special couriers, armored guards, and express services.

As luck would have it, Marino found out that one of the refineries employed an uncle of Joe Provost. Every day, like clockwork, a truck from the Federal Express Company would stop at the refinery and pick up gold dust. The truck would make some other stops before making its final stop at the airport, where an airplane would take some of what the truck was carrying out of the state.

Marino wanted to hijack the gold-dust load, but before he did, he wanted to go over his plan with me and have me check out the location and the truck movements to see where the best place to hit would be. Included in this heist was to be a fourth man, "Frankie M."

Frankie M. was a real knockaround guy who, until he teamed up with me and some of my crew, had worked for a gypsy crew of street toughs until the guy who ran it got gunned down on the federal courthouse steps in Brooklyn just as he was about to appear before a federal judge. After the shooting Frankie M. figured it was safer to do business with someone who had "friends" in the mob than someone like his ex-boss.

Anyhow, we watched this Federal Express pickup operation at the refinery in Providence for a little more than a week. Then we mapped out what we were going to do and decided to hit it. I was going to drive an old clunker of a car that would be the crash car—the vehicle that would crash into any police vehicle or other car that tried to follow the crew that handled the stickup and got off with the loot.

We followed the Federal Express truck from the refinery to its next stop. The driver gets out, makes his pickup, and as he comes out, Frankie M. and Provost take him—push him into the truck and they take off with Provost driving. We're all heading, now, for the drop where we agreed to meet, and I'm following them, when all of a sudden state troopers are coming up fast behind us. It seems a woman saw the holdup and abduction take place. She had a CB radio and called in the state cops.

Provost and Frankie M. reach the drop area, push everything out—whatever was in the truck—and take off. Behind us is a state trooper, and I'm supposed to jam him, crash into his vehicle, only I'm too afraid. What am I, stupid—me, Joe Cantalupo, plow an old clunker into a state-police car from another state? Not me, Charlie Brown.

I pull this clunker into the parking lot of a bowling alley

where I left my Lincoln Mark IV. Screw this! I'm heading back to the bar where we all started. As I do, I can hear, wherever I go, the sirens and loudspeakers of the state-police cars. "He's going down this way," one loudspeaker said. "He's going that way," another broadcast.

I drive back to Marino's club, and I wait for hours. No Marino, no Provost, no Frankie M. Finally, I decided to head back to Brooklyn. At about 4:00 A.M., I got a call from Frankie.

"Frankie, where the hell are you?" I half-shouted.

"I'm home," he said. "You're home—you're all right?"

"Yeah, sure," I answered. "What the hell happened?"

"They chased us to a dead-end street—the cops, right?" he said. "We jumped out, threw our guns away, and took off through the woods. I don't know what happened to Provost or Marino. All I know is, I crawled through those fuckin' woods until I got to an Italian barbershop. I got him to help me. He cut off all my hair so the cops couldn't identify me. Then I caught a train home."

Provost, we learned later, had also escaped through the woods, eluding the police search. Marino, who had been waiting at the drop with a station wagon to make the pickup, watched the cops race after the Federal Express truck, and then quickly gathered up everything that had been tossed from the truck to the drop area.

The next day, Marino called me to meet him at Frankie M.'s house. When I got there, he had everything laid out on a table— 520 one-ounce jars of pure gold dust. At the going rate of $110 an ounce, we were looking at more than $57,000 of gold dust!

I had a buyer, "Johnny Tips," a soldier in the Gambino crime family who ran a Brooklyn bar on New Utrecht Avenue by day and a gong show for queers at night. Between the two, he often came up with enough information to provide me with tips on possible scores. When things worked out, he'd get a piece of whatever action we had.

So I went to "Johnny Tips" with the gold deal, and I was careful to explain to him where it came from and how we'd gotten it. After a little haggling, "Johnny Tips" offered me $80 an ounce, or $41,600.

I went back to Marino and Provost and the rest. "I can only get sixty-five dollars an ounce," I told them.

"Sixty-five bucks!" shouted Marino. "Shit, this is pure gold. You can't go wrong with pure gold. It's all in one-ounce jars. We gotta get more than that, Joe—it's worth more than that."

Frankie M. and I were partners and Marino and Provost were partners in the deal. We were supposed to split everything down the middle, fifty-fifty, and then split with each partner. Frankie M. knew what I was doing.

"Look . . . they know it's hot, man," I said.

"Ah, shit," said Provost, "tell them to shove their sixty-five dollars. Let's peddle it ourselves."

"Use your fuckin' head," I snapped. "You ain't gonna peddle this stuff yourself. You'll just get in trouble. Let me go back, try again, see if I can move them up some. Let's not get the wrong people mad at us. I don't need that, man."

So I faked going back. Frankie M. went with me, to make it look good. When I returned, I told Marino and Provost that the final offer was seventy dollars an ounce, and if we didn't take it, we could be in big trouble.

Everyone agreed. Frankie M. and I brought the 520 ounces of gold to "Johnny Tips" and got the money. They got $35,000, which was split four ways; each share was $8,750. Later, Frankie M. and I also split the other ten dollars an ounce, which amounted to twenty-five hundred dollars each. Three or four months later, the price of gold went from $110 an ounce to nearly $400 an ounce. The big winner was "Johnny Tips."

14

BODY MIKE

I n the fall of 1976, there was an in-house power struggle between the New Rochelle office of the FBI and the New York office over how I was to be used. Because of its size and, I guess, the politics of the FBI, it was inevitable that New York would win. I didn't know it then, but in the long run, I would eventually lose not only my informant status, but my identity as a human being because of that power clash.

Instead of continuing to make successful cases for the office in New Rochelle, I was told that I would be primarily working for the New York office, and they would pay me the approximately fifteen-hundred dollars a month I was receiving for providing the Bureau with intelligence.

Up to that point, I had provided information that resulted in recovery of stolen goods amounting to more than $1 million for the Bureau, and there had been the recovery of stolen U.S. Army C-4 plastic explosives that could have caused a disaster, both in damage and death.

In addition, agents had made cases involving drugs sales, interstate thefts, and robberies against a half-dozen individuals, including Gredda, Johnson, Marino, Provost, Miguel, and others. Those cases had been put on a shelf to await prosecution when I surfaced. I didn't realize it then, but I had a maximum of five years of anonymity left to me from the time I'd made my first case. No one told me when they recruited me and squeezed me to work those cases that there was a statute of limitation of five years. If they weren't prosecuted within that time and I wasn't surfaced as a witness, the Gredda drug case would automatically be dumped—dismissed unless the subject of the case was a fugitive. Unknown to me, there was a time clock set in motion when I participated in the Gredda case. The Bureau and prosecutors would have to break my cover by 1978 unless they decided they could fry bigger fish by continuing to use me. To do that, however, they would have to dump the case, and write off the expense of gathering evidence against Gredda.

From the Bureau's point of view, the cases in New Rochelle that were in the bank, so to speak, were still pretty small time. They weren't high-profile mob cases, and that's what the Bureau wanted the most—cases like the one I'd helped them make against Colombo's sons and their underlings, where thousands of dollars in gambling receipts had been seized and hundreds of thousands of dollars in gambling action had been disrupted.

All that had cost them less than twenty thousand dollars in informant fees, and that was only the tip of the iceberg that they considered was within their reach as long as I was under their control and on the hook to the mob loan sharks.

The flea market had become a treasure trove of information about the business politics of the mob, about how three crime families—the Colombo, Gambino, and Genovese families—worked together, made concessions and decisions to make money in the market I created. Meetings were observed, photographs taken, evidence gathered, that would be useful later in major federal cases against mob bosses. It was a mother lode the Bureau was going to mine, and it was spelled out to me in a Manhattan meeting with one of their agents.

The Bureau was aware of my debts to mob loan sharks almost from the moment Alfred Gallo died. They were also aware of my financial problems in setting up a new real estate office and my mob partnerships in the flea market. All of that provided the Bureau with an agenda of cases that they knew they could make against ranking members of different crime families. Since all of those cases were in Brooklyn, it stood to reason that they would concentrate my undercover work there, where they could make the greatest impact.

"You're gonna have to work for us in Brooklyn, Joey," explained Frank Lazzara, an agent who worked out of the New York office. Lazzara had taken over as my control agent from Cullen and from Charles Domaro in New Rochelle, where I had been working.

"What kind of cases, Frank?" I asked.

"Loan sharks . . . extortion . . . cases like that," he answered.

"Against who?" I asked.

"The people you're in hock to—Mike Bolino, Johnny Russo, Allie Boy Persico—all of them," he said.

"How we gonna do that?" I asked.

"You're being squeezed because you're having trouble paying the vig, right?" he said. "They say they're going to work you over unless you pay up."

"Right," I answered.

"Well, we'll help you pay your vig," he said. "We'll give you the money to pay the interest—only you pay it when we want you to, when we think it has the most effect. We'll have you pay some one week, wait a few weeks before you pay more. That way you get the threats—you get the pressure we need, Joe, to make a case. We gotta bait the hook to catch the fish."

He paused for a long moment, then threw in the kicker. "When you pay them, we want you to record what they say," he said. "You're going to have to go in wired for sound."

"Jesus, Frank," I said, "you know what you're asking me to do? These people find a wire, they kill me . . . there, then, no if, ands, or buts . . . they cut my balls off and stuff them down my throat."

"It's the only way, Joey," he answered. "Besides, we'll be around to help if you're really in trouble."

"And if I don't?" I asked.

"Then you're on your own, Joey," he said. "We have to cut you off. No more money, no help with the vig, nothing. You're on your own. They'll carve you up for being a deadbeat, anyhow, and we won't be around to help."

He was right, of course. Without the nearly fifteen hundred bucks a month the Bureau paid me for information, I was dead meat. It wasn't much, but it was helping keep the wolves from my throat. With the added vig money he was offering—the money that would pay the interest on some loans but not the principal, which Lazzara made it clear I was responsible for—I might survive. But for how long?

I knew that by paying the vig on the Bureau's schedule I would get in deep trouble with the loan sharks for not making payments on time. They wouldn't just yell and scream at me—they might belt me around a bit, and I'd have to take it. I was going to be the ball that everyone batted around. I was going to have to live with crapping in my pants out of fear. I could already feel my head throbbing, my heart pounding! I was already shaking inside, and I couldn't control it. I wanted to run, but there was no place I could run to, no place I could hide . . . not then.

Lazzara didn't say if the Bureau would call in the cases that were shelved and make me testify, but I knew that would probably happen. I also knew that they'd find out or maybe already knew about scores I'd already made with others to help pay the mounting loan-shark bills. That meant jail; that meant being at the mercy of these animals when they knew I had been informing on them. At that moment, I was on the verge of panic. Somehow I kept my cool.

"What about the New Rochelle office?" I asked.

"Forget about them," he said. "You work for me now . . . for the New York office."

I shrugged. "What choice have I got, Frank," I sighed, "what choice have I got? When do we start?"

"Soon, Joey, soon," Lazzara said. "We got a lot of work to do."

When the phone rang in my real estate office, my secretary answered, buzzed me, and said a Joe Moser wanted to talk to me about a new rental. I could feel my gut start to churn as I picked up the phone.

"We gotta meet, Joe," Lazzara said. "Same place, nine o'clock tonight."

The meeting was at the same restaurant we had met at earlier in midtown Manhattan. Lazzara was with his supervisor. It was getting close to showtime. At the meeting, arrangements were made to wire up my leased car, which they were paying the monthly tab for, and my home, for meetings I might have with Bolino and others who sometimes stopped by to make collections.

"When we want you to go to a meeting wired," Lazzara explained, "we'll arrange to meet you at a midtown hotel off Broadway. We'll tell you what room to go to, and you'll be taped up and everything tested up there. Believe me, Joey, no one will ever know. Trust me."

That was the way it worked. They would call me or I would call them about a meeting with a particular person they wanted evidence on or I had to pay vig on a loan to.

The code name on every call was, as it had been before, Joe Moser. Usually, it would be Lazzara. When I answered on the phone, he would tell me it was "showtime" and then give me the room number, usually at a hotel off Broadway in the theater district.

I'd take the car to a parking lot, then I'd grab a subway or a cab to Forty-second and Broadway. From there, I'd walk to the hotel, making sure I wasn't followed. Once inside the hotel, I'd sometimes go to the theater-ticket counter and check out what plays they had tickets for. When I was sure no one I knew was around, I'd walk through the lobby to the elevator, get off at one floor and take another elevator to the floor I wanted to go to. Then I'd knock at the door, and the agents would be there waiting to let me in.

"Okay, Joey, strip," one of them would say, with a smirk, and while I took off my suit, shirt, undershirt, and pants, they'd make wisecracks about all the hair on my chest and stomach, or my back or legs.

"Joey, you're gonna love this when we get finished," one would say. "Yeah," another would crack, "and you'll get a real kick when we take it off."

That usually meant they were going to enjoy my agony when they stripped away the adhesive tape they used to hold the microphone. When I would finish with the recording session and return to the hotel, they would lose no time in ripping off the adhesive and whole clumps of my hair as they did it. Sometimes I felt some of them showed an almost fiendish delight in ripping that adhesive off and watching my reaction. Sometimes I'd grit my teeth and curse under my breath, other times I couldn't help but yell from the pain. When I did yell, I'd get a chorus of, "Come on, Joey, be a man—don't be a crybaby."

"You bastards!" I'd yell. "Gimme a break. Let me take the tape off . . . please!"

"Oh, no, Joey," they'd laugh. "This is our job. We gotta do our job."

"What are you, fuckin' doctors?" I'd shout.

More laughter. They had no mercy, these agents. They'd just laugh.

By a strange twist of fate, the first time I recorded a conversation for the Bureau, I didn't have to go to the midtown hotel to get taped up, they had to come to my apartment to wire it up.

As I look back, I think under normal circumstances Lazzara and his men would have preferred to wire me up in the hotel. It certainly would have saved a lot of aggravation and eliminated a lot of risks, but Lazzara wanted me calm, in familiar surroundings, in a place where he and his men could react quickly if they had to if things went wrong—and as it turned out, things went wrong.

The first objective was to get my wife out of the house. Veronica knew I was working for the Bureau. She didn't like the idea, because she was afraid of what might happen to me if I was discovered. She also worried about the kids, but I had promised her, as had the Bureau, that if anything happened, if what I was doing was ever uncovered by the mob, she and the kids would be moved, and above all would be safe.

As a result, Veronica sort of accepted what I did without talking about it much, and when I told her that I wanted her to go and play bingo with the kids somewhere while I conducted business at the apartment, she left without too much comment, just as she did when Colombo wanted to use our apartment for a Mafia Commission meeting.

That was the way things were done in Brooklyn in those days. The wives, the women married to guys in the mob or guys close to the mob, accepted things. They didn't question. The husband was the boss, and that was the way it was. That doesn't mean she was meek and mild. She had a helluva temper when I did things that were wrong, and she had her suspicions about the women I was fooling around with, but she was still a woman who did what she believed was best for her husband and her family. So when I didn't want her around for meetings or I didn't want her to interfere with what I was doing, I'd tell her and that was that. That's not saying it was right, and it sure as hell isn't the way things are now.

Almost immediately after my wife left, Lazzara and his agents came to the apartment dressed in workmen's clothes, carrying a beautiful artificial elephant-leaf plant. Inside the pot for the plant, at the bottom, was a Nagra. Behind the couch in the living room they installed the Kell to broadcast the backup to the conversation to a parked Bureau car, where a tape machine would make a twin recording of what was said. Before they left, they activated the recorder in the plant.

"Okay, Joey, everything is set," one of the agents said. Then they were gone.

My nerves were razor thin at that moment. I was cold with sweat, and I popped a Valium to calm down, waiting for Michael Bolino to arrive. The last thing I had ever thought I'd have to do was bug a conversation with Michael. We'd been close for so long, but he'd turned our friendship into business and he was bleeding me the way all the loan sharks were—worse, he was the guy who'd set me up with the loan sharks, and he was very close to the Persicos. So he was a natural target for the Bureau. I had no say in the selection.

I turned on the television to keep my mind off what I had to do, when suddenly this plant started to shake. Now what the hell am I going to do? Nobody told me what to do when something like this happens. How do I get the goddamn thing to stop? There was no number to call the Bureau and get them in a hurry, so I did the next best thing: I leaned over the couch and spoke into the transmitter behind me.

"Frank, give me a call . . . fast! I got . . . we got a serious problem!"

Within a minute, he was on the phone, and I told him about the dancing plant.

"Frank, you gotta do something about this goddamn thing," I said. "It's jumping and shaking like it has the Saint Vitus itch. Jesus . . . Michael will be here any minute."

I had barely hung up the receiver when two agents were at the door, knocking. I let them in, and they went to the plant and deactivated the recorder, but there was no time to take the plant out or put in a new recorder. Everything would have to be recorded by the Kell. They had to reset the Kell higher up the back of the couch, tape the wire, and cover all of it in a way so it wouldn't be seen. My biggest problem now would be to make sure that I kept Michael close to the couch when we talked.

There couldn't have been five minutes to spare before Bolino walked in. The first place he went was to the plant, admiring it, wondering where I'd got it. I told him a friend of Veronica's had given it to us, and let it go at that.

That first recording with Bolino was made the early evening of October 28, 1976. It was an important tape for several reasons.

First, it established the business participation of Johnny Russo, Lou LaRocca, Allie Persico, Bolino, and myself in the flea market and in the pinball machine business at the flea market—all of it got on tape, including Persico's and Bolino's having 10 percent of the market's ownership. It provided the Bureau with recorded evidence that Persico was going to steer mob clients to the new real estate office I was planning to buy—the same office the Bureau had said they'd invest ten thousand dollars in before some idiot bureaucrat in Washington nixed it. It also established, out of Bolino's mouth, the power of Allie Boy Persico to keep loan sharks from my throat—not just Colombo family loan sharks, but Genovese family loan sharks, like Russo.

Making that first tape was like making my first jump out of an airplane, when I was certain I was going to get killed. Before the meeting, before the plant started shaking and jumping, I whistled a lot. You don't hear it on the tape, but when I'm particularly nervous, I whistle a lot. Once Michael and I started talking, all those problems seemed to fade into the background.

The only thing I was conscious of was what Michael and I were saying, what I had to get him to talk about on tape, and staying near the couch. It was like . . . lights, camera, action . . . let the tapes roll. And they did . . . in the car where Lazzara and his buddies were monitoring and recording what we said:

JC: How you doing?

MB: All right.

JC: Are you squashed?

MB: Of course . . . fucking tired and sick. Sick and tired.

JC: You're sick and you're tired? Where were you when you called me?

MB: Downtown.

JC: You were downtown when you called me? You got here fast. Did you order twenty [pinball] machines?"

MB: I don't think Johnny wants twenty machines.

JC: You don't think Johnny Russo wants twenty machines. Does he want ten machines? Does he want fifteen machines?

MB: I don't know. Why don't you talk with him?

JC: I'm telling you what I want. I told you the other day that I want twenty machines for here. This is what I was told in the beginning. In conjunction with the discotheque.

MB: All right.

JC: Now they're opening the fourth. I need them for the third.

MB: Yeah, but maybe he's getting 'em someplace else. Is that possible. Huh?

JC: I was told.

MB: By who?

JC: Louie LaRocca. To go to Allie Boy and ask him for the machines.

MB: All right.

JC: Some things are important to me—

MB: Yeah.

JC: —Aren't important to you.

MB: What's important now is that you keep them off your back until you go into the real estate office.

JC: It's important, yes, okay? Now the other thing that's important is the market. My twenty percent.

MB: Um-huh. So, Joey, let me put it to you this way. You wanna be left alone, you want 'em to get outta there so that you have a chance to earn. So what the fuck do you wanna do with it now? [unintelligible] If they wanna push you out, that's the best thing that ever happened. I'm telling you. It's the best thing that ever happened to you.

JC: My point. I have ten percent. I gave you and Allie Boy ten percent.

MB: Right.

JC: All right, now they're gonna make money.

MB: I'll talk to Allie Boy about it. I told you that Allie is going upstate. He is supposed to come back tomorrow. He won't. He ain't coming back until maybe Saturday or Sunday. I didn't forget.

JC: It's important to us.

MB: Of course it is. I understand.

JC: 'Cause now when they see they're earning . . .

MB: I understand.

JC: You know, they're gonna throw me out. I mean, you might stay in. You might say all right, go ahead and throw him out. I have to have the answers.

MB: The answer you want is for them to leave you alone.

JC: The answer . . . the answer is if you or Allie Boy will say, Listen, leave him alone, he'll start making payments in February. Right? With Johnny Russo . . .

The conversation didn't end there. We talked about my debt to Russo, who I still owed twenty thousand dollars on a knockdown loan. Now a knockdown loan is what you still owe after the loan shark agrees you've paid enough vig—that you can't pay any more vig, and that everything you pay after he says it's a knockdown goes to knocking down the principal you still owe him.

I had paid Russo three hundred dollars a week in vig for more than a year on fifteen thousand dollars I'd borrowed. He had already collected more than the original fifteen thousand dollars, so he agreed to the knockdown and, in doing that, he said what I still owed was twenty thousand dollars, only I wouldn't have to pay vig on that twenty thousand dollars. That meant by the time I got through paying off everything he wanted, I would have paid him more than thirty-five thousand dollars on a fifteen-thousand-dollar loan. He wasn't doing me any favors. He just knew that he had milked the cow dry.

We talked about a seventeen-thousand-dollar loan I had with Cockeyed Allie that was now down to fourteen thousand dollars, and then we discussed a ten-thousand-dollar debt I had with Allie Boy Persico. There was one big problem about that debt. Persico thought the money had been borrowed by someone else.

It all began in the summer of 1976, with a pocketbook manufacturer from downtown Manhattan, a man named Eddie Edelman, who Peewee Campagna had sent to me when he was looking for mortgage money. Edelman was a very, very wealthy man. He owned a pocketbook business, apartment houses, and other investments, but he had a problem—a ten-thousand-dollar cash-flow problem and trouble with some wiseguys in Manhattan who ordered pocketbooks from him and wouldn't pay for the merchandise.

When Edelman told me about the problem, I went to Bolino and I told him about Edelman.

"This guy needs a rabbi, Michael," I said. "He's got big bucks, but he needs a little help. Allie Boy helps, maybe it turns out to be a good thing for him."

After Persico checked out Edelman through Campagna, a meeting was arranged and Persico told Edelman, although he later denied it to federal prosecutors, that he could be assured he wouldn't have trouble collecting on pocketbook sales to the wiseguys again.

"Whatever happened before," Persico said to Edelman, "people ripping you off for pocketbooks, I cannot help, but you can be assured if it ever happens again, I will take care of it."

So there was a friendship made then—at least for the moment—and Persico felt he had a piece of this guy. He didn't, but he felt he did.

Edelman also had this penthouse apartment for rent. It was a beautiful place overlooking Manhattan. All he wanted for it was one thousand dollars a month. I took Persico to see it. He liked it, but all he offered was $750 a month. Edelman turned him down.

Then came Edelman's cash-flow problem, a sudden need for ten thousand dollars, something he denied ever asking for, but he did. I went to Persico and got the money, and he personally handed me the ten thousand dollars cash. Interest was to be 2 percent a week.

Now Persico figures he's in to Edelman, and I figure I've done a favor for Persico that he'll remember . . . until I see Edelman.

"Joe, I don't need the money anymore," he said.

"Jesus Christ, Eddie," I said. "I went through all this shit to get you this money—now you don't even want it?"

"I don't need the money now, Joey," he said with a shrug. "Some people paid me money they owed me. . . ."

So there I am, stuck with the money that Allie Boy gave me to give to Edelman. I can't go back to Allie Boy and tell him Edelman doesn't need the money. I figure he'll break my skull. So I keep the money and I give five thousand dollars to my uncle Sal to hold and I take the other five thousand dollars to pay my shylocks.

A week later, I give twenty-five hundred dollars plus two hundred dollars interest to give to Allie Boy. Now I owe Allie Boy $7,500, and the interest is $150 a week. I pay . . . and I pay . . . and I pay, and after about a month I finally tell Bolino that Edelman never took the money. He tells me not to worry about it—as long as I keep up the payments, Allie Boy won't get upset.

Just before the holidays, Persico tells me to go see Edelman and get twenty pocketbooks so he can give them out as presents for Christmas to his friends.

"Don't worry about it," I said, "I'll get them for you from our friend." And I did—only I had to pay for them. Edelman wanted cash on the barrel for them, so while Allie Boy thought Edelman gave them to him, I paid for them, and I was sucking wind getting the money to cover the cost, which was about a thousand bucks.

The Bureau wanted that on tape, and part of it, at least, came out as the agents listened in as Bolino and I talked in my living room. A partial transcript of what we said follows:

JC: . . . I might be able to give you another five hundred dollars until I go into business [real estate] again.

MB: This I never told him [Persico]. He still thinks the guy, the Jew, got it. I'm tellin' ya right now.

JC: You never told Allie Boy.

MB: No, because you never told me.

JC: 'Cause what?

MB: 'Cause you never told me. If I ever tell him that . . . He don't know you and your uncle got the money.

JC: What would he say?

MB: He'd be very upset.

JC: Well, does he ask ya?

MB: No. As long as I pay him. And when you . . . when I have to press you for his money, it means I don't want him to ask me for it."

JC: What about the other thing, the real estate business?

MB: I told you as soon as he comes back Saturday, Sunday, whenever it is. I will definitely take care of it.

JC: The only reason . . . I wanted it was because before I go into Fortway [real estate], I want to know that—

MB: Nobody's gonna bother you.

JC: And also that whatever . . . I know about you . . . but whatever business you got you're gonna send to me.

MB: Of course.

JC: Same with Allie.

MB: Why not?

JC: The same way . . . the same thing with Johnny.

MB: Yeah.

JC: The same thing with all these people. That's what the important thing is. To know that—

MB: I understand. I know what it is.

JC: Yeah? What is it?

MB: Just so they all get . . . everybody leaves you alone so you can start earning your money, and by February you start making payments. . . .

We talked for another fifteen or twenty minutes, and then it ended; Bolino left, and for the next ten minutes I couldn't stop shaking. I changed my clothes, which were ringing wet, and waited.

The phone rang. It was Lazzara. "It went great, Joey, just great," he said reassuringly.

"I'm numb, Frank, and I'm ringing wet," I answered.

"You'll do just fine, Joey," he said. "You got a talent and don't know it. By the way . . . my men should be knocking on the door just about now. They're going to clean everything up." And they did. They removed the plant and the Nagra, and they stripped the Kell from the back of the couch. It was over—at least for a few days. . . .

15

THE DIPLOMAT—
SEAT OF POWER

There was nothing distinctive about the exterior of the Diplomat Social Club. It was a simple one-story brick building located at Third Avenue and Carroll Street. Its double doors and three large front windows gave it the appearance of a typical Brooklyn neighborhood bar. It wasn't.

While the Diplomat was always busy, always filled with lots of people, strangers were not welcome. It was, after all, the hub, the headquarters of the Persico group. It was a place where goodfellows, family associates, bad-asses, and even drug dealers who dealt with the Persicos hung out, not a place for some Joe off the street to sip a beer and pass the time. The uninvited quickly were told to leave, and when you're in the lion's den and he roars, you leave . . . in a hurry.

Behind the double-door entrance was a large L-shaped bar, about forty feet long, with stools. In the back was a kitchen and a bathroom. Next to the front windows were booths with tables and chairs where guys would play pinochle or some other card game for hours. To the immediate right of the entranceway was a cigarette machine, and down the center of the forty-feet-wide-by-eighty-feet-long room, were tables and chairs, a jukebox, and a couple of arcade game machines.

Among the tables at the center, near the rear, sat Alphonse

(Allie Boy) Persico. He sat there like a king on his throne, calling members of his court to his table to talk, to transact business, and to deal with the daily problems of the mob that he was running for his brother, Carmine Persico.

More often than not, either by his side or in his immediate vicinity, were Hugh (Apples) McIntosh, a bodyguard and vicious enforcer; Alphonse (Little Allie Boy) Persico, Jr., the son of Carmine; Jerry Lang (Langella), the underboss, and Bolino. There were others there at one time or another . . . Joey Brancato, Carmine (Tutti) Franzese, the sons of Joe Colombo—anybody who was part of the Persico faction or had to deal with that group. Sooner or later, they all show up there.

No matter who was there, everybody in the place was always whispering, afraid that what they talked about might be bugged and overheard by some law-enforcement agency. I often thought it was a miracle that any of us could overhear anything anyone said because of the noise in the joint. It was always filled with noise—loud music, the ringing of arcade machines, the clatter of glasses being set up or cleaned up by the bartender or sometimes barmaid. Dimly lit to begin with, it was even harder to see through the clouds of cigarette smoke that choked the lungs and burned the eyes.

The Diplomat was a place where everything happened and everyone was seen. It was a place where you quickly learned that some of the established Mafia family rules applied only for those who didn't have the power.

I remember I had always been told by Bolino and others that drugs and drug dealers were not tolerated in the Colombo family. But when I worked deals with Gredda and came with him to the Diplomat in 1975 while he paid debts he owed, I saw men who I knew—who all the mob knew—were coke and heroin dealers hanging out in the Diplomat, talking and working their business deals with Allie Boy and others. That's when I knew the rules were for those who looked up the ladder, not those who looked down and set the rules.

It was a place where Jerry Langella, decked out in a $600–$700 suit, would sit in a barber's chair in the middle of the floor getting a haircut from his barber, who had been called to the club. It was crazy. It was as though he was trying to mimic Albert Anastasia, who got knocked off by the Gallo gang and Carmine Persico in a barber's chair back in 1957.

The Diplomat was a place you wanted to be seen, to be remembered, because it was the seat of power—ultimate power—in the Colombo family. Those who were seen there were people who were accepted, people with some stature, maybe small, maybe large, but some stature.

It was not the kind of club you would want to go to record a conversation. Just the idea of going to the Diplomat to do such a thing was enough to make a man think about going back to church and preparing for his last meal.

On November 3, 1976, my wedding anniversary, that was exactly what the FBI said I had to do—record a shylock payoff I was about to make to Bolino and anyone else who might be there, especially Persico.

I didn't normally tell Lazzara and Bureau agents about every meeting I had with Bolino. I couldn't. It was too dangerous. They would have had me running around carrying a bug every day, every time I met someone. But I told them I was meeting Bolino on November 2 at his house because he had wanted to talk to me about the flea market and my shylock-debt problems, which I had discussed in a conversation previously recorded for the Bureau in my home. They wanted me to record the follow-up conversation, and I agreed, letting them tape me up at the Manhattan hotel. This time I was at his house wearing both the Nagra and the Kell. The Nagra was in my boot, and its mike was taped at my belly. The Kell mike was taped at my side.

It was a short meeting, lasting maybe fifteen minutes, but to me it felt like hours. I was sweating like a pig.

Now at the time I'm wearing this suit with a vest, and across the vest I've got a gold strap attached to a watch with a twenty-dollar gold piece on it. It was on the opposite side from where the microphone was hidden under my clothing.

As we talked about my coming to the Diplomat the next day

to make a payment to him and find out if Allie Boy Persico is going to get me the reprieve from the loan sharks, Bolino stopped, walked up to me, and grabbed the gold coin watch.

MB: . . . Is that fake gold?
JC: No, it's real.
MB: Gold plate?
JC: It's a twenty-dollar gold piece.
MB: How much they ask for this?
JC: Give me a value.
MB: (unintelligible) What could it be worth . . . three hundred, four hundred dollars?
JC: Probably.

As he fingered the gold piece and looked at it, my heart pounded and I could feel sweat dripping from my armpits, around my gut, down my leg. I was certain, absolutely certain, he was going to discover the bug. He didn't, and the meeting ended with my promise to bring the money, the vig I owed, to the Diplomat at 2:30 P.M. the next day.

I walked out of the house whistling, relieved that I hadn't been discovered. I drove back to Manhattan, parked, took a cab to the hotel, and let Lazzara and his agents strip the tape from my body, gritting my teeth as they ripped whole clumps of hair from my belly and chest and my leg.

"You're going to have to do this again tomorrow," Lazzara said.

"You're crazy," I said. "No way am I going to wear this stuff at the Diplomat. Christ . . . someone's bound to spot it, especially in there. They're paranoid about bugs . . . they're always checking for bugs."

"They won't spot anything—I promise ya," Lazzara insisted.

"I don't care, Frank . . . fuck it . . . I don't care!" I yelled. "I don't wear this Nagra, no way. What happens if they spot it, or this transmitter? What happens to me?"

"You just say, Help, help, help," he said. "Say help three times and we come running from the car."

"Bullshit, Frank. I'll never get to the second help," I said.

"Someone behind me will take me out. I'll be dead meat . . . dead meat."

"We'll get to you, Joey," he insisted. "I promise you."

It was cold and miserable the next day, and I was talking to myself as I went to the hotel in Manhattan once again, asking myself why the hell I was doing this thing. I was almost convinced that this was to be my last day on earth, the last day I'd take a breath. I was certain I was about to be killed, because I was sure Bolino and Persico and all the others would discover I was wearing a body mike.

I went to the hotel room and told Lazzara I couldn't do it. He told me I could. Unlike Tallia or Cullen or Domaro, he didn't threaten me, didn't tell me that the Bureau would blow my cover if I didn't go into the lion's den that afternoon. That's probably why I went, but I was still dying an inch at a time as I arrived at Third Avenue and Carroll Street wearing the Kell.

I popped two Valiums, ten milligrams, this time to calm me down. I should have been mellow, floating, by this time . . . but I wasn't. I was a wreck. I had this equipment on me, this Kell body mike, and I was convinced that everybody in the Diplomat would know I was wearing it. The first people I saw as I started to open the Diplomat's door were Anthony and Joe Colombo, Jr. They said hello and kept walking.

I stepped inside and walked straight to the end of the bar closest to the door by the cigarette machine. The smoke was so thick I could barely see Allie Boy, sitting at his round table at the rear, talking with some people.

The place was packed. I could see Vinnie Moon, a coke dealer, there. Jerry Lang was there too. The music was blaring loudly from the jukebox, so you could hardly hear yourself think. How the hell were the agents going to hear what I was saying in their car around the corner? I didn't know. I just stood there momentarily, waiting . . . wondering if everyone knew I was carrying this goddamn thing, wondering who was going to grab me first and punch out my lights permanently.

Suddenly, Bolino appeared out of the crowd and walked up to me. I handed him the $320 I owed him for vig—$150 on the

Edelman loan, the rest interest to other loan sharks like Cock-eyed Allie. We talked about Lou LaRocca, who, he said, had been to see Persico earlier about his investment of eleven thousand dollars in the flea market with his son, and the problems we were having in making money to pay the bills. We talked about Johnny Russo and my money problem with him.

Bolino said, "Explain to Allie. Don't make Allie think that John is such a bad guy. Say the truth now—it ain't a bad deal at all. Johnny has been very, very patient over here. The man is right. Am I right or wrong? Very patient. No . . . don't make it sound as if Johnny wants to break your legs. It's wrong."

I didn't realize it then, but our conversation was breaking up on the microphone. The agents were only getting part of what we were saying. Meanwhile, Persico walked over to join us. For some strange reason, he didn't make me come to his table, he just walked to the bar to join Bolino and myself.

"How are ya, Joey?" he said.

Before I could say a word, Bolino shows him the money I just gave him. "Here, Allie, he brought in some money . . . he made his payment," Bolino said. "Joey, explain to Allie what you want to do and what's going on."

So I did, believing all of it was being recorded. It wasn't. "I just need a break. I need your help . . ."

While I'm talking, I'm scared as I look up at Allie Boy, who towered over me. He stood about 6'2" and was hefty and very tough. I'm about 5'10" and no slouch, but he had a reputation as a deadly killer. I mean, there were guys on the street that just shit their pants when they heard his name spoken, and here I am in his backyard, his club, with about forty of the toughest, meanest bastards you ever want to know about from Brooklyn's mob, and I've got a bug on me—not a very good one, but if they find it, I'm dead on the spot. No place to run and I know goddamn well the FBI isn't going to get to me in time . . . no way.

His eyes, I swear, were looking right through me. Cold . . . deadly . . . evillike, looking straight into my eyes. I thought I was looking into the eyes of the devil—if I looked enough, I was going to see the devil.

Suddenly, he spoke in a carefully modulated voice—nicely, but in a way I felt was cutting into my brain with a razor-sharp knife so I wouldn't feel the pain until it was too late. . . .

" . . . if you're afraid Johnny is going to break your legs—I'm gonna break your head. All right?"

He was saying that if I screwed this reprieve up—if I didn't make good in the real estate office and pay off all my debts—he would make what Johnny Russo wanted to do with me look like kindergarden stuff. I got the message.

When the conversation ended, when he guaranteed my reprieve from paying the shylocks from the two families until February, I left and walked out of the Diplomat to my car, which was parked next to a fire hydrant. As I'm walking, I'm whistling, because it is such a relief to get out of there without being discovered. When I reached the car, I started muttering, "I hope it was worth it. I hope you guys got what you wanted."

Lazzara and his men put me on the cross for that—they ate my ass up one side and down another. By saying what I did, I could have screwed up their tape. Luckily, they hadn't recorded it. The taping ended when I walked out the door of the Diplomat.

We didn't go back to the hotel. It was cold as hell, but they decided they didn't want to go back to the hotel. Instead, it was decided that we all go to Staten Island, to the Verrazano Bridge. We all stopped on the left-hand side, at a Department of Transportation parking lot. There, I climbed into their car and they made me strip, in the cold, down to my bare chest. I sat there crouched, shivering in my underpants, while they ripped the adhesive holding the transmitter and the battery pack to my body.

I was nearly frozen by the time I got dressed and returned to my home. The agents had their recording and their Kell, and although the tape wasn't great, it proved to be invaluable evidence against Persico at his trial several years later. I got my reprieve—it wasn't much—and Russo still broke my chops, because Bolino often spent the money I gave him to pay Russo.

To make that reprieve work and pay some of the shylocks what I still owed while keeping Persico happy, I had scores to work—and, unexpectedly, another case to set up for the New Rochelle office, a case that eventually would lead to my becoming a federal witness and a man forever on the run.

The card in my mailbox was from an old friend of the family, a wealthy Jewish shopkeeper named Harry Berger. It read simply, "Please call. I need help."

Harry and his wife, Tillie, had been friends of my grandfather and my father. They had been guests at my wedding, and he had done business with our real estate office for years—nothing great, but the kind of business that is bread and butter to a real estate office. He was a quiet, gentle man, not a man familiar with the violent world that I lived in or the people that I dealt with. He was, in fact, the last person I would have expected to become involved with the mob.

He and his adopted son operated a popular glass store, B&E Glass, in a downtown Brooklyn neighborhood a block from the Nestor Social Club, where a lot of mob people hung out, particularly Anthony Scarpati, a captain in the Colombo family under Persico. Scarpati, or Scappy, as he was known on the street, was a tough loan shark with a reputation for a short fuse with those who borrowed money and didn't pay. He didn't waste time with his victims—just beat the hell out of them to keep collections coming in.

Berger didn't realize it, but his son, Murray, was a gambler, who, when he couldn't get money from the business, went to Scappy and another loan shark to borrow money.

By late December, Murray owed eighty-seven hundred dollars and was paying three points a week for that loan—nearly three hundred dollars in vig. By early January, Murray was falling further and further behind in his payments, and Scappy was threatening to break his legs or worse. Murray finally became so desparate he told his father. That's when Berger came to me, and I answered his note for help.

"I need your help, Joe," Berger said. "I don't know who to turn to . . . how to help Murray. He says they've threatened his life if he doesn't pay up, but I don't know if that's all they want."

"Let me see what I can do, Harry," I said. "Maybe I can take care of it."

I left Berger, and I went to see Scappy, who I'd known for more than a decade from the days of Colombo at my father's office, and I tried to buy the loan from him—cut a deal and get Harry's son off the hook.

Scappy wasn't selling. It wasn't just his loan; part of it belonged to another shylock, so it had to be paid in full.

"Look, Joe, this kid's behind in his payments," Scappy said. "He owes us eighty-seven hundred dollars. We want the money. No deals . . . just the money."

I thanked Scappy for talking to me and explaining things, and I left.

Now, up to this point, I had not told the Bureau what was going on, but because I couldn't do anything for Berger, I figured I'd bring them in on it and see what they could figure out.

The agent assigned to the case was Charles Domaro from the New Rochelle office, and almost immediately he wanted me to record everything. First we made tapes of conversations with Murray and Harry Berger about the loan and about the threats, and about Harry's willingness to take the eighty-seven hundred dollars from a bank and let me pay off Scappy. Arrangements to collect the money and pay off Scappy were made for January 6, 1977.

"You're going to have to go in with the recorder," Domaro said.

"No way," I answered. "I'm not going into the Nestor Social Club wired for sound. That's suicide!"

"The hell you're not," he said. "If you don't, we take everything off the shelf."

"You do, I get killed!" I protested.

"Your call, Joe," he said matter-of-factly. "You gotta work to make your keep."

No offer of protection, no "We'll take care of you, Joe," just walk the hot coals again. Not much choice. If Allie Boy or the others found out what I had been doing, they would have chopped me up in pieces . . . while I was still breathing. At that moment, I hated Domaro.

Back to the hotel room . . . back to a Kell transmitter taped to my belly . . . back to a Nagra in my boot and wires taped to my leg and up my crotch to a microphone near the Kell mike.

With Domaro and other agents following, I first met Berger and went with him to the bank, where he withdrew the money. Then we went to talk to Murray. Finally, it was time for me to go belly-to-belly with Scappy at the club.

The Nestor Social Club was located on the first floor of a small two-story building located at Fifth Avenue and Carroll Street. It was a crummy place with a small bar, a few tables for card players . . . maybe half the size of the Diplomat.

I stepped from my car and walked toward the club. It took everything I had to control the panic I felt inside. I walked into the darkened club and saw Scappy.

We shook hands, and I handed him the money. "Here's the eighty-seven hundred dollars, Scappy," I said.

"Thank you, Joe, thank you very much," he said.

"Count it, Scappy," I said, pointing to the wad of bills. "Make sure it's all there."

"Ah, Joe, I don't have to with you," he said. "I trust you."

"Count it, Scappy," I said again. "I don't want no more comebacks on this kid. So count it . . . and please, Scappy, don't give him no more money. If you give him more money, I won't be responsible."

"Joe . . . don't worry about it," he answered, counting the money as he did. "He will not get any more money from me . . . from anyone."

"Thank you, Scappy," I said. Then I left, walked across the street, and met Berger and his son.

"Okay, Murray, you're clear. They won't bother you, only don't try to get more money from them. They won't give it to you."

Both thanked me for the help, and Harry sent me a case of scotch. Domaro and the agents met me at the hotel room, collected the Nagra and the Kell, and enjoyed themselves ripping off the adhesive. The case, like others behind it, was put on a shelf to await federal prosecution later . . . or so I thought.

I didn't always tell the FBI what was going on, particularly when it involved a score, a job I thought I'd make money on to help me pay the shylocks. If the Bureau knew what I was doing, they never tipped their hand. They were interested in just one thing—making cases against the big shots in organized crime.

There was one case they didn't know about that they would have loved to have been in on from the start. It involved Gregory Scarpa, a captain in the Colombo family and one of its biggest money-makers. Scarpa had been busted for everything from bookmaking to fencing stolen bonds, and he was involved in the sale of weapons to Middle East arms dealers. He was also a shylock with peculiar hang-ups.

I had told Scarpa about a big Chinese New Year's party that my friend Wah On Lee was throwing, an annual affair that brought in buckets of money from gambling. There would be a minimum of a couple of hundred thousand dollars in cash, not to mention the jewelry people would be wearing. It was ideal for a heist.

Scarpa thought it was a great idea, particularly because I could be used as the inside man, since I had tickets. He organized his crew, fourteen of them, for the job. All of them, including his son, Greg Junior, had a reputation for hustle and daring. They were tough street people.

It was a crystal-clear night when we met on the corner of Thirteenth Avenue and Eighty-sixth Street. Scarpa and I sat in a car watching as four guys walked toward the door of the Hong Pan, the restaurant Wah On Lee owned. Under their topcoats, two of them carried old Thompson machine guns, the tommy guns the Chicago mob used during Prohibition.

Everything went sour when a patrol car drove by on Eighty-sixth Street, and the gunmen found the door locked. That's when Scarpa decided to call the whole deal off. "It don't feel right, Joey," he said. "We're gonna put it off till next year. I don't wanna do it today," he added, looking at the clock.

"Why?" I asked.

" 'Cause now it's Saint Valentine's Day," he said. "That's when all them guys got killed in Chicago. I don't want no Valentine's Day massacre here."

So a couple of hundred thousand dollars went down the tubes because Scarpa was haunted by a mass mob murder. Who could figure that?

Michael Bolino and I pulled off another successful scam that I didn't tell the Bureau about until long after it was over. The target of the scam was a young guy I'll call Mikey Sach. That's not his real name, but he's been through enough with wiseguys—why make it worse now?

Mikey was really a nice guy, a humble young man who ran a liquor store with an apartment in the back on Bath Avenue. He also ran a small supermarket next door that his father left him. Soaking wet, he carried about 130 pounds on his 5'5" frame, and he lived alone.

Mikey was the kind of guy all the wiseguys took advantage of—a sort of Casper Milquetoast who never raised his voice to anyone. They would come to his store, fill up bags of groceries, and walk out, telling him, "I ain't gonna pay you." Mikey would just shrug and walk away, mumbling to himself.

Joe Notch saw him as a sucker, and played him. One day he went to Mikey's liquor store with a case of Cutty Sark quarts. "Mikey," he says, "I've got a hundred of these cases. I'll give them to you for fifty dollars a case."

Mikey thought that was a good deal and gave Notch the five thousand dollars. Needless to say, he never saw the hundred cases.

Across the street and down the block from Mikey's stores was a social club run by a guy known on the street as Patty Boxcars. Patty was nearly sixty and had spent almost thirty of those years in and out of jail. He also had a son who thought he was a real tough guy and was constantly going into Sach's store and shaking him down for money or taking money out of his cash register.

Things finally got so bad that Mikey couldn't take it anymore and went to see a neighborhood lawyer, who sent him to see me. I checked out his problem and found that he was considered ripe for a rip-off by Bolino.

"We want some big money out of this guy, not the penny-ante stuff," Bolino says. "Tell him we want ten thousand dollars."

So I went to Sach and told him that I could keep the wolves off his back, but it was going to cost him ten thousand dollars.

"Let me think about it, Joe," he said. "That's a lot of money."

While he thinks about it, Bolino sends in the troops to Sach's store while it's filled with regular customers, and the troops begin cursing and yelling and knocking things over. Sach got the message, took out a bank loan, and paid me the ten thousand dollars. I gave it to Michael, and he split it up—two thousand dollars for me, two thousand dollars for Michael, two thousand dollars for Allie Boy and two thousand dollars each to Patty Boxcars and his boss, Charlie Moose Panarella.

A little time goes by, and Bolino comes to me and tells me they want to do another number on Mikey Sach.

I protested. "Hey, Michael, give this kid a break," I said. "He's a hard-working kid. He's in that store early every morning, and he leaves late every night."

Bolino shakes his head. "Its time, Joe," he says. "You gotta pay bills, I gotta pay bills. We all need money."

So they start harassing Sach again, and, as expected, he comes to me. "Joe . . . I paid for this to stop," he pleads. "I paid them ten thousand dollars . . . so why are they doing this to me again? Please, Joe . . . help me."

Bolino and I have another meeting, and a new deal is set. The plan was simple. We were going to have a meeting with Boxcar's kid, myself, and Sach. Boxcar's kid would wear an army jacket with big pockets. Inside those pockets, he would have bags of blood. "You're gonna have an argument with him, get so mad you stab him in front of Sach, and he's gonna see all that blood," Bolino said. "He's gonna pay to get out of a murder case."

I didn't like the idea much, but that's the way Bolino wanted it, and that's what happened. I stabbed Boxcar's kid with a small knife, the blood poured out, and Boxcar's kid fell to the floor, apparently dead.

Sach was sitting across the room and turned white as a sheet. He ran to the bathroom and started tossing up. I yelled to him, "Hey, Mikey . . . we gotta do something! This guy is dead."

"Oh, God, Joe . . . what are we gonna do?" he gurgled from the sink.

"I got a friend I can call," I said.

Everything was arranged. Bolino arrives with a van and he and I load the "body" into the van and he drives off. Then I go back to deal with Sach, who is babbling like a baby.

"What am I gonna do, Joe?" he cries out. "I'll lose everything, everything my parents left me, everything I've worked for all these years."

"Look, Mikey, you're an accessory to murder," I said, "but for ten thousand dollars maybe we can fix things. I'll get out of town for a while, and I'll give some of the money to my friend for taking care of the body."

Sach pays up, and, once away, Bolino does the split, laughing all the time at how simple the sting was.

About six months later, Boxcar's kid shows up at Sach's little supermarket. The kid nearly had a breakdown. He sold everything he had and moved out of town. That should be the end of the story, but it isn't. Two years ago, I learned that Sach had moved back to Brooklyn and set up a candy store. He was supposed to be under someone's protection. As sure as I'm sitting here telling this story, he's being shaken down again, and no one will help him They are just going to milk him until he's dry. It's the American mob way.

16

THE BEGINNING OF THE END

"**A**llie Boy wants to see you at the club, around one o'clock. Be there."

The voice was Michael Bolino's, and there was something strange about the way he sounded, something that I couldn't put my finger on as I put the telephone down. I remember thinking, Why now?

I was paid up on most of my loans to shylocks in the Colombo family, and I had made a special effort to keep up with payments on the Edelman loan. So why would he want to see me?

The truth was, there had been something strange about Michael Bolino since April 17, when I saw him at Tomasso's restaurant, a popular mob hangout and a great place for parties in those days. Next door was a mob social club, the Veterans and Friends Social Club, where Gambino capo Jimmy Failla and his new family boss, Paul Castellano, hung out. Nine years later, Frank DeCicco, a new Gambino underboss, would die there, blown apart by a bomb placed in his car.

The party on the evening of the seventeenth was very special. It was a "members only" party for newly initiated soldiers of the five Mafia crime families of New York. I wasn't among those invited to the blowout. I arrived by accident, and what I saw I would later have to testify about at several federal trials.

The mob in New York had opened its books for new members for the first time in years, and the bosses and the newly made members, as well as their sponsors, were at Tomasso's celebrating with a party that all involved would remember.

Young Allie Boy Junior, the son of Carmine, was there with Allie Boy, who was then the acting boss of the Colombo family. Bolino, Anthony and Joe Colombo, Jr., and Shorty Spero were all there, celebrating their initiation into the Colombo family with Allie Boy Junior. The Gambino family was represented by the new boss, Castellano, who was there with Failla and newly made Gambino recruits. I saw Christie Tick Furnari, who was then a captain of the Lucchese family, at the party. Lou LaRocca and Johnny Russo of the Genovese family were there. If there were people from the Bonanno family at the party, I didn't recognize them, but there were a lot of people there that I didn't know.

As soon as I walked in and saw what was going on, I turned on my heel and left. It wasn't a place for the uninvited to hang around. A few days later, both Bolino and Joe Junior explained what the party had been about, although I had suspected as much.

For a decade, the membership books of the five families had been closed to new members. I had no idea why, but there were a lot of people that I knew, including Bolino and Spero, who were waiting for the day when they would open the books . . . allow new members to be initiated into what informer Joe Valachi called "Our Thing," or Cosa Nostra.

To be a member gave the new goodfellow stature and power on the street, as well as supposed access to money. It really didn't, but a lot of people thought it did. What membership did do was provide an edge of protection to the deals those involved cooked up. They had to share their profits with their superiors, but they were usually safer from threats by members of other families than people like me were. Members also had to do, without question, what their bosses told them to do—murder friends, relatives, whoever the bosses fingered. The *"famiglia"* was the mob, not the immediate family. I could never have lived with that.

I'm told that the ritual of initiation also requires that new members tell all, bare their souls, at their ceremonies. They could keep no secrets from their sponsors and from the members of the family who sat in at the ceremony. That proved to be a problem for me, as I was soon to find out.

I congratulated Bolino and Joe Junior, but at the time, Bolino seemed cool, and he seemed just as cool and distant when he called me on the phone to come to the Diplomat on April 22.

I did not call the Bureau about my scheduled meeting with Persico, because I didn't know why I was being called in to see him. I also didn't want to face him wired for sound again. I just knew I wouldn't survive another facedown like that with him. I had, however, told Lazzara about the Tomasso's initiation party, figuring it would give the Bureau and its agents something to keep them busy checking on. That way, they'd leave me alone, at least for a little while.

At 1:00 P.M., I arrived at the Diplomat with Frankie M., who was a member of my crew and who offered to drive me there. When we got to the Diplomat, I noticed the streets were strangely empty. There weren't a lot of cars parked outside as usual. That should have set off warning bells in my brain, but it didn't.

Inside, I saw Bolino, Allie Boy Persico, and Hugh (Apples) McIntosh, Persico's bodyguard. They were sitting at a table . . . alone. There was no one else, no blaring jukebox, no clouds of smoke—the place was empty except for them.

Without a word, Bolino stood up, walked over to Frankie M., and said, "Frankie . . . do me a favor. Wait outside."

Frankie M. looked at me and shrugged. I nodded, and he stepped outside. There were, after all, things that they might want to say to me that they didn't want Frankie M. to hear. He wasn't responsible to any of them, he wasn't someone they trusted.

I stepped toward the chair where Allie Boy was sitting and reached out with my hand to shake his. I remember his eyes were flashing as he stood up. His hand reached out—not to grab my hand but to grab the collar of my suit jacket. Then he started punching me and punching me and punching . . .

"I want all my fuckin' money, you hear me?" he shouts. "I want all my fuckin' money—and I want it now, you son of a bitch!"

I fell to the floor as he let my jacket go. My face, my nose, my mouth, were all bleeding. Blood was all over my suit jacket and my shirt as I lay there on the floor with Persico standing there, glaring down at me. Out of the corner of my eye, I could see Bolino. I thought for a minute he was going to join in the fun and belt me a few times himself. He didn't; instead, he reached down to pick me up, then he helped me outside, around the corner, where he took the handkerchief from my jacket pocket and soaked it in some water from an outdoor faucet and washed off my face.

"Why, Michael . . . for Chrissake, why?" I asked.

"He found out you used the money you got from him for Edelman," he answered. "You didn't tell him the truth, and he's mad."

"But how?" I asked. "You said it was all taken care of, he'd never know as long as I paid. . . ."

"Don't worry about it, Joe," he said. "Just get his money, the money you owe him from Edelman."

"Yeah, sure, Michael," I said. "Fuck you . . . don't worry. I'm getting a beating, and you say don't worry. You just stand there and say don't worry."

But I did worry . . . I was scared to death. I felt my life was hanging in the balance, and no matter what Bolino said, I was in deadly danger.

It's not an everyday thing to be beaten up personally by a family boss in his club. When news of the beating hits the streets, it spreads like wildfire, and I knew I'd be out there naked, stripped of protection, a target for every creep in the neighborhood unless I got things straightened out, and fast.

I was a mess, but I staggered over to my car, where Frankie M. was waiting. "What the fuck happened to you?" he asked.

I told him. "Take me to Jan's home," I said. "I can't go home and let my wife see me like this."

When I got to Jan's—she was my girlfriend then—she washed me, cleaned me up, and gave me a drink, and when I told her the story of what happened, she got nervous, went out and borrowed some money—twenty-five hundred dollars—so I could pay off Allie Boy.

A week later, I met Bolino and gave him the money Jan had raised for me. "Give it to Allie Boy," I said. "It's all I could raise this week."

Bolino promised to take the money to Persico. In the meantime, he said I'd have to come up with the remaining five thousand dollars . . . fast. "I'll try and buy you some time with this payment," he promised.

What Bolino didn't tell me—and I suspected had happened—was that when he got initiated into the family as a made man, he had to tell all his secrets, and one of those secrets was how he'd let me keep the Edelman money and pay back in installments without ever telling Allie Boy. That was an embarrassment to Persico, who thought he had his hooks into Edelman when he really didn't.

Even though payments were being made on time and he was collecting his interest, Allie Boy lost face as a boss. He'd been suckered by his own soldier and his soldier's associate. Since he needed Bolino more than he needed me, he vented his spleen on me, and in a sense he was right. The trouble I had with that was that I was following Bolino's instructions, and Bolino never told him that.

There was one other problem that possibly added fuel to the fire in Allie Boy's belly the night of the Tomasso dinner—a bungled shakedown plan by my crew that involved my old friend Al Wasserman.

Some of my crew members had come to me with a scheme to extort Wasserman for $100,000, using fear and violence without actually hurting him physically. The idea seemed reasonable to me, but I knew that before I put the wheels in motion, I would need permission from Persico, so I went to Bolino. The surest way to win permission for such schemes is to share the wealth, and I promised Bolino that he and Allie Boy would get 10 percent of whatever I got from the scam. Bolino in turn gave me his word that the shakedown had been approved by Allie Boy.

The first thing the crew and I did was shotgun Wasserman's office in Brooklyn. As expected, Wasserman called my father, who, on instructions from Bolino, advised him to talk to me.

I met with Wasserman and told him there were members of this gang who wanted to hurt him because he had cut them out of some profitable painting contracts on his apartment buildings. If he didn't want to get hurt, I said, he'd have to pay $100,000.

"Oh, my God," he said, and started spitting—he has a space between his teeth and when he gets excited he starts spitting as he talks. "You tell these punks I'm not paying, Joey."

The next move by the crew was an arson. We all went to his apartment house at Sea Cliff Towers on Staten Island, the same building my father lived in. We doused the elevators with gas, pushed the "up" button, and lit the gas. One problem. The elevators have sprinkling systems, and the fires were doused.

Wasserman contacts me the next day and offers to pay twenty-five thousand dollars. I tell him it isn't enough. He has to come up with $100,000. This time he retreats, saying he has to think about it. The next day, he and his wife go into hiding and the crew strikes again. They burn down two model homes he has on display for a development on Staten Island.

Once again, Wasserman comes to see me. "Please, Joe," he says, "make them stop."

"Al . . . pay them what they want," I say. By now, I'm getting pissed off at his stalling.

"Let me think about it, Joe," he answers.

Again he disappears, and again the crew strikes—this time at his home on Ocean Parkway in Brooklyn. One of the crew tosses a can of gas through a glass door and burns the place to the ground. A victim of the fire is Wasserman's favorite French poodle.

The result was that Wasserman sought help from the Gambino family, and Paul Castellano personally intervened, turning up at Allie Boy's home in the middle of the night to tell him to keep us away from Wasserman. Allie Boy was furious. Bolino had never told him of the caper, so he couldn't argue with

Castellano, who had collected the twenty-five thousand dollars we were originally offered to halt the shakedown.

We didn't talk about the beating for quite a while after it happened—in fact, it wasn't until June 9, 1977, that I made a point of bringing it up. This time Lazzara was aware of what had happened—we'd talked about it—and I was wired for sound at Bolino's house, talking not only about the beating and how much I still had to pay Persico, but also about the disappearance of Sally Albanese. This is what was recorded by my body mike:

MB: What's this?

JC: This? A watch—Frankie gave it to me. It's not, whatchacallit, solid gold.

MB: Better be careful.

JC: With my watch?

MB: With what you're carrying. There's a hundred agents in this area, every day.

JC: Yeah?

MB: There gonna be for the next three weeks.

JC: Why?

MB: Because they're looking for Sally Albanese.

JC: [Later] Did you speak to Allie Boy, Mike?

MB: Yeah, and you got until before the Fourth of July.

JC: Before the Fourth of July?

MB: Yeah . . . *Capisce?* Five thousand.

JC: Is he still upset with me?

MB: Yeah, yeah. Don't say . . . don't say he said it's okay. It's okay.

JC: Who am I gonna say it to? I got no one to say it to.

MB: All right. This way you got a whole . . . almost a whole month. You do what you gotta do to keep your commitment. All right?

JC: Have you seen Johnny Russo?

MB: Johnny Russo . . . I told him you was in Rhode Island. He wants your phone number.

JC: He wants my phone number?

MB: I didn't give it.

JC: As soon as I get some money, I'm gonna give it to you.

MB: I know. Johnny wants his money. . . .

JC: No, thank you, Anna [turning down a drink from Bolino's wife].
    What's the problem with Sally [Albanese]? If it's not my busi-
    ness . . .

MB: He's gone [murdered].

Later in the conversation, Bolino told me Persico had ordered
him to stay out of my problems with Russo. Up to the time Allie
Boy had beaten me, he had arranged to keep loan sharks from
other families at bay, guys like Russo, as long as I paid them
through Bolino. Now, things had changed.

MB: I told Johnny you were in Rhode Island. He says, Just give me
    his phone number. I said, I ain't got it . . . it changed. Allie—
    Allie told me don't make, don't make trouble, you know, don't
    make a fool of yourself, don't make Johnny ask you this, that,
    and other things. If Johnny wants you [unintelligible], get his
    money.

JC: Yeah, but I'm supposed to be with you [under his protection].

MB: You gotta call Johnny back. You know, like I told you. . . . The
    next time you got two hundred dollars, give it to me. I'll give
    it to him.

Our conversation shifted to the problems that the Bureau was
causing in the neighborhood, problems that had prompted both
him and Persico to put their homes up for sale.

JC: I saw Allie Boy's house is for sale too. So everybody is moving
    out.

MB: I'm telling you—the neighborhood is very hot. Nine guys
    walked into the . . . nine agents walked in on us last night. Nine
    agents!

JC: I got a message the Chinaman wanted to see me.

MB: What Chinaman?

JC: Hong Pan [Wah On Lee].

MB: Don't go see him. Don't go see him.

JC: I went to see him.

MB: You did?

JC: He said he went to the grand jury, and they gave him immunity
... and they asked him about me ... if I ever gave him any
money, or anything like that. Do I come in there? You know, me
and a lot of other people. But he came to tell me that. Is he
[Persico] still mad at me? I'd love to go down there one of these
days.

MB: Eventually, you'll be paying everything off. Don't worry about
it, Joe. You don't have to go down and see nobody. What do you
have to see him for?

JC: I'm talking about Allie Boy. Is he still mad at me?

MB: Don't worry about Allie Boy anymore.

JC: I'm worried.

MB: I'll take care of it.

JC: The thing that still sticks in my mind—

MB: Keep your commitment, Joe, just keep your commitment
... and don't worry about it.

JC: Because from the side of my eye I could see ... I don't know
if I explained it to you ... I would do the same thing ... you
were standing there, like if you had to do it, you would have hit
me too.

MB: I picked you up.

JC: I know you picked me up. But if you had to do it, you would
of did it.

Fear had become a daily event for me. The shylocks made it
that way, and the Bureau compounded it by making me go
belly-to-belly with them. Without the protection of Bolino and
Persico, I would drown, I would die with broken arms and
broken legs, I would die in pain on a street somewhere and
nobody would give a shit ... nobody would be there to help.

Outside of Persico, the man I feared most and the man the
Bureau made me face the most was Johnny Russo. He was an
animal. Persico, until the beating, had at least treated me with
some measure of respect. But Russo ... he didn't care about
anything except collecting money.

It seemed as if whenever we met, Russo was threatening me.
If I went to his home to pay past-due interest, he spat on me and
threatened to beat me up. On the day Persico promised me he

would convince Russo to wait for his loan payments, Russo showed his contempt for the agreement by threatening me.

We met by accident that day at a luncheonette at Bay Eighth and Eighty-sixth Street maybe twenty minutes after Persico had guaranteed my safety from Russo. I was still carrying my Kell— the transmitter—after the meeting with Persico, but the Bureau was nowhere in sight. They had left for Staten Island, where I was supposed to meet them. I had stopped for a quick cup of coffee.

"I'm gonna break your fuckin' legs . . . I'm gonna put you in a fuckin' hospital unless you come up with the money!" he shouted in the luncheonette. "You got until tomorrow." The next day, with a tape running, I paid him five hundred dollars.

In February 1977, he came after me . . . at my home. Bolino was the problem. Part of the arrangement worked out with Persico was that I pay Bolino what I owed Russo, $320 a week, and he, in turn, paid Russo. Only he didn't. Bolino liked gambling, and he was a loser. He'd lose everything on some nag and never give it to Russo, and Russo would come looking for me . . . just as he did in the middle of the night at my home on February 25.

Russo was supposed to be paid three days earlier. I'd given Bolino the money, but he never paid Russo.

It was late. My wife and kids were in bed, and I was lying down watching television. My doorbell rang, and there was Russo, resting on a cane. I thought he'd hurt himself and needed the cane because he was limping.

"Where you been, you cocksucker?" he screams. "Why didn't you bring the money?"

"I gave it to Michael, Johnny. A week ago . . . honest!" I said.

"I'm gonna break your head with this!" he shouted, raising the cane in the air.

"Please, Johnny . . . I paid. So help me Christ, I paid Michael," I pleaded.

"I find out you didn't . . . I don't get my money, Christ can't help you, nobody can help you," he growled.

He turned to leave, then he stopped and looked at me with those piercing brown eyes of his. "You love your wife?" he asked. "You love your kids?"

"Come on, John, you know I do," I answered.

"You better get me my fuckin' money, or you ain't never gonna see them again," he said, shaking the cane at me.

That kind of threat scared me more than any. I feared for my own life, but I feared more for that of my wife and kids. I told Bolino that; I told the Bureau that.

Bolino's attitude was, don't worry about it . . . he'd take care of things. Take care of things—this was my so-called goomba, the man who promised to protect me but who was milking me dry, putting me on the hot seat not just with Russo but with Allie Boy, with other loan sharks, with his lies and the spending of the money I gave him to pay off my debts. He was putting me deeper and deeper into a hole, and I, in turn, was turning more and more to robberies and thefts, which he profited from. He was taking food off my table, endangering my family. In the end, that's why I agreed to go against him for the Bureau. He'd have had me killed sooner or later.

When I told the Bureau of Russo's threats because I was late on payments, they would make me hold back on my payments to Russo, to provoke him, to make him make threats that could be recorded. They would hold out money they promised to give me to pay him, forcing me to avoid him and then later confront him when he was angry.

The worst of those meetings came on March 7, 1977. I met Lazzara and his men at the hotel so they could wire me, and then I drove to Ro-Sals restaurant and lounge at McDonald Avenue and Avenue X. Russo would usually be there to count the take of the bookmaking operation he ran for Tieri. I had five hundred dollars with me to pay Russo—part of it vig money the Bureau had provided after making me stall about paying Russo for several weeks. The money I had was less than half of what I owed him for those weeks.

Russo was standing at the bar as I walked in. "You got my fuckin' money, Joey?" he growled.

Now when Russo growled, he was difficult to understand; that's how he got the nickname "Mumbles"—because no one could understand what he was saying half the time.

"John, I ain't got the payment," I said.

"What'd ya say?" he asks.

"John, I ain't got the payment. I haven't got all the money," I answered.

Suddenly, he jumps up. "Whaddaya fuckin' wired up!" he shouts.

Russo is hotheaded, and when he loses it, people can get hurt.

My mind is telling me to stay calm, keep your cool, don't panic. My butt is telling me something else. I'm about to shit all over myself.

"What are you talking about, John?" I said.

"I said, are you wearing a fuckin' microphone?" he said grabbing my jacket.

"Hey, John," I answered, as coolly as I could, "if you feel that way about it, John, I won't even talk to you, you know?"

He comes right back, forgetting all about what he said, and shouts, "Joey . . . I'm gonna break your fuckin' chair over your fuckin' head. God can't help you . . . all right. I want my fuckin' money."

I reached in an gave him the five hundred dollars. It was all I had. Then I left. After that, I had to depend on Bolino paying Russo and keeping him from my door and the promise of the Bureau that they would not let me be hurt by him.

That tape and the others I made with Russo for the Bureau later resulted in his conviction for extortion—for loan-sharking. It was the beginning of the end for him and for a lot of Brooklyn Mafia people.

17

BILLY WAS JUST A KID

I thought the outside door to my apartment was going to come off the hinges from the pounding. It was nearly 10:30 P.M., July 25, 1977, and for a minute I thought it was Russo trying for another collection. When I learned it wasn't him, I released the electric lock, and in staggered my half-brother Anthony.

He was sobbing uncontrollably as he reached the staircase leading to my upstairs apartment. Slowly, he crawled up the stairs toward me.

"It's Billy . . . he's dead," he cried. "They killed him, the bastards . . . they killed him."

I ran down to help him up the stairs. He looked like he'd been run over by a truck. I found out he'd been thrown off the second-story balcony of the Aloha Motel in Seaside Heights, New Jersey, the night before—thrown from the balcony onto the windshield of a car parked below by some young punks he'd argued with when he saw them hit a pregnant girl. He survived the fall, shattering the windshield without serious injury, but while he was getting off the hood of the car, our brother Billy had been stabbed.

"What the hell are you talking about, Anthony?" I said. "What do you mean Billy's dead?"

"He's dead, Joey," he said. "Some guy stabbed him in the side and he fell on the bed and he died in the room. He just sort of faded away before help got there. . . ."

Billy . . . Billy . . . Billy, my handsome twenty-two-year-old half-brother William Cantalupo. The happy-go-lucky party kid. Billy dead? Impossible. Who the hell would kill Billy? He was just a kid. He was just a fun-loving kid who never did anything to anyone.

He was the brother I loved playing football with. The kid I played handball and stickball with. The boy who grew a mustache so he'd look like his father. The brother I'd shared intimate moments with, including the night he lost his virginity with a hooker I procured.

I looked at Anthony in shock. "I'm gonna get my crew," I said. "We're going back to Jersey."

"Wait, Joey, wait. Let's talk to Dad first," he said.

Billy and Anthony had been sent to LaSalle Military Academy on Long Island, where my father believed they would get a good education. He must have spent more than $150,000 educating them, sending them to the best preparatory schools and colleges, dressing them in expensive clothes, providing them with cars . . . whatever they wanted.

It was at LaSalle that they met the grandsons of Carlo Gambino and Paul Castellano, as well as the sons of prominent foreign diplomats. It was there Dad hoped they would learn a different way of life. LaSalle was a kind of Catholic finishing school for boys, a prep school that led to places like West Point, Congress, even jobs in the White House.

As in all schools, some kids do well, some don't. Billy was among the also-rans. He graduated from LaSalle, where he made a lot of friends, then went on to Catholic University, where he tried but could not make the grades to get into law school. When he came back to Brooklyn, he went to work for my father as a salesman, doing the job I once did, only without having to contend with Colombo and the world of the Mafia at the front desk.

Billy liked parties, and when there was a reunion of some of his LaSalle classmates at a motel in Seaside Heights, New Jersey, he was one of the first to say yes. Anthony was not far behind.

It was apparently a great party until two men started hassling a pregnant girl at a soda machine on the first floor of the motel. Then one of them slapped her. Words were exchanged, threats made, a free-for-all took place, and Anthony was thrown from the balcony and Billy was stabbed in the side. Police were called to the scene, and so was my father.

When I got to my father's office with Anthony, I was ready to go after whoever was responsible for Billy's death. My father stopped me. He didn't want me involved in any attempt at vengeance. Instead, he wanted my help in arranging the wake and the funeral.

The funeral took place at the Terragrossa Funeral Home in Bensonhurst, and Billy was buried in a plot on Staten Island that was donated by a friend of the family. The wake and the funeral were attended by people both in and out of the mob, not because they knew Billy, but out of respect for my father. The Castellanos, the Gambinos, the Colombos . . . all those people my father knew or had helped in real estate and mortgages, all those whose kids went to school with Billy, turned out. It was a Who's Who of Brooklyn's business world, politicians, and organized-crime figures. Everyone rubbed elbows; nobody gave a damn about where you came from or who you were.

Police, meanwhile, waited a month before charging a twenty-eight-year-old man named Richard Sabatino with throwing Anthony off the balcony, and nobody had been charged with Billy's stabbing. The Ocean County Prosecutor's Office had also indicted another man, Joseph Chilli, for perjury. They said he had lied when he said he wasn't around when Billy got stabbed. Anthony didn't know who was involved or who had thrown him from the balcony the night he came to see me.

That's where the case would normally have ended, except for a conversation that Joe Notch Iannacci had at the Hong Pan with a relative of Sabatino. In that conversation, they confirmed what some suspected—that Sabatino was covering up the identity of the person they said was the real killer of Billy, the son of a Fulton Fish Market wiseguy in the Joseph Bonanno family.

Killings like that are not forgotten in the mob, and particularly in the Gambino crime family, which counseled patience, promising that in time all wounds would be healed. A sitdown was held, and a pledge made to make the one responsible for Billy's death pay.

Sabatino, who worked in the Fulton Fish Market himself, changed his story in July 1979, and pleaded guilty to stabbing Billy. The charges of throwing Anthony from the third floor were dropped, and he was sentenced to an indeterminate jail term in New Jersey on a manslaughter rap. He was back on the streets in the Fulton Fish Market a short time later, and married into the family of a Genovese family wiseguy.

It took nearly seven years before the remainder of that pledge was supposedly fulfilled. In January 1984, the bodies of two men were found in the trunk of a car in Manhattan after they had been shot. One was Joseph Gerald Chilli, the son of Bonanno soldier Gerald Chilli, who had lost his head and stabbed Billy at the party. Police wrote it off then as a narcotics murder. I was told his death was a payback for Billy's untimely death. I would like to believe it was true, but I can never be certain. They don't send out certificates of proof for things like that—just a whispered word.

There were other repercussions. On April 5, 1989, Gerald Chilli, his brother Joseph Chilli, a Bonanno captain, and his son, Joe Junior, were indicted on racketeering charges for trying to murder two men who they believed killed Joseph Gerald Chilli. One of the accused shooters, Anthony O'Connor, survived five shots, while the second man, Anthony Bonventura, has disappeared.

The old Mafia dons really wanted their kids out of their way of life. They didn't want them to follow in their footsteps. Three Finger Brown's kid made it out of that world and went on to West Point.

Gambino's sons, Tommy and Joe, stayed pretty straight. They ran a trucking business and a sweatshop in the garment center; they still do. I can remember Joe Gambino, up to his elbows in piecework, with sweat dripping from his forehead and his shirt, busting his chops from dawn to dark at a miserable Brooklyn clothing sweatshop that he ran for his father. The Gambino boys always helped their old man—but then, that's what a son's supposed to do.

It didn't hurt their career or their business success that their father was a boss either; but then, it didn't hurt the Rockefeller or the Kennedy kids that their old men hustled oil or liquor and used some muscle doing it. Unlike the Rockefellers, of course, whatever the Gambino kids did drew a lot of attention from cops and agents, and I guess they will always be under the microscope of law-enforcement people who think they're hustling even if they aren't.

Paul Castellano tried to do the same with his kids. He didn't want them in the mob, doing the things his soldiers did. He wanted them in business, moving up in the world, breaking away from the tradition of the Mafia. They got into the fat-rendering business, they ran chicken distributors, and they ran restaurant franchises, like Bobby Rubino's, and they stayed legit, or at least the feds and local law enforcement haven't ever laid a glove on them.

Joe Colombo really wanted the same for his sons; I know that because he made a point of trying to keep them out of things. The only thing he did get them involved in was the Italian-American Civil Rights League, and that was because Joe Junior was under fire from the feds.

They didn't listen. First they got into the bookmaking business, which, as far as Colombo was concerned, wasn't all bad, because everybody bets. But he wanted them to concentrate on catering houses, nursing homes, and restaurants, and he was willing to finance them there. When he was shot, they turned to other things, maybe just to survive, but things that would have made the old man come unglued if he'd known about it.

I became aware of some of the things they were involved in while I was on the street—the bookmaking, the loan-sharking, vending-machine rackets, running their own crews to commit crimes to get money and position themselves to become made members of what had become Persico's crime family. I had no idea, however, of how far they had broken with the traditions and values of their father until the federal government and the Suffolk County District Attorney's Office tried to tap me as a witness against them in a racketeering case in 1985. I refused to get involved. I might have informed on them in the gambling case, but I told the feds from the start I would never testify against any of the Colombos. We'd been too close.

According to the evidence the feds and the district attorney had, the Colombo kids—particularly Anthony—were behind a crew of thieves that raped, robbed, and murdered victims in their homes from Newburgh, New York, to Kings Park on Long Island.

Their gang was, in many respects, a lot like the gang that I ran. They went for coin collections, drug rip-offs, unprotected card games, insurance scams, and high-roller casino-junket players who were suspected of having large stashes of cash. I could understand that. That's survival in the family. They were soldiers, and they had to produce revenue, not just for themselves but for their bosses and their crew members.

Sometimes the traditions and values of their old man got lost along the way. The discipline and self-control, values I know Joe Colombo tried to teach them, were history.

A year after their arrest, Anthony, Joe Junior, and Vinnie pleaded guilty to the federal racketeering charges, but they denied they had anything to do with murders or rapes. I don't know if they were telling the truth. I do know what I was told their crew members did. The Colombo kids just admitted to racketeering charges involving gambling and the bribery of a cop. Anthony got fourteen years and was fined $500,000 as the ringleader. His brothers got five years each. The federal judge, Henry Bramwell, said Anthony's problems partially came from "his being brought up in a house headed by an organized-crime figure . . ." Anthony's attorney, Barry Slotnick, disagreed. He said if Joe Colombo had lived, "Anthony could probably be going to take his seat in Congress instead of going to prison."

The judge did have a point. Living in that environment, with all the power their father had, with all the crime people who were in and out of their home, part of their everyday life, the odds were against them from the start just like they were for kids like Little Allie Boy Persico, Carmine's son, or Greg Scarpa, Jr., whose father was the loan shark's loan shark.

Little Allie Boy was part of a dynasty that Carmine was building, the way Profaci did. Profaci tried to have his brother-in-law, Joe Magliocco, run a lot of family enterprises, like liquor distributors and linen suppliers for restaurants. Joe eventually became the boss, and his brothers and sons and nephews were left to run those businesses. Profaci's son, Salvatore, took the olive-oil business his old man controlled and became a capo who ran the New Jersey branch of the family.

Persico wanted his son and his relatives to do what Profaci wanted his family to do—control the Colombo family, become its leaders, and strengthen his power while he was away in jail. It didn't work the way he planned it to any more than it did for Profaci.

Little Allie Boy tried, but he got caught up in the FBI sweep of the Colombo mob, and he got convicted with his old man as part of the rackets conspiracy to run the Family. He was running the pinballs and loan-sharking with me in the flea market, so he wasn't any better than the rest. In fact, he was worse. He also got involved with narcotics, which really brought him down.

That's what ruined Scarpa's operation and damn near started a gang war a couple of years ago. Greg Scarpa, Sr., was one of New York's big-time loan sharks. He could move millions of dollars in hot securities, handle trainloads of stolen goods or shiploads of arms for the Middle East. He was tough and mean, but I never knew him to deal in narcotics. He was respected by Colombo and Persico alike, which is why he became a capo. In 1985, he came down with cancer, and Greg Junior took over running his crew. Instead of sticking with what his old man made a bundle at, Greg Junior went for the big money that narcotics brought, and he was eventually busted by the feds for operating a cocaine ring after being a fugitive—one of the feds' ten-most wanted criminals—for a year.

But his arrest in 1988 by federal agents didn't come until there had been a whole lot of grief for the mob—fights over turf in

Brooklyn and lots of publicity on television and in the newspapers.

The turf war led to killings of some rival narcotics dealers. Before it was over, more than a dozen had been killed, including Greg Scarpa, Sr.'s younger brother, Salvatore. On January 14, 1987, Sal was gunned down in the Wimpy Boy Social Club on Seventy-fourth Street in Dyker Heights, Brooklyn, where young Scarpa was supposed to run the narcotics operation from.

That would never have happened if Scarpa Senior had been on the street. He never wanted anything to do with narcotics, and he sure as hell didn't want his kid involved in it. Things just got out of hand as they usually do when the old-timers aren't around running things. The new bosses don't have the control or the discipline of the guys they replaced.

18

SHED NO TEARS FOR JOE ONIONS

Joe "Onions" Scanlon was big, stupid, and violent, but when it came to dealing with his buddy Andy Merola, he was a pussycat. In his stocking feet, standing on his tiptoes, Merola was only 5' tall, but he had a vicious streak, and for some reason he terrified Joe Onions, who, at 6'3", 260 pounds, towered over Andy.

I met them both through Mike Marino, and now and then they would come to Brooklyn to party after doing a job in Rhode Island or New York. I had used Merola on New York heists, and, when he had some stolen stock to sell, I had arranged a taped meeting on the Belt Parkway during which he sold the hot stocks to Frank Lazzara.

The stocks, about twenty thousand dollars worth of bearer bonds that Merola and Joe Onions had stolen from a home in Providence, were worth only two thousand dollars to Lazzara, who chiseled Merola down and down until they settled on the price.

When the Bureau money greased Merola's palms and Lazzara collected the stock, he and the Bureau put that case on the shelf to keep my role as an informer secret and waited to see what else might develop with Merola, who was a very active operator with strong organized-crime ties to the Raymond Patriarca crime family in Rhode Island. Of course, I didn't tell them that Merola and I were doing other things together that brought money in to help me keep the loan sharks from my throat.

While Merola was a cool operator with ice for blood, Joe Onions had a temper that he had a tough time keeping in check . . . except when he was with Merola. It was amazing to watch this Mutt-and-Jeff combination. With the flick of his hand, Joe Onions could have broken Andy in half like a toothpick. That should have made Andy pause before he went at Onions, but it didn't. In fact, the reverse was true. Whenever Onions got out of hand, it was Merola—all 130 pounds of him—who put him down. When Merola got nasty with him, Joe Onions would start to cry. That's how he got his nickname. In tight situations, Joe Onions would cry like a baby.

In November of 1977, the same time I arranged the stock sale for Lazzara, I brought Andy and Joe Onions and some other Providence gang members to the Golden Gate Motel to party with some girls and Brooklyn members of my crew. It was a blast I thought was needed to take off some of the tension that had resulted from a series of blown jobs.

As usual, Joe Onions got drunk and loud and abusive. None of the crew could control him. It was so bad that finally little Andy bellied up to him—that is, he got his nose to just above his belly line—pulled Onions down to his level by grabbing his shirt, and slapped him back and forth across the face.

Joe Onions turned red in the face, he was so mad. For a moment, he lost all control. He called Merola a midget, a lousy midget. He could have squashed Andy like a grape, but all that comes out of that big mouth is, "Andy, you are a fuckin' lousy midget." Then, instead of pounding Merola into salt, he took it out on the walls of the motel, punching more than a dozen holes in them. He must have caused $300–$400 in damage, smashing his fist into the walls.

Merola was wild. Nobody had ever dared call him a midget and gotten away with it. At first I thought he was going to kill Onions, but when he lost his temper and began screaming at him, he turned Onions into a shaking, shivering ash-white giant, who stood there babbling like a little kid, absolutely helpless and terrified by what Merola said. The threat was so real to Joe

Onions, it so scared him out of his wits, that he hired a car service to take him back to Rhode Island. It cost him two hundred dollars . . . and eventually his life.

Although they worked together on the job, Merola and Joe Onions were still having problems. The next thing I heard was that Joe Onions had gone into hiding in Connecticut, certain that Merola was going to kill him.

With Merola no longer his buddy, Joe Onions went out on his own, getting involved in a string of robberies of drugstores where he stole both cash and pills. The pills were his undoing. He sold them to some undercover Providence cops who used that sale to turn him into an informer.

While Joe Onions worked as an informer, he turned on the guy he cherished the most, Merola. He told the cops that Merola had explosives and blasting caps hidden in his Club 21 at 140 Knight Street, on Federal Hill in Providence. The cops then raided Merola's place, found what Joe Onions had told them about, and busted Merola. Once again Joe Onions went into hiding.

Now I didn't find out about all this until May 5, 1978, when Merola called me from Providence to tell me he was coming to Brooklyn to talk to me. "You know that problem we had with Joe Onions?" he asked.

"Yeah . . . what about it?" I said.

"Well, you don't have to worry about that anymore," he said. "He's gone."

When he arrived at my house, it was about 11:00 P.M. With him was another of his crew members, a French-Canadian friend of his named Morris LaBlanc.

"What the hell's this about Joe Onions?" I asked.

"We had to kill him," Merola said matter-of-factly. "I told you he was a rat, and we found out he was."

I couldn't believe my ears. Here I am in the frying pan again, right in the middle of a murder I had nothing to do with. I had no bug to record what he was saying; I had decided not to call Lazzara because I didn't want him to know about my role in a coin theft we had done in Rhode Island.

"What the hell are you talking about?" I asked.

"He was a no-good fuckin' rat . . . a fuckin' stool pigeon," he said. "He got me fuckin' busted on the explosives by telling the cops where I had things stashed. I figured it was only a matter of time before he threw us all in the bag on the coin job."

Merola had plans for another killing. "I need your help," he said. "I gotta dump another body. I figure I dump the body here—in Brooklyn—nobody cares. There are so many shootings here, they'll figure it's just another mob hit. They're always dumping bodies here."

Who did he plan on killing and why?

Merola explained it all during a two-hour talk we had in my apartment.

He said that after Joe Onions had disappeared, he and Nick Pari had contacted Joe Onions's common-law wife, Sandra Surprise, and a close friend of Onions's named Eddie—Edwin DiFonzo. Merola said he convinced them to lure Scanlon to his club to patch over their differences.

"I told her, 'Sandy, we want to see him,' " explained Merola. "I said, 'We don't want to hurt him, we just want to talk to him, get things back they way they used to be. Tell him we're not gonna hurt him, we just want to talk to him, and everything will be okay.' "

Joe Onions showed up. With him were his girl, Sandy, and their baby, and Eddie. Pari and Merola were in the club waiting.

The Club 21 was a regular mob-style social club with a bar, with tables and chairs to play cards, and a bathroom and a kitchen. There is also a back staircase that leads up to two apartments on two floors above the club. It's the kind of place where things can happen and nobody will be the wiser. It's also the kind of place someone like Joe Onions would consider safe.

There was no way Joe Onions could have thought anything was going to happen. I mean, here he was, with his wife, his newborn baby in her arms, and his trusted friend who was godfather to his child in a club that was familiar to him.

Merola said Joe Onions was scared . . . really scared. "He starts begging me to forgive him," Merola said with a smirk, "then he says to Nick and me, 'Listen, give me a beating—I deserve a beating for what I done.' " Merola said Pari asked him why he'd brought a knife to the meeting with him, and Joe Onions pulled his knife out and put it on the table that all of them were seated around.

"He kept saying, 'Go ahead . . . beat me. Why don't you just beat me up for what I done?' Merola told me. "So we did . . . sorta."

Merola said Pari hit him in the mouth, and as he did, Merola said he jumped up, drew his gun from his holster, and shot Joe Onions in the head. The bullet went through the head, he said, and hit Pari in the finger.

Meanwhile, Merola said that as a result of the shooting, the club was a mess. They got some plastic bags, stuffed Joe Onions's body in it, and he and Pari got rid of it. They also broke up the gun in pieces and got rid of them in safe places. The club was a mess, blood all over the rug and the floor.

First he had DiFonzo clean up the carpet with soda water and soap, then he ripped up all the carpeting and got rid of that. Now, he didn't trust DiFonzo.

I asked them why the hell they killed Joe Onions in front of all the eyewitnesses.

"We didn't have no choice," Merola said. "It was the only way we could get him there. He'da never come there without Sandy and the kid . . . never. Sandy ain't gonna talk, she's a stand-up gal. It's this Eddie I'm worrying about. He's the weak link. We gotta get rid of him."

First he wanted to shoot Eddie and leave his body in the trunk of some stolen car on a side street in Brooklyn. "Hell, they're always dumping bodies around here," Merola said. "Nobody will notice one more."

I shook my head no. Then he wanted to take Eddie out into the middle of Sheepshead Bay in some boat, weight him down with cement or anchors or something, and dump him. Again I shook my head.

I told Merola I didn't want to get involved in any hit on Eddie, but I'd see what I could find out about dumping the body here, whether anybody in the families might get hot about it. "We gotta coordinate things so nothing goes wrong," I told him. "I don't need more trouble right now. Leave Eddie for now."

For the next three days, I agonized over what I knew I had to do. I had to tell the Bureau, but I was afraid it would make things worse for me. If I didn't tell them, I could become an accessory to murder. So on the third day, I called Lazzara and told him everything that had happened.

We arranged to talk to Merola by phone, on toll phones, and record the whole story. For the moment, the case was put on a shelf, but arrangements were made to protect DiFonzo and, later, Joe Onions's girlfriend. They wound up testifying nearly a year later, as did I. They never found Joe Onions's body, although the cops and the feds tore up the floor of Club 21 and looked down a lot of deep pits and wells that Merola had talked about before.

Without a body, without any physical evidence of the murder, the cops and the feds didn't think they had a prayer of winning the case. But strange things happen. Sandra and Eddie became federal witnesses and testified.

After a lot of negotiations with the state, the feds ordered me to testify. They didn't want me to testify because of other cases they were more interested in and thought more important, but they finally agreed to have me testify.

Rhode Island, the Merola-Pari case, was my first courtroom test in a case that everyone said would never make it. But in July 1979, the jury listened and believed, and both Pari and Merola were convicted of first-degree murder. It was the first time in Rhode Island state history that anyone was ever convicted of murder without a body. They were sentenced to life in jail, and I thought that was the end of it. I was wrong.

Two years later, Merola, who had gone to jail in Texas for a theft, and Pari won an appeal of the case because the judge didn't let their lawyers question a state trooper who was running around with Sandy and might have challenged her credibility as a witness.

Prosecutors said it was because of my testimony they were convicted and jailed. That may have been great for all the prosecutors, but for me it was a downer. There they were on the street, and I was the prisoner—in hiding under a different identity to stay alive.

In 1982, Merola and Pari cut a deal with the State Attorney General's Office and took pleas to second-degree murder and manslaughter, respectively. The state supposedly felt it couldn't retry the case because DiFonzo had died. He'd gone in the Witness Program, got involved with drugs, and died from an overdose in South Carolina. That's the story everyone was told, but I've always wondered about that; I always wondered whether Merola's friends got to the kid.

Merola got twenty-five years—ten in prison, and fifteen years suspended sentence and probation. Pari got twenty years, seven years in jail and thirteen years suspended sentence and probation. Part of the deal was to admit where they'd dumped the body—in the ocean off Narragansett. Maybe, but the body was never found, and they had told me they dropped it off some rocks into a pit of some kind in the same area.

I really get ticked off when I think how I'm still on the run, in hiding, and these two clowns are back on the street.

19

LET'S MAKE A DEAL AND A BUCK

It was less than a month after I told Lazzara about the Joe Onions murder that he told me I would have to meet with federal prosecutors Tom Puccio and Ed McDonald. Puccio was the boss of the Brooklyn Strike Force, and McDonald was his new chief assistant, a naive young lawyer who I sized up as likable but not streetwise. Puccio was tougher, more experienced.

We met at the Roosevelt Hotel in the same room where the FBI had taped me up so often to record conversations, and it was at that meeting that they offered me immunity from prosecution for any past crimes I had committed. They didn't know what those crimes might be, and I didn't offer to tell them, because it was all talk, verbal promises, nothing in writing. I had learned long before that you can't bank promises unless they are in writing.

The immunity meant that nobody would be able to prosecute me for past crimes—not the feds, not any state, or any local law agencies. But there was a hitch. I had to agree to go belly-to-belly with a hidden microphone again against Allie Boy Persico, against Funzi Tieri, and against a lot of capos and soldiers in several crime families who I had access to, who I could make deals with and borrow money from. They wanted the flea-market operation, the real estate deals, every kind of business operation I could get them to talk about on tape.

I got very nervous when they told me that, and I got even more nervous when they said that eventually I might have to go into the Witness Protection Program, move from Brooklyn, and change my identity. That just didn't click then; it didn't register in my head. I figured I'd have years to make money on the street. Witness Protection . . . that was only something they'd do if my role as an informer was uncovered. No one really said, Joe, you're going to have to become a witness and testify at trials against these people. I guess it was implied, but I didn't look at it that way. I looked at it as a way to make more money by providing them with more information, more intelligence.

As worried as I was about wearing a body mike against all the bosses and capos, I reluctantly agreed to the deal they were offering. I'd been involved in a lot of burglaries, robberies, loan-sharking, and other crimes with a lot of people. Without immunity, sooner or later someone would blow the whistle, or I would screw up and get caught and then I could wind up in jail for a long time, only I'd be without any protection.

"I want it in writing. I want this agreement in writing before I say anything," I told them.

"Okay, Joe," Puccio said, "in writing when the time comes. Meantime, you work for us on these people—and you don't do anything that's illegal anymore. Understand?"

I understood, but when I walked out of that hotel room, I fully believed I was going to be on the street, doing my thing, for years.

I wasn't thinking of that agreement when Jerry Gordon and Frankie M. came to me in April 1978, with four bank passbooks in various denominations—$15,000, $7,000, $5,000, and $3,000. They were for the bank accounts of an elderly scrubwoman who had died in a Brooklyn apartment house.

Her body had been discovered by her building superintendent, who stole the books and gave them to Gordon, who promised him money if he could tap into her accounts.

"We got these bankbooks, Joey," Gordon said. "You know

about banks. You got contacts. How do we get this money?"

"I don't know, Jerry," I said. "Let me check around."

Once again—I should say, as usual—I was desperate for money, and my desperation was magnified by a meeting I taped with Bolino for the FBI on March 31, 1978. The meeting was about my loan-shark bills, which I had scaled down, using money from various capers to pay back the principal and some FBI money to pay back the interest. Of the original eighty thousand plus dollars, I'd probably paid back a couple of hundred thousand, but the loans were causing me problems even with the feds giving me the money to pay my vig.

The conversation first centered on my debt to Russo, the way he kept harassing me and my interest in paying off the loan balance, which was down to $16,800:

JC: Let me ask you . . . you know what I owe Russo?
MB: No, I don't. I am worried about that, Joe. If you need me tomorrow . . ."
JC: I wanna pay it off. I wanna pay it off.
MB: Let me see.
JC: Can you give me a price?
MB: Do ya want to make a deal? He won't make a deal unless you come up with the money.
JC: Michael, I have to make a deal. If you were to talk to him . . .
MB: I can talk to him. I can do anything I want to.
JC: Talk with him. Joey owes you. I must owe about sixteen eight [$16,800]. What can I buy it for? Just in conversation.
MB: Yeah, but, Joe, you don't understand. I'm a goodfellow. He's a goodfellow. If I say to him, What could I buy it for, he says six, seven, eight thousand, or half the money. What am I going to say?
JC: I'll see what I can do. Can't you do that?
MB: Yeah.
JC: You can.
MB: I'll talk to him.
JC: And the . . . and the sixty-five hundred dollars? . . . You can talk to him . . . to Allie Boy?
MB: Seven thousand dollars.

JC: Seven thousand dollars . . . can you talk to him?

MB: Yeah . . . but, Joey, I can't . . . I can't . . .

JC: Give me a price, so I know. . . .

MB: I just gave this to Allie Boy—this seven thousand dollars— that's why it isn't a question.

JC: I been paying a long time.

MB: You been paying him since November.

JC: Will he take four thousand dollars?

MB: No. No, that's out of the question.

JC: You think Russo will take seven?

MB: Russo . . . Russo. We can talk to Russo. I can talk to Russo. No question about it. Matter of fact, I will. I'll talk to Johnny about it. But Allie Boy . . . you can't, because he just got it. It's new. You can't knock him down three thousand dollars. What are you, crazy? What's the difference if you pay him off? That's your ace in the hole. Then, if you want anything, you got it. You'll never get it [loans] for a point. Where are you going to get money for a point after this? Allie will give it to you for a point after this. You got it beautiful . . . to kid Allie Boy . . . why? You miss a payment?

JC: I miss nothing.

MB: Ain't it better you got it for a point from him . . . and you don't have to see nobody no more? You got a fantastic record. I'm telling you . . . Joey, believe me, I'm telling you.

JC: All right, Russo. Russo's the one.

MB: But meanwhile, you're still paying. You're still paying one twenty-five a week here . . . I mean that.

JC: All right. Give me a figure, that's all.

MB: I get ya . . . I get ya a figure.

The deal was almost set. All I had to do was pay off everything I owed Persico and he would let Bolino arrange the knockdown loan with Russo, cutting what I owed him in half. He would also, according to Bolino, lend money to me at goodfellow rates—one percent per week.

All I had to do now was get the money to pay them off, and I would be free of the loan sharks; I would no longer be stealing from Peter to pay Paul, hustling on the street, plotting, and doing all sorts of capers to raise cash. Once paid up, my credit and my standing with Persico would grow, and I would be in a position to do a lot of the things that the Bureau, Puccio, and McDonald said I'd have to do if I wanted to survive with immunity.

I had no second thoughts about taking the dead woman's money. If there was a way to get my hands on it and use it to my advantage, I thought, why not? So I took the bankbook Gordon gave me with the fifteen-thousand-dollar account in a Brooklyn savings bank, and I went to the home of friend of mine and my father's who was a vice-president at the Brooklyn Savings Bank. I asked him what I could do. His answer was to give me a sort of road map to cash in.

First I had to send a letter to the bank. The letter, he said, would have to be written by someone who could fake the handwriting of the dead woman, signing her name and requesting that the bank release her funds in a bank check so that she could deposit it in a local bank. The reason for the change was that she could no longer travel to the bank where she kept her funds because of illness and wanted a bank closer to her home.

I took the idea to a girlfriend, who practiced signing the woman's name and imitating her handwriting, using as a sample the signature in her passbook. When she had the handwriting down pretty well, we drafted the letter and sent it to the bank.

Meanwhile, Jerry alerted the building superintendent where she lived to flag any mail the postman might bring in for her.

A little more than a week went by when the check turned up in the mail. The superintendent gave it to Jerry, who gave it to me.

I lost no time bringing it to my banking friend, who told me to open a joint savings account in a branch of the same bank in a shopping center. The names to be used were the dead woman's name and that of Joseph Casera.

I chose to use Casera because it was the name on my driver's license, a license that the FBI had supplied me with in 1975 when I lost my driver's license because of speeding tickets and parking fines that I hadn't paid.

At the bank, I opened the account with a signature card that had the dead woman's signature forged on it by my girlfriend and that of Joseph Casera. The bank check made out to her was deposited in that account. I then had to wait ten days for the check to clear before I could touch anything.

Every few days, I would draw some money from the bank, a few thousand at a time. Sometimes a week would go by before I withdrew anything, and then I'd take out five thousand dollars. In a matter of weeks, I had taken all but eight hundred dollars from the account, which I decided to leave in and not touch. Most of the money went to pay off the loan sharks, especially Persico's seven thousand dollars, which had to be taken care of before July 4.

I gave Gordon and Frankie M. a couple of thousand, which they had to share with the superintendent. When they wanted to know why that was all they got, I told them I had to take the money out slowly, not all at once. Privately, I had no intention of sharing anything more with them. Hell, I'd done all the work. They never did get another dime.

No one got charged in that case—not me, not Gordon, not Frankie M. or the superintendent. My banker friend lost his job for showing me how to strip the account when the feds learned about it later, but that was the extent of it.

In years to come, that caper, which I eventually got immunity for, became a prime target for defense attorneys attacking my character on the witness stand. They would all look at the juries considering the charges against the mobsters, point to me, and tell the jurors how I robbed the dead.

20

PROTECTED WITNESS

"**I**'m sick of it, Joey. I'm sick of your affairs. I'm sick of you running around. I'm sick of the calls from the women you were with."

My wife's voice was shrill and sharp with anger; she was angrier than I had seen her in years. Our marriage had been a marriage in name only since 1975. After the birth of our youngest son, there was virtually no sex.

I don't know why, but it had always been difficult for me to make love to Veronica. She was a gorgeous creature—beautifully built, sexy—but for some reason, we always had problems. She enjoyed sex, just as I did, but she never turned me on. I liked my matinees during the day. She didn't. I liked sex in strange apartments with other women. Maybe it was the excitement of doing what I shouldn't be doing. Maybe it was the thrill of turning on and being turned on by other women. I enjoyed that . . . hell, I loved it. By the time I got home—and I was always home before midnight—I wasn't ready for more sex, least of all with my wife.

Maybe it was out of a feeling of guilt because I'd been jumping in bed with other women, but I couldn't be aroused by Veronica, and she knew it. She just never said anything about our problem, about the other women, until after I'd met with Puccio and McDonald and told her about the possibility we might have to leave Brooklyn and live somewhere else under a different identity.

"Screw you, Joe," she said. "I'm not going into any government witness program with you. I'm staying here, with my two boys. You go, damn you. You go—and take your goddamn girlfriends with you."

She changed her mind, but only out of desperation, for the safety of our kids, her parents, and herself. Our marriage was, as I said, a marriage in name only.

In late April, I was fed up with the yelling and screaming and the fights, so I decided on a change of scenery. Without another word, I walked out, got in my car, and headed toward Long Island, to my hometown in West Islip where I'd grown up, attended school, and played football—where I hoped I'd get some relief from the pressure and frustration I was feeling.

I wonder, I found myself thinking, if my old girlfriend is still around? It was a wild thought. I had not seen Rachel since I was getting ready to go into the army. We had been close, good friends, but there had been no sex, just that sort of puppy love you feel when you are a kid in school.

I stopped at the Colonial Inn on Higbe Lane, West Islip, where we used to hang out before I went into the army. As I sat at the bar, toying with a drink, I asked the bartender at the inn if he knew where she was.

"Yeah," he answered. "She's divorced now . . . living at home with her mother. I see her every now and then."

My bartender friend came up with her phone number, and I called. Her mother answered, and I left a message with the number of the Colonial Inn and my name. I don't think I honestly expected to hear from her at all, but within an hour she returned my call and we arranged to meet at a bowling alley we often went to.

Rachel kept a diary from the day we met, and that diary recalls that moment better than I ever could.

When I returned the phone call exactly at 6 P.M., he just said, 'Hello.' I knew who it was and I froze completely for a minute. My whole body was shaking.

His voice was very deep and sexy. The feelings that I experienced right then on the phone and the rest of the night were unreal. My head started spinning with all kinds of thoughts going through it. I was at a loss for words, but when he spoke, he invited me to dinner and I accepted.

We met at an old hangout, the local bowling alley. As I sat in the bar waiting, I felt like a teenager on her first date. I was nervous . . . my stomach was aching and I was shaking.

After I ordered my drink, a few minutes had passed before I looked up at the door to see this handsome-looking gentleman enter with a smile. I thought my heart stopped. Never before did I experience the feelings that I did at that moment.

In my own way, I felt exactly the way Rachel said she did in her diary. I was like a kid again—excited, nervous, and a little shy. I hadn't felt like that with any of the women I'd been with . . . not in all the years in Brooklyn, not even when I first met Veronica.

From the bowling alley we went to dinner at the Captree House. That night, April 27, was the beginning of a new relationship for both of us, one that eventually led to our marriage after dozens of secret, often dangerous, meetings in motels and hotels across the country.

As my marriage went downhill, my meetings and relationship with Rachel escalated. We dined in Port Jefferson restaurants, stayed overnight at the Holiday and Ramada Inns in Suffolk and Queens, and took a three-day trip to Pennsylvania and Ohio.

Near the end of July, my wife and I and our boys went to stay with my sister. I used the visit as an excuse to get away for a family vacation. The truth was, I was ducking Jerry Gordon and Frankie M., who were looking for me to collect more money from the check-cashing scam.

Our vacation suddenly became a nightmare in early August when my father required bypass surgery on his heart and I had to go to Mercy Hospital to see him.

"Hiya, Dad . . . how you feeling?" I asked as I bent over his bed to kiss him on the cheek.

He was weak and tired from the operation and the medication, but he was alert and there was a coolness in his manner and in his eyes that chilled me.

"What are you doing with the FBI, Joey?" he asked sharply.

I was stunned by his question, but I reacted calmly. "Nothing, Dad . . . I'm not doing anything. Why do you ask?" I said.

"Carmine Lombardozzi came to see me yesterday," he said slowly, watching me for any reaction. "He said Harry Berger came to see him, and Harry said the Bureau had you on tape with him over the Scappy situation."

I was shocked, absolutely shocked and near panic, but I managed to contain my feelings as I answered him. "I don't know who is spreading this crap," I said, "but I'm gonna find out."

"Joey, be careful," my father said, showing a depth of concern I hadn't seen in him for years. "I just lost one son a year ago. I don't want to lose another now."

It was his way of warning me that my life was in jeopardy. If Lombardozzi knew and told him because they were close and in the mortgage business together, others knew and would be looking for me. He didn't know I was working for the Bureau, but he figured I might have been wiretapped or someone had bugged our conversation. He never dreamed I was carrying a bug, recording conversations with his friends and with mob figures he knew. If he had known, I'm not sure he would have warned me the way he did.

My immediate reaction when I left his room was to run like hell . . . but where? How? With what? The first thing I did was call Lazzara after I left the hospital. He wasn't at the office, and I couldn't reach him by phone. I learned he was in a hospital in Nassau County recovering from a hernia operation. I did the next best thing; I drove out to the hospital where he was staying just outside of Valley Stream to see him.

"Frank . . . what the fuck are you doing to me?" I shouted. "Are you trying to get me whacked on the street?"

Frank looked at me as if I were crazy. He put his fingers to his lips and then waved me toward a chair next to his bed. "Calm down, Joey, and lower your voice," he said. "This is a hospital, you know. Now what the hell are you talking about?"

"They know about the Berger tape," I said. "Lombardozzi told my father I was on a tape with Berger. That makes me a dead man."

"Jesus . . . I don't know anything about it," he answered, "but you get off the street and stay off the street until I find out what's happened."

I headed back to my sister's home in West Islip alone, and waited.

Lazzara, meanwhile, got busy on the phone and learned through his supervisor that Charles Domaro, from the New Rochelle office, had gone to see Berger . . . to make the case against Anthony Scarpati. The problem was, he never bothered to tell the New York office or anybody else until it was too late.

When Domaro met with Berger, he told him that the Bureau had a taped conversation between him and me discussing the Scappy loan deal with his son. He wanted Berger and his son to testify against Scappy.

Poor old Harry was too scared to testify. He was too afraid to do anything but run to some wiseguy and tell him what he'd been told by the Bureau. He paid a helluva price for that tip. His son disappeared after that and was never seen again. Scappy's people had taken him out to protect Scappy.

With the story that my cover as an informer had been blown verified by Lazzara, there was a lot of scrambling inside the Bureau and the Eastern District Strike Force.

I hadn't finished all the jobs—all the body-mike, belly-to-belly tapings they had planned to have me do. They had made no plans to put me in the Witness Protection Program. It was too early. Nobody planned anything like that before 1979 or 1980. Worse, they hadn't presented any evidence, any testimony, before any grand jury against any of the major people I was taping.

"You're gonna have to sit it out out there, Joey," said Lazzara. "You gotta stay where you are until I can pick you up. You've gotta stay invisible. We'll try to keep an eye on things until we see you. Meanwhile, stay out of Brooklyn and stay off the streets."

So there I was, out on my own, my family—my wife, my boys,

even my sister and mother—at risk, because no one in the Bureau and no one in the strike force was ready to take responsibility for protecting us. As far as I was concerned at that moment, all those promises made for years didn't mean a goddamn thing. All they were worrying about was covering their own asses.

The next call I got was Lazzara. He said Frankie M. and Gordon had tried to take out my former girlfriend, Jan. They had gone to her home and told her they wanted to take her for a ride.

"We know where Joey is," Gordon was supposed to have told her. "He's out on the Island. Why don't you take a ride with us to see him . . . help us get things straightened out."

Jan was smart enough to realize that any ride she took with them was going to be permanent. She figured that Frankie M. and Gordon had decided she knew too much about them and their relationship with me and wanted to eliminate her as a potential witness. The idea that they knew where I was was strictly a guess. Long Island is a big place—over 3 million people live there in dozens of towns and villages spread across hundreds of square miles. They hadn't the faintest idea where my mother lived, or my sister, and they knew the last place I'd go to was my grandmother's, where they had been before. So they were just guessing.

When Jan refused to go, Gordon tried to force her out of the house. He kicked her hard—so hard that she went flying down the stairs, breaking her leg. They couldn't carry her, and with her screams she was attracting too much attention, so they couldn't kill her there either. They took their only alternative. They ran. Jan got medical help and then called Lazzara, who, with the Bureau, provided her with protection for years. For some reason I never understood, they never had local police charge Frankie M. and Gordon with assaulting her and attempting to kidnap her. I didn't see her again until I was called to testify against Allie Boy Persico.

Life in West Islip was confining, and difficult. It was tough for my sister and mother; it was tough for Veronica and the kids. It was hell for me, because I couldn't see Rachel.

There were meetings, three or four, with Lazzara and his supervisor and other agents. They came to West Islip and tried to work out what would be done and how. There was a lot of finger-pointing, a lot of excuses at those meetings, to explain why my cover was blown. But all the finger-pointing, all the explanations, in the world wasn't helping me or Veronica come to grips with what lay ahead. We were going to have to be moved to a new area. We were going to have to have our identities changed . . . our whole lives changed. There would be no contact with friends or family, no return visits to our home, no school with their old friends for the kids. I'd have to start a whole new way of life. While I was doing that with my family in some strange community I'd never seen before, I would have to be returning to Brooklyn under protection to testify against some of the most powerful criminals in America.

Veronica, at first, wouldn't even consider leaving the area. It was just too overwhelming for her and for the boys. Starting life in some strange place without friends or family is a frightening thing to face for a woman who has hardly ever left the confines of her hometown, even when that hometown is a borough of the City of New York like Brooklyn. When she finally agreed, it was only if the government would agree to move and relocate her mother and father. That presented problems, but the government did agree.

I had no choice. If I didn't go, if I didn't agree, I knew I'd be killed. So I agreed, but I still told them nothing of what I had been doing, because I had no immunity in writing yet. I also had to figure out ways and means of seeing Rachel. This wasn't a quickie relationship. It was very special, something I couldn't part with and survive.

On August 31, 1978, the Bureau finally acted. For a month, my family and I had been hiding out at my mother's and sister's; now, it had to end. It was too dangerous, too confining. Everyone was getting short and testy with everyone else. It was too much to ask of my sister and her family and my mother.

So the Bureau moved us about ten miles from where we'd been staying, to the Ramada Inn where Rachel and I had spent several nights.

Veronica, the kids, and I had a couple of rooms with a sitting room. Veronica and the kids slept in one room; I slept in another. In adjoining rooms were agents assigned to protect us, about half a dozen agents from Lazzara's office.

The agents went where we went. If we went to the supermarket, they were with us. If we went to dinner or breakfast, they were at our table or a table next to us. They were our shadows, day and night.

For the next ten days, I was back and forth to the FBI office in Rego Park, Queens, trying to negotiate a deal with the government. The biggest hitch was over my wife and our rapidly deteriorating marriage. I wanted the government to agree to provide protection and subsistence for Veronica and my sons, as well as myself, if we got a divorce.

There was no way, I told Puccio and McDonald, that I could be expected to testify against all the racketeers they wanted me to go against if I wasn't guaranteed protection for my family, whether we were together or split up. And I wanted that protection to continue until my court appearances ended.

Puccio and McDonald were agreeable, but they had to get final approval from Gerald Shur, who was then the Justice Department's overseer of the Witness Protection Program. For a while, Shur, I was told, was opposed. Finally, McDonald told me, Shur relented, and the Justice Department agreed to the deal I asked for. I never, however, spoke face-to-face or even by telephone with Shur. All the negotiating was handled by the strike-force attorneys, who I had to depend on.

They wouldn't, however, budge from the monthly subsistence allotment . . . $980. For all of us, that was a shocker. After living the way we had, spending $7,000, $8,000, and $9,000 a month just to live—forget what I had to do to pay the loan sharks—I couldn't begin to understand how I was going to live on $980 and pay for our housing, food, clothing, and other essentials. In the years that followed, I had to come up with enterprising ways to supplement that income to meet the bills of everyday living.

After ten days at the Ramada, we bailed out in a caravan of Bureau cars. Left behind was my rental from Terragrossa Leasing—a Cadillac the Bureau paid me to lease that had been bugged to record conversations with mob associates and loan sharks. The Bureau stripped the car of the eavesdropping devices, and later, I was informed, Terragrossa sued the Bureau unsuccessfully to recover leasing payments that were not paid after I had to go into hiding.

The caravan of Bureau cars took Veronica, the kids, and myself, as well as all our luggage, to the Southern District headquarters of the U.S. Marshals Service WITSEC (Witness Security) Office. There, I met with Inspectors Jack Walsh and Alfie McNeil.

Before a word was said, the FBI agents left. By law, they could have nothing to do with the next stage of our life, the Witness Protection Program. That was handled exclusively by the U.S. Marshals Service. Lazzara shook my hand and handed me an envelope with several thousand dollars in it, money that the Bureau owed me for my work as an informant.

Veronica and I stood there, looking at each other and the kids, wondering what the next hours and days would hold for us. Little was said until finally a deputy, who was to be our escort, came over to us and told us to pick up our bags and follow him and several accompanying deputies. There were fourteen bags among us, and none of the deputies would help.

Once we loaded everything, they drove us, using two cars, to Newark Airport, were we were instructed to take a flight to Milwaukee, Wisconsin, and then pick up another flight to Minneapolis-St. Paul, Minnesota, where we were to be met by Deputy Marshal Michael Ball.

Minneapolis-St. Paul! Minnesota! Where the hell was that? To four people who'd lived their lives in Brooklyn and had never gone beyond Pennsylvania and Ohio, it was the end of the earth. They might as well have told us we were going to Moscow!

Neither Veronica nor I knew where Minnesota was or what to expect. One day you're on the streets of New York City, the city that never sleeps, the land of hustle . . . the next day you begin a whole new life in a place they call the land of the Vikings. When we landed in Minneapolis, I felt like a Sidge getting off the boat from Sicily. I felt out of place, I looked out of place, and I was convinced that the mob would find me in a minute. I wasn't far wrong, as events later turned out!

Mike Ball and a female deputy were at the airport, and they, unlike the deputies we dealt with in New York, helped my wife and kids with the bags. They took us to a Holiday Inn for temporary lodging in a community called, of all things, Brooklyn Park. Nothing like the originality of the marshals. Put a mob guy and his family from Brooklyn in a place called Brooklyn Park, Minnesota.

In the hotel, Ball explained that for the next thirty days we would use the Holiday Inn as our temporary home until we found a home that we could live in. The marshals would pay for the rooms and all our meals, and they would help us get transportation. The help was in the form of giving us a phone book to look up car-rental companies. We had limited resources—less than twenty-five hundred dollars between us. Veronica, however, is a master of stretching a buck, and she arranged for us to lease an old used station wagon from a company called Rent-A-Relic. The cost was $60 a week rental, with an option to buy for $450. What we leased was just that, a relic, but it ran.

On the second day in Minnesota, the marshals took us to get our driver's licenses. The marshal inspector in charge was Dan Dodge, and he gave me instructions that floored me. In Minnesota, you have to take an eye test, a written test, and a driving test.

But before we took any of the tests, he told me to pick a name that I could use on the license. I did. I picked Joseph Tali.

"If they ask you why you don't have a driver's license," he said, "just tell them you've been in jail for the last twenty years, that you've been serving time for murder."

Was this guy for real? At first I thought he was kidding, but he wasn't. Then I remember thinking, He's crazy. Wrong again. I found him to be brighter and more concerned than most about witness security. He just thought telling a clerk you were a convicted killer would so stun him that he'd do what you wanted . . . no questions asked.

Stupid . . . crazy . . . reckless! I don't know, but I do know that I was lucky that the clerk never asked me about what happened to my past license.

If I thought Dodge's instructions were strange, I learned in the months and years ahead that a lot of the deputies I had to deal with were a little on the strange side. Security wasn't exactly their strong suit, yet that was what the government had put them in charge of—the security of the lives of thousands of witnesses.

There was one deputy, an inspector in the WITSEC Program, who had a strange habit and a morbid sense of humor. His name was Eric, and he lived, at the time, on Staten Island. He loved to keep canaries. I mean, his house was like Parrot Village in Florida, except it was Canary Village. All told, he had about thirty of them. The strange thing about them was that he named them after each witness he handled. Every time he would get a new witness, he would get a canary and name it after the witness. He named one of those damned birds after me. Then one day he called me to tell me one of his canaries had died.

"Oh, yeah, Eric?" I said. "Which one?"

I almost knew the answer before he opened his mouth.

"It was Joey," he answered, chuckling to himself, "the one I named after you. You better watch your step, Joey. That might be a warning about the future."

A few days after we arrived in Minnesota, Eric had to fly out from New York to see us, hand-carrying a Memorandum of Understanding that we were supposed to have signed in New York but didn't. The marshals discovered they'd screwed up by flying us out so fast. In the rush to get us out of New York, they had forgotten to have us sign a Memorandum of Understanding, the agreement that every witness has to sign when he accepts government protection as a witness.

The Memorandum of Understanding sets out the rules that witnesses and their families have to live by. You get to read it once—that's it—then you sign it, and the government, the marshals, keep it. The witnesses and their families receive no copies, supposedly for security reasons, because it lists your WITSEC number and some other vital information that killers might find useful in searching for you.

Without the signed memorandum, the marshals and the government weren't covered if anything happened to us, so they sent this inspector, Eric Jergensen, by plane to see us with a copy of the memorandum to sign. The marshals, particularly Eric, were all ticked off about that.

What the marshals were supposed to do, and didn't, was explain to us our rights as witnesses, what we were entitled to. We were entitled, for example, to five hundred dollars to help us buy a car. There was also government funding to help pay for a witness's auto insurance and his license plates. No one told us that. We had to lay out the five hundred dollars out of what little money we had on the station-wagon rental. In fact, there were a lot of things I later learned we were entitled to that the marshals never bothered to tell us about.

When I read the memorandum, I noticed that the agreement on a deal to provide for my wife and children in the event of separation or divorce wasn't in there. So, despite Jergensen's objections, I wrote it in by hand.

Within a week after arriving in Minnesota, Veronica had to fly back to Brooklyn, meet some deputies, and go to our old home on Eighty-third Street in Brooklyn, so that a mover, assigned to do the job by the government, could pack up everything we owned and move it out. I was nervous about her trip, and I called Lazzara to ask him to go to the house with the deputies to be sure she was safe.

She arrived early in the morning, and by afternoon she was on a plane back to Minnesota, while our furniture and personal possessions were on a van to somewhere in Virginia. There, they would be transferred to another location and stored for thirty days, and then sent to whatever home we had decided to rent.

Renting in Minnesota, as I learned elsewhere in the country, meant we had to play by rules that some deputies established to fill their own pockets. Luckily, for us, Ball and Dodge weren't among those lining their pockets, but we found in areas from Minnesota to New York, from Iowa to Washington, that there were deputies who used the secrecy of the witness program to fatten their own wallets.

We ran into deputies who directed us to rental locations that normally charged, say, $350 for an apartment to the average person, then upped the ante to $400 when the deputy informed him he was renting to a government "undercover man." The deputy would get the lion's share of the increase, and the landlord would get the guaranteed government rental—particularly a cut from the government-witness fund for housing that provided the security down payments that witnesses defaulted on time and again because they had to be moved in a hurry, without the required notice to the landlord. There were also schemes for other kickbacks to deputies that could amount to considerable amounts of money that the witness never saw—money from other special-witness funds for insurance, prescription drugs, and moving costs.

With the wagon, Veronica and I and the kids went house-hunting, and finally came up with a place we found acceptable in Maple Grove, a small, pleasant suburban community that was about a thirty-minute drive away from Minneapolis.

There was nothing elaborate about the house. It was a two-bedroom, one-family house with a basement, a two-car garage and an 80' × 100' plot. The rent was $450 a month. It was a tight squeeze with a $980 allowance, but we were willing to make sacrifices, and I figured I could hustle some extra money from the government on travel expenses and other costs.

Before we could sign anything, Ball had to see it and meet with the landlord. He instructed me to say nothing about what I did until he saw the landlord. When he did, he told the landlord that I worked for the government in an undercover capacity. The rent stayed the same; there were no under-the-table payments in that transaction.

For the time being, I settled into the life of a dedicated family man in Maple Grove, coaching one of my son's football teams, manicuring my lawn, and building a small family garden in the back. I was just that newcomer from the East . . . that dark-skinned Italian who moved into Maple Grove.

The school principal where my boys attended class was informed that I was an undercover operative for the government to prevent too many questions about my sons' school records and my movements and employment. My neighbors knew I worked for the government, but they didn't know what I did, and I never took time to explain my job to them.

Life at home with my wife was still difficult, particularly since I had to fly in and out of Minneapolis to New York to meet with Puccio and McDonald for debriefings. She suspected, rightly so, that I used the flights to New York to arrange secret meetings with Rachel.

21

TRUST NO ONE IF YOU WANT TO LIVE

Almost from the start, my life as a witness was placed in jeopardy by the U.S. Marshals Service in New York. The reason was simple. They had no criminal intelligence and no understanding of the mob people they were facing, the people they were supposed to be protecting witnesses like myself from.

If you are going to protect someone from assassins, you should know something about the assassins, the people behind them, who they associate with, and where they hang out.

Most of the people I ran into in the Marshals Service had no experience with organized crime. Worse, they didn't seem to be interested. They didn't ask the witnesses they were protecting any questions about what might be dangerous about the area they were going to or coming from. They didn't have mug-shot files relating to people the witness was testifying against or the people they employed, and they didn't talk to other agencies, like the FBI, unless they had to. And when they were in public places, some of them had a tendency to talk too much about who they were protecting.

There were exceptions, of course, like Inspector John Partington of Rhode Island. Partington was the witness-security chief for New England, and he provided protection for me when I had to testify against Merola and Pari in Providence. It was obvious from the start that he knew what he was doing. He knew everything about Merola and Pari—their habits, their friends, their associates, and their connection to Raymond Patriarca. He knew about their hangouts and, most important, he knew the danger zones around the courthouse in Providence where I had to testify.

On the day I testified, he had me inside before anyone arrived at the courthouse, and when I completed my testimony, he sent a double out with deputies to draw the press and flush out any potential hitmen. While they watched the obvious, Partington slipped me out the rear in a car where I lay down on the floorboard in front of the rear seat so I couldn't be seen.

Partington, however, was special. He was too good. That's probably why he didn't survive with the service and win promotions to the top. He wasn't a politician. He was a security specialist who believed in helping witnesses and keeping them alive.

The majority of the inspectors and deputies I ran into in the Marshals Service Witness Security Program knew enough about the mob to put in a thimble. I learned that almost immediately in my first trip from Minneapolis to New York.

For most people, traveling from Minneapolis to New York is at most a three-hour flight, barring air-traffic delays or airline screw-ups. For a witness like myself, a trip like that took eight hours or more. As a security measure, the marshals required me to fly an irregular schedule over a circuitous route. The routes I flew to get to New York were pure torture, and they were torture for the deputy who accompanied me on the first few trips. It seemed to me that I flew to more cities to make more flight changes to get to the same place than any man alive. Safety and security were the prime directives for travel. I couldn't and didn't argue with that reasoning. It made sense.

What didn't make sense was assigning deputies to protect me who didn't have the faintest idea of who or what to look for. I mean, there weren't a helluva lot of Brooklyn Mafia figures in Minnesota, and the deputies, while nice guys, didn't know a mafioso from a pig farmer.

My eventual destination was always New York, but I might

land in Newark, or Philadelphia, and on occasion at LaGuardia.
In between, there might be stopovers and flight changes in
Milwaukee, Chicago, and other cities. If I wasn't with a deputy,
a deputy would meet me and escort me to the new flight . . . at
least in the beginning.

The first time I came in, I was met by a deputy in the early
evening, taken off the plane, and hustled to a side entrance of the
LaGuardia terminal to a waiting car. From there, we went to the
Marshals Witness Security Office in Manhattan before we
headed for a "site" hotel where the marshals were going to put
me up for the night until they could take me to the Eastern
District Strike Force headquarters at Cadman Plaza in Brooklyn.

"Site hotels" were supposed to be safe locations where the
marshals could house one or more witnesses on a particular
floor. The marshals had them all around the suburban areas of
cities around the country, and in New York they had them in
Long Island, New Jersey, and Connecticut, as well as Manhattan and Staten Island.

From the time I left Minnesota to the moment we headed
across the Verrazano-Narrows Bridge, no one had said a word
to me about where I was going to stay for the night. Finally, fed
up with wondering and guessing, I turned to the very quiet
deputy who was behind the wheel.

"Mind telling me where we're going?" I asked.

He half smiled before answering, and then identified a particular hotel on Staten Island, part of a national chain of hotels
often used by tourists.

"You've got to be kidding," I said. "I can't go there."

"Why not?" the deputy answered.

"Because Sally Profaci operates there!" I said. "He has a piece
of the bar. A lot of the mob guys hang out there. I used to hang
out there. They'd spot me in a second."

As we got through the tollbooths, the deputy pulled to the
roadside. "Jesus," he said. "I gotta check with office. You gotta
talk to Jack Walsh."

Why, I wondered, hadn't we done that while I was in Manhattan?

Walsh was the inspector in charge of witness security for the region and had an office in the Southern District. He supervised the movement of witnesses in and out of New York, deciding on where and how they would be protected whenever they were in the area to testify or meet with federal officials. Generally, he was better than most, having learned his trade with Partington. But you are only as good as your information, and he wasn't informed about this location.

"Why didn't you tell us about the hotel before, Joey?" he asked.

"How the hell could I tell you?" I answered. "Nobody bothered to tell me where I was going until we were crossing the bridge and I asked the deputy here."

"From now on, Joey," Walsh said, "you've got to tell us the hot spots, point people out to us so our people know."

"By the time I tell you it's Sammy the Syrian or Allie Boy Junior or whoever, I'm dead and so's your deputy," I said. "Why don't they know who to look for? Don't you guys talk to the Bureau? Don't you check out the area before you bring people in?"

Walsh didn't answer, but he told the deputy to take me to another "site hotel" in New Jersey, checking with me first to see if I knew of any problems at that location.

In late September 1978, I arranged through Alfie McNeil to stay for a night in Waterbury, Connecticut, at the Red Bull Inn. At the same time, I arranged to have Rachel drive up to meet me and stay with me. Alfie knew about Rachel, and he agreed to the meeting as long as security wasn't broken and Rachel was aware of the dangers and the need for absolute secrecy. It wasn't by the rule book, but sometimes rules are bent a little to keep witnesses happy—ready to do what they have to do and not constantly thinking about the dangers they face, about the bleak future they have waiting for them.

I rented the room directly beneath mine for her while deputies checked me into the hotel with instructions not to leave unless they were notified. I had no intention of leaving, just of staying in the room making love to Rachel on a waterbed, with ceiling mirrors reflecting our every movement. It was wild.

A day later, I was moved to a "site hotel," a Holiday Inn

where the marshals could control movement in and out of an entire floor through a command post they set up to provide security for a number of witnesses they had staying at the "site."

I was furious when I saw the "site" hotel room—a small hole-in-the-wall, with a single bed, some nightstands, and a TV set. It was called the Skyline Hotel in Manhattan.

"Do I have to stay in this little fuckin' room all the time I'm here?" I asked the deputies.

"Oh, yeah," explained the head of the detail. "You have to stay here when you're not with us. You can't go out without us. We have the key. If you need soda or ice or something else, you call us. Don't leave your room. If you do, you lock yourself out, and you'll get in a whole lot of trouble."

He was grinning from ear to ear as he said it, as if he was enjoying my discomfort. "We'll be down the hall in our command post . . . our room," he added. "If you need something, dial this room number." He handed me a slip of paper with a number on it, turned on his heel, and left.

Another deputy was still there.

"How the hell am I gonna see my girl?" I asked. "I thought everything was taken care of."

The deputy shrugged. "Don't know about that, but I'll give you an idea about how you can get ice during the night if you want it without locking yourself out."

I smiled. "I'll be your friend for life," I said.

"Hey, I know this isn't easy," he said. "I've been on these details before. Just remember, we're here to protect you. We don't want you to get hurt. So don't take chances . . . don't go wandering around."

"I promise," I answered.

The deputy handed me a roll of tape. He showed me how to tape up the door lock so the lock wouldn't engage. "Carry an ice bucket with you, so if you're spotted, you can say you were just going to the ice machine," he explained. "Otherwise, get back to your room before we come to collect you at six."

Because of that understanding deputy, I managed to breach security and slip into a room I arranged to have Rachel rent on the same floor. For the next three nights, we tried to make up for the time we'd lost since I'd gone into hiding when Agent Domaro blew my cover in Brooklyn. The danger of our meetings added to the excitement of the moment for both of us, but Rachel was still tense, fearful that something might happen to me.

Rachel's diary reflects the tension and the concern we both felt. She wrote, "A cautious man . . . a man who takes risks while taking precautions. I know what was happening . . . the danger he was in, the risks and all the protection, but it wasn't going to change my love for him . . . or stop me from seeing him . . ."

Each day, literally from dawn to dusk, I spent long, tedious hours being debriefed by McDonald at strike-force headquarters in Brooklyn. At 6:00 A.M., the deputies would come to my room to escort me to McDonald's office. That meant that at 5:00 A.M., Rachel and I would have to get up, get dressed, and I'd have to slip her out to a room I had reserved for her on another floor, return to my room, and quickly get ready for my bodyguards.

It was nerve-racking—a helluva way to make love, to be with the woman I wanted to be with, but it was worth it . . . every minute of it. It was a plan we tried to follow, not always successfully, not always without incident, each time I came to town.

In early March 1979, there were problems. We were at a "site hotel" in Kenilworth, New Jersey. Rachel had rented a room on the floor beneath mine, and for several nights I had slipped from my room, taped up the lock, and spent the night with her.

It had been particularly difficult to slip away because the command post was located next to my room, and deputies had checked several times to see if I was in my room. Each time they had checked, I was there.

The marshals were nervous about the arrangements. They had six witnesses on the same floor. One of them was a black girl who was a witness in a drug case. She got loose one night and went back to her old stomping grounds in Harlem. When she came back, they caught her before she got back into her room. She started cursing and screaming at them. It took them an hour or more to calm her down.

The deputies took a lot of abuse, there's no doubt about it. Some knew how to handle it; some didn't.

One of them who didn't was the head of the detail, Eric, who had been on my case since he had to fly to Minnesota with the Witness Memorandum of Understanding for me to sign. We didn't hit it off then, and we hadn't hit it off during the months I had to fly in and out of New York for meetings. He was always watching me, badgering me, breaking my shoes.

This time he caught up with me, figured out what I was up to. The evening after the black girl got caught, the deputies had announced that this would be the last night at the site.

"We're moving outta here tomorrow," Eric announced. "The site's been compromised; we're going somewhere else."

"Where?" I asked.

"You'll know when we get there," he answered.

At about 10:00 P.M., I put my clothes on over my pajamas, snuck out of my room, and took the stairway down to Rachel's floor and her room, carrying the ice bucket with me. At seven in the morning, a little later than I usually went up, I returned to my room. It was locked! The tape had been removed, and it was locked.

I went, bucket in hand, to the command-post room. Eric greeted me with a smirk.

"Where the hell you been since 10:00 P.M., Joe?" he said.

"I been with someone I want to be with," I said. I looked around. All my clothes, my bags, were in the command post.

"Well, you won't be seeing her anymore," he snapped. "You're going back to your room . . . and you're gonna stay there. We're gonna lock you in without your clothes until we have to leave. You got that?"

"I got it!" I yelled back, "and I'm gonna see some people about this. What you're doing isn't right, and I'm gonna get this straightened out once and for all."

"You do that," he said quietly. "You just do that, Joe. You'll learn you don't run this operation."

I never thought I did. I thought things had been worked out before with Alfie. I was wrong. I went back to my room, and they locked me in. I called Rachel's room on the phone and told her what happened.

"What are we going to do, Joe?" she said, trying to hold back the tears. "I don't know what I'll do if we can't be with each other."

"Don't worry, honey," I said, "I'll get something worked out. I'm going to have a sitdown with McDonald and the marshals. I'll get this worked out."

"Where are they moving you to now, Joe?" she asked.

"I don't know . . . but I'll call you as soon as I can," I said. "I love you, Rachel. I promise I'll get this worked out."

I watched her as she left. It was raining and miserable. She looked up at my room and waved before stepping into her car, driving off. She tried to hide it, but I could see she was crying.

It took two days before I could arrange a sitdown with the necessary people. McDonald, Walsh, McNeil, and Frank Lazzara were all there for the meeting at the strike force.

"Look, I can't do what you want me to—concentrate and tell you everything I know, prepare for the cases you want—and live like a fuckin' mummy in some fuckin' rathole of a hotel without seeing my girl," I said.

"It's against the rules, Joe," McDonald said.

"Sure . . . so's a lotta things," I said, "but let's face it—the rules are stretched or broken all the time. I've been meeting with Rachel for months. Why, all of a sudden, is it a security risk? That's bullshit, and you know it."

After a lot of hassling back and forth, they struck a deal. They would fly me in to New York and take me to Waterbury, Connecticut, where I would stay at the Red Bull Inn. Rachel could have an adjoining room, and deputies would have a command-post room nearby. The government would pick up the tab for the rooms and the meals. Rachel would have to arrange her own transportation, and security would have to be tight. She could tell no one where she was going. She never had, and she never did.

Eric was not a forgiving guy. He was a by-the-book type of inspector, and when the rules are bent, something has to be done. In May, it became apparent something had been done.

I had been having a particularly bad time with my wife. She had discovered some makeup on my clothes when I returned from a trip in early May and was convinced I was meeting with my old girlfriend Jan. Veronica was so convinced, in fact, that she had located Jan's phone number through some records I had and called her in Brooklyn, screaming at her, telling her to stay the hell away from me. We had a battle royal, a real blowout. Life with Veronica had become a living hell.

Out of desparation, I called McDonald to see how soon I would be able to get away from home and return to New York and Rachel. That's when the bomb dropped.

"I'm sorry, Joe," McDonald said. "When you come East, you won't be able to stay in Connecticut."

"Why not?" I said. "We had a deal!"

"I know we did," he said, "but someone has written to Washington to complain about you. He's complaining that you're not staying on site like other witnesses, that you're treated different. Washington's raising hell about this."

"Who wrote the letter, that inspector . . . Eric?" I shouted.

"I can't tell you, Joe," McDonald said. "They just said someone wrote, they didn't say who."

I knew it was Eric. He had told me I hadn't heard the last of it when the deal was cut.

I called Rachel from a phone booth to tell her what had happened. I didn't want Veronica to know about her or where she could reach her. I was depressed, I was angry, I didn't know what the hell I was going to do, but I told her that if I had to, I'd leave the witness program before I'd stop seeing her.

It was hell for Rachel as well. In her diary, she recalled how she felt after I called to tell her:

> I was sick all Tuesday night. I cried myself to sleep. I couldn't talk . . . I was so choked up and I was worried sick about Joe and what was going through his mind. What hurts is knowing how strong this order came down from Washington and what can be done. If nothing can be done and Joe has to go back to the same locations as the programs and be locked up in a room . . . if we can't see each other, it's going to be hell.

I was badly shaken when I returned to New York. I was mad at McDonald, mad at the Marshals Service, and particularly mad at the inspector who I was convinced had written the letter to Washington.

I wanted out—any way I could get out, I wanted out. I had planned doing a book with *Newsday*'s organized-crime investigator Tom Renner, but that was down the road. We had met at an FBI office and we had talked, but our understanding was clear— no book until I was through testifying. So there would be no money coming in from any book for maybe years. There was no way I could know how long it would be before I would be finished testifying at trials. I had to go against a lot of people . . . if I testified.

I had talked to my father by phone a number of times, using a federal telephone system that couldn't be traced. Up to that point, Persico and Bolino had not been indicted, but they knew I was ratting on them, telling the feds everything.

Each time my father and I talked, he urged me to make a deal with Bolino. "Joe," he would say, "call Michael. They want to make a deal. Work something out with him." The last time I called him, he said it might be worth $300,000 to them. Later, at Allie Boy's trial, he denied making the offer, acting as an intermediary. He testified I was trying to extort the money from Bolino and Persico. That wasn't true, and the jury didn't believe him. If they had, they wouldn't have convicted Allie Boy.

Anyhow, I had a number of phone-booth numbers I could use. When I called my father, I told him to tell Michael Bolino I would call a particular booth number that we had agreed to use in the past.

I called him. "Michael, this is Joe," I said.

"Yeah . . . I know," he answered.

"Look, Michael. Go to the phone booth on Fort Hamilton Parkway tomorrow morning," I said. "I'll call you."

The next day, I dialed the number from another phone booth. I didn't tell the FBI or McDonald what I was doing. I'm not sure I knew what I was doing. I just knew I was desperate . . . looking for a way out. In my heart, I guess, I knew this wasn't the way, but I had to try.

"Michael . . . it's Joe again," I said. "My father says I should talk to you. So talk."

"Joey . . . what the fuck are you doing to me, to Allie Boy?" he asked, knowing full well what I was doing. "You know what's going to happen here . . . the position you put me in? All these fuckin' people you're going to hurt?"

"Yeah, Michael, I know," I said, "but I gotta survive, and you people aren't going to let me."

"Joey . . . listen. They want to make a deal," he said. "It's worth three hundred thousand dollars to you."

"Really," I answered. "Michael . . . I'll tell you what. We . . . you don't trust me, and I, I don't trust you. The only person that I can trust is my father, and if we're going to do something, we're going to do it through him. If we make a deal, I want absolution. I want absolution from Allie Boy, from Carmine, from Funzi, from Johnny . . . from all of them. You get me the absolution, I'll get back to you."

I hung up. I knew at that moment it would never work; I could never trust Bolino or anyone. I couldn't even trust my father. My plan was to give him fifty thousand dollars to pay back money I owed him and use the rest to run off with Rachel. It was stupid, and I knew it. My father would have been forced to set me up. That's the way the mob works. They make family set up targets they want to hit. So I did the only other thing I could do; I told the FBI and I told McDonald. I told them part of the story . . . not all of it.

I told them I had been offered $50,000, not $300,000. I'd let them set up the mob and take them down on the payoff. I'd pocket the $250,000, pay my father what I owed him, and keep the balance. What was the mob going to do—say they'd paid me $300,000 instead of $50,000? They would have convicted themselves by admitting to that.

My condition was that I didn't want my father charged with anything; I wanted that guaranteed, but first I wanted to meet with my father, eyeball-to-eyeball, to work out the deal. The feebs reluctantly agreed.

The meeting was set up at the FBI's offices in Rego Park, Queens. It was June 1, my father's birthday. The timing couldn't have been worse. It was the same day Rachel was to come to the FBI office. I had been staying at another witness-program hotel "site" on Staten Island. I considered it dangerous, and I told the marshals. They just told me to stay in my room and everything would be cool.

I wasn't very cool about anything. Rachel was just an hour away, and I couldn't see her. Finally, we decided to chance it. Instead of my sneaking out of my room to hers, I would sneak her into my room—a real violation of the security rules. The witness program permits no visitors to any witness room. It was the kind of violation that could result in termination from the witness program—a loss of all subsistence, everything. I was still willing to chance it.

Just as Rachel was ready to drive to the site, the marshals decided to do what I said they should do all along. They moved me and other witnesses from the Staten Island site. This time we were moved to New Jersey.

I was wild. I blew my top. It was Alfie who finally cooled me down and worked out an arrangement. He would agree to let Rachel and me meet at a hotel in Philadelphia, but I would have to pay all expenses. I didn't have the money, but Rachel did, so we arranged for a pre-trip meeting at the FBI office. It took place the same day my father arrived. He was an hour late. Rachel was on time.

Rachel described what happened in her diary:

I got into Queens about eleven, parked the car and went up (to the FBI office). I was nervous, but all I wanted was to see Joe and touch him.

When I got out of the elevator, I told the woman who I was and who was expecting me. I sat down and had a cigaret. As I was sitting there, a man walked over to the same woman. Before he even spoke, I knew who he was. For a minute, I felt like my heart had stopped.

I couldn't believe what was happening. The gentleman that was standing no more than ten feet from me was Joe's father. The resemblance was there . . . white hair. He sat in the chair next to me. I was breaking out in a sweat.

Dan [Reilly, an FBI agent] walked out [from the Bureau office to talk to the receptionist]. He had the same expression on his face that I did . . . that "I don't believe it" look as he looked first at me and then at Joe's father.

I told Dan I would wait. He took Mr. C. in first. A few minutes later Dan came out and suggested that I go for coffee for about twenty minutes. We were both a little worried. We didn't want his father to remember my face or my name.

My father didn't recognize her, although he had seen her once or twice in the summer of 1978. We met in a private room the Bureau provided for us.

"I talked to Michael, Dad," I said. "How can this possibly work out? They'll box you in . . . they'll squeeze you."

"There's no way it can be worked out, Joe," he said matter-of-factly. "I'm not joining you, and you can't come back. There is no absolution."

I told him that Wayne Orel and some other Bureau people wanted to talk to him privately. They talked. He admitted nothing. Since I wouldn't testify against him, they had no case. So he left. Later, when the trial of Allie Boy and Bolino took place, he testified for them. It didn't work.

After he left, Rachel and I met in an office. We made arrangements to take the same flight to Philadelphia. She could only get a reservation for one night at a hotel in New Hope. I managed to stretch it out for another night before I returned to Minnesota.

Veronica was more reasonable when I returned home. I had managed, with the help of McDonald and McNeil, to win approval of an agreement by the government to take her parents into the program. Her father had retired, and they had no one except for Veronica and their grandchildren. Washington agreed to the move because of the possible danger to them by the mob. They hadn't been threatened, but with the latest attempt to compromise my testimony, anything was possible. The marshals moved Veronica's folks out of Brooklyn to a house that I had found near ours in Maple Grove.

With her parents near her, Veronica grew to love Minnesota, and I have to admit, I had grown to like the area myself. The people were friendly, my kids loved the school, and the town was quiet and kind of homey. Veronica would have been content to live out the rest of her life there. I think I might have too, if I could have figured a way to bring Rachel there to live with me.

In July, I testified in Rhode Island against Merola and Pari, and both were convicted on murder charges. In November 1979, Allie Boy and Bolino were arrested on a six-count indictment in which Persico was accused of lending me $43,500 at 2 percent a week—loan-shark rates. Newspapers were filled with stories about my working with the FBI as an informant for years, supplying intelligence and other information while I was taking out shylock loans and recording conversations with those who gave the loans to me.

On February 20, 1980, I was given the written immunity I had been promised in a document signed by McDonald and countersigned by me. The document guaranteed that I would be immune from prosecution or any crimes I committed as long as I told them about all crimes and testified against Persico, Bolino, and whoever else they wanted me to.

It read in part:

This agreement will not prevent the Government from prosecuting you for perjury should it be discovered that you have given false testimony in connection with this matter [the Persico-Bolino case]. In addition, in the event that you do not fully comply with all the other terms of this understanding (full disclosure of all criminal activity on the part of Persico and Bolino, full disclosure of your own criminal activity, testimony, etc.) this agreement will be abrogated. Should this occur, the Government will be free to prosecute you with regard to any and all violations of the federal criminal law in which you may have participated, and to use against you any and all statements made by you and testimony you have given prior and subsequent to the date of this agreement.

Just before signing the agreement, I had to tell McDonald about my aborted plan to scam the mob for $250,000. He was furious. Lazzara and Walsh literally had to hold him. McDonald was taller than I was, but I was huskier, stronger, and tougher at the time. That didn't stop him. He was still ready to beat the hell out of me, and they were holding him down in his chair as he cursed and yelled at me like some wild man. He said that he was convinced defense attorneys had bugged my conversations with Bolino.

On February 15, 1980, Persico's attorney, Frank Lopez, had leaked a story to the *New York Post* claiming I had tried to extort $300,000 from Persico and Bolino. My father was asked by reporter Jerry Capeci, then of the *Post,* if they had tapes of the so-called extortion attempt; he wouldn't comment. But Lopez did. "There is a tape recording relating to the extortion attempt," he said. It was pure bullshit . . . a bluff. They never produced it at the trial, but they faked McDonald out.

"You fuckin' asshole!" he shouted. "You could have blown five years of work. Why the hell didn't you tell me the whole story . . . why tell me fifty thousand dollars instead of three hundred thousand dollars?" he shouted.

"It's your fault!" I shouted back.

"What the hell do you mean . . . it's my fault?" McDonald asked.

"It's your fault, because you know what a bad guy I am," I said. "I needed the money."

He shook his head, half laughing at what I said. Walsh had a smirk on his face; so did Lazzara. But I very nearly lost my opportunity for immunity that day. McDonald was ready to throw me to the wolves—case or no case—just for a moment.

The timing of Lopez's disclosure to the *Post* was interesting. It had come less than a week after federal prosecutor Joel Cohen had filed affidavits charging that a Persico associate, Victor Puglisi, had offered fifty thousand dollars to an IRS undercover agent for an advance look at the strike-force files on Persico and Bolino and at the transcripts of the tape recordings I had made with Bolino and Persico. The agent had also taped bribe offers of $250,000 by Carmine Persico and Hugh (Apples) McIntosh, Persico's enforcer and a paralegal for Lopez. That bribe was supposed to pay off a judge. Clearly, the Persicos were worried about my testimony. Puglisi disappeared after that, and was never heard from again. The street word was that he was "gone," buried by the crime family. Carmine was sent back to jail because of the bribe offer to the judge.

The first trial ended in a mistrial when a juror admitted during jury deliberations that he had read a newspaper article that prejudiced him against Persico. The net result was a new trial ordered by Judge Jack B. Weinstein. Persico and Bolino were convicted on May 2, and my troubles began all over again, this time because of the loose mouths of some deputy marshals in the courtroom.

I was in Maple Grove when it happened. Persico and Bolino, following their conviction, were handcuffed and led off to jail to await sentencing.

I didn't realize it, but just before I left, before I had finished testifying, a couple of deputies were overheard in the courtroom talking about me during a recess. They were among a group of deputies who knew me, who did favors for me, and who I often played cards with, drank with, and had pizza with. The result was that too many deputies knew where I lived, when I arrived, and where I was going.

Sprinkled throughout the courtroom audience along with deputies were a lot of wiseguys from the Colombo family. One or more of them were listening as the deputies talked about me near the courtroom doors.

"Well, Cantalupo's got nothing to worry about when this is over," one said to the other. "Yeah," answered the second deputy. "As soon as he's finished testifying, he'll go back to Minnesota."

That got back to Persico, who was in jail, fuming about being locked up, temporarily unable to get out on bail. He was yelling and screaming about me, calling me every name under the sun. "I'm gonna get that motherfucker!" he shouted. "He's in Minnesota, and when I get outta here, I'm gonna get him. If it takes me my life, I'm gonna find and get that bastard."

In a cell next to his was a prisoner who listened and talked to the marshals, looking for a favor in return for his information.

The marshals contacted Lazzara, who by then had become a lie-detector expert. He questioned the prisoner, gave him a lie-detector test, and determined he was telling the truth.

"You're going to have to move Joey and his family," Lazzara said. "We can't take any chances."

I got a call that afternoon. It was Dodge and Ball in Minneapolis. "Pack your bags, Joe," Dodge said. "Take the kids out of school, call your mother-in-law and father-in-law. You all gotta move."

I couldn't believe what I was hearing. "Why? What the hell is going on?" I asked.

"Allie Boy knows where you are," Dodge said. "We'll be out to pick you all up. Have your bags packed."

22

ON THE ROAD AGAIN

The move from Maple Grove in June 1980, was very upsetting, very traumatic for Veronica, myself, and the kids. We had grown to love the place, the people, everything about it, including our rented home and the small garden I had cultivated and worked in. We were comfortable living in Maple Grove. We didn't have much money, but we weren't starving either. The kids loved the school, and they'd made a lot of friends. Most of all, we had grown close to many of our neighbors, who were genuinely nice, often generous, and willing to share. They made us feel comfortable . . . safe . . . at home.

Now, we had to leave, and we weren't permitted to say good-bye to friends. There could be no explanation of our sudden disappearance to neighbors. We couldn't even tell the teachers at the school why we had to pull the boys from their classes. The order was just to pack everything and leave when the deputies arrived. For all of us, that was the most difficult thing . . . leaving without explanation.

Our old recently bought Rent-A-Relic station wagon was stuffed to the roof with every piece of luggage, every toy, every essential we could call an essential. Veronica's parents' car was equally jammed. And before we left, the car that Dodge and Ball had arrived in had been turned into a traveling clothes closet.

On the front seat of my car and that of my father-in-law were our loaded guns. They were legal. In Minnesota, citizens were allowed to carry guns in their cars as long as they were in plain view. Since our temporary destination was nearly a hundred miles away, in a hotel in Eau Claire, Wisconsin, and all our traveling was by car, my father-in-law and I wanted to be ready for any possible trouble. Two deputies wouldn't be enough if there was a firefight.

We locked up the houses and left without incident, and several hours later, our three-car caravan arrived in Eau Claire.

We lived like sardines, crammed into small hotel rooms in Eau Claire, while the marshals tried to figure out where they would move us to next. Everyone was unhappy. My wife's mother bitched constantly. She wanted to go back to Brooklyn. That, of course, was impossible.

Veronica and I didn't sleep together, and the close quarters made us barely civil. We were always sniping at each other, while the kids were constantly fighting. It's a lousy way to live under the best conditions. Living together while a time bomb ticks . . . well, things do get touchy. Meanwhile, during those two weeks, I had to return with the deputies to Minneapolis several times.

The first time was to supervise the removal of everything from the house by movers sent by the marshals. I remember standing in front of the house, sifting through letters I'd pulled from my mailbox that were from my neighbors, my friends, and the school, bawling like a baby as I watched the van pull away and disappear in the distance.

The letters all had the same message: "Why did you leave us? Is there anything we can do to help, so you can stay? Why aren't the boys in school anymore?" Everyone was concerned for our safety. Everyone was upset that we hadn't been able to say good-bye.

I climbed into Dodge's car, still crying, and looked out at the homes around me. The timing had been perfect for the move. Everyone was at work. The neighbors didn't even know I had returned, packed, and was leaving once and for all. It was the hardest thing I had ever done, harder even than leaving my friends and family in Brooklyn. For some reason, Maple Grove had become something very special for me and for my family.

My last trip from Eau Claire to Minneapolis was to meet with the marshals, pick a new name for us to live under, and sign a new Memorandum of Understanding with WITSEC. The meeting took place at the city zoo, the Como Zoo.

"What name do you want to use when you leave here?" asked Dodge.

I looked up at the sign and answered without hesitation. "Como . . . let's change the name to Joseph Como."

Dodge grinned from ear to ear. "Like the zoo?" he asked.

"Like the zoo," I said with a chuckle.

Joseph Como and his family were driven to the Minneapolis-St. Paul International Airport. As they left the zoo, the family of Joseph Tali and his family disappeared. The only reminder that they had been there was their abandoned Rent-A-Relic wagon, left in the tourist parking lot at the zoo.

The new Como family entered the airport terminal with two deputies through a side entrance, and boarded a flight bound for Denver, Colorado. Several hours later, we boarded another plane operated by another airline. Destination: Boise, Idaho, and a new life.

Putting a New Yorker in Boise, Idaho, is like putting a round peg in a square hole. Neither one fits. Putting an Italian from Brooklyn in a place like Boise is even worse. It says something about the brains of the people who were pushing the witness pegs on their national checkerboards at the WITSEC headquarters in Falls Church, Virginia. What it said to me was that they didn't know much about people.

New Yorkers live in a state where there are lots of people. There are something like 350 residents per square mile living in New York. In Idaho, they tell me about there are about twelve people per square mile, so someone from out of town, particularly an Italian someone from Brooklyn, New York, stands out like a beacon in an empty ocean. I am still amazed that the mob never located me there—but then, who the hell in the mob went to Boise in those days?

Most likely the main reason I survived for the year I was in Boise was Inspector Walter Belveal. Walter—or Waldo, as he was called by his friends—was a monster of a man. He was about 5'11", maybe a couple inches taller when he was wearing his cowboy boots, and he weighed in at 320 pounds. Each of his thighs was the size of two of my legs, but they weren't flab; they were hard muscle.

Boise, besides being the capital of Idaho, is its biggest city. At the time, I think the population was nearly one hundred thousand. You would never have guessed it. It was a small town trying to be a city, a pretty community nestled in a valley beneath snow-capped mountains. The people were friendly and helpful, and I guess for the first time in my life, I realized Idaho was more than just a place where they grew potatoes sold in supermarkets in Brooklyn. It was dairy and cattle country . . . with a capital Brrrrr. It could be beautiful in the summer, which seemed short to me, but in the winter . . . I never knew a place could get so cold or be covered with so much snow. All in all, though, I liked it, and so did Veronica and the kids. The rodeos, the western style of dress, the easy, walk-don't-run life-style, the rugged countryside . . . it was a way of life that could put an end to ulcers for a guy from New York. My in-laws didn't appreciate it. They were bored, but then I can't remember any place pleasing my mother-in-law except Brooklyn.

Waldo did manage, however, to impress my mother-in-law. He got her a driver's license—something she had never been able to get in any state before. Unlike Minnesota, there were no tests, no long waits. Not for Waldo. He had the right connections. He just took us in to the Motor Vehicles Bureau, got our pictures taken, and we all walked out with our driver's licenses.

Waldo was unlike any inspector we had dealt with before in helping us get settled. In the past, the deputies had just left us in a hotel and told us to get a car and hunt on our own for a house. Not Waldo. He was concerned about us. He wanted us to adjust. Once we had driver's licenses, he helped us find a car, an Oldsmobile station wagon that cost us fifteen hundred dollars. The government paid five hundred dollars, and we put up the balance.

Once we had the car, Waldo went house-hunting with us, taking us from one neighborhood to another until we found a beautiful three-bedroom home with a two-car garage and a fenced-in backyard that we were able to rent for $550 a month. He checked everything out, made sure that there would be no problems, and arranged for approval of our lease.

Because we had moved to a new area, and because the government had increased the allowance to witness families, our monthly subsidy went from $980 to $1,200, just enough to cover the increased rental costs.

We had barely settled in when word came from New York that shook all of us. Allie Boy Persico was missing. He and Mike Bolino were scheduled to appear for sentencing June 23. Bolino showed and got five years in prison. Persico never appeared. He was among the missing, forfeiting his bond of $250,000, which had been secured by his home and his thirty-eight-acre horse farm in Saugerties, New York. No one knew where he was, but a month later, just as the government was about to seize all his properties, a former business partner of his appeared at the federal courthouse with $250,000 cash, preventing the seizure process from continuing.

I knew one thing. Wherever he was, Allie Boy was thinking about me and how he was going to kill me. It wasn't until years later that I learned that there were times when we were probably only a few miles apart when I flew to Connecticut to be with Rachel at the Red Bull Inn in Waterbury. Unknown to us and to the feds, Persico went into hiding in Hartford, Connecticut, under an assumed name just as I checked into Waterbury's Red Bull under an assumed name. While the government was helping me live under a new identity because I'd testified against him, the New England mob teamed up with Allie Boy's people to help him live under a different identity to escape jail while they tried to hunt me down.

Almost from the beginning, Waldo knew about Rachel, and he did what he could to arrange for us to meet. The arrest of Frank "Funzi" Tieri on June 30 by the FBI in New York provided Waldo with a vehicle for those meetings.

Shortly after Tieri's arrests, arrangements were made for me to meet with the prosecutors on the case, Nathaniel H. Akerman and Barbara Jones, both assigned to try the case in the Southern District of New York.

The case against Funzi was a landmark case. It was the first time a boss of a Cosa Nostra crime family was being tried as a boss, for directing the operations of the family and its criminal operations for more than a decade, from the mid-1960's to 1980.

There were a number of protected witnesses being used in the case. The best known and most significant was James (Jimmy the Weasel) Fratianno. He was a confessed killer, an admitted member of Cosa Nostra, the American version of the Mafia, and a crime captain of the Los Angeles crime family. He had testified in Los Angeles against leaders of the Los Angeles branch of Cosa Nostra, and now he was supposed to testify about the structure of Cosa Nostra and how bosses run their families. He was also supposed to testify about how Tieri and some of his top captains voted to have a guy hit and how they plotted to bankrupt the Westchester Premier Theater.

My testimony was more limited in scope, but nevertheless important. Prosecutors were using me to show the continuing domination of Tieri from the early 1960's, when I first met him at my father's real estate office, through the period I ran a flea market with him in Brooklyn.

I had to testify about the meeting of the bosses, including Tieri, at my apartment in Brooklyn in 1968. I was to testify about our partnership in the flea market in Brooklyn, the loan-shark rates he charged me for money to continue the business, and the deals cut with other family bosses and the meetings between Tieri and other leaders, including Allie Boy Persico. I was also to testify about Tieri's threatening the life of my uncle Sal if he didn't stop selling pizzas from Eddie Arcaro's and competing with the business of Allie Boy's relatives at Sbarro's.

To meet with the prosecutors required travel to various locations—Salt Lake City, Oklahoma City, Minneapolis, Manhattan, and Waterbury, to meet with the prosecutors and go over what I knew about Tieri. Some of the travel was at government expense, some was at the expense of Rachel.

I arranged with Waldo to call me at home at various times to notify me that I had to go out of town for a debriefing with a prosecutor. In the instances where I was legitimately meeting with prosecutors, I arranged to have Rachel fly out to the city where I was to meet with Jones or Akerman and stay with me at the hotel. There were other times, however, when I would pass some money to Waldo to pay for my airfare to Salt Lake City. The money was provided by Rachel. I didn't have enough money to pay for our meetings. What little money I had paid for the food and housing of my family. Any use of that money or what little we had managed to save, Veronica would have noticed immediately. So Rachel paid the freight.

In November, Tieri went on trial, and I was brought to New Jersey to a WITSEC hotel site under very tight security. There could be no meetings with Rachel while I was testifying.

The rooms of the hotel had paper-thin walls, and the guest in one of the rooms next to mine was Jimmy the Weasel. We never met, but he probably caught a lot of aggravation and complaints for his excessive phone bills because of me and because we were lodged for that short period in the same witness site.

The Weasel, like most of us who become witnesses for the government, was a prolific phone user. He called people from one side of the country to the other. Of course, he didn't have the bucks to pay for those calls any more than I did. What he did have—just as I did—was the office phone number of the prosecutors. He had the numbers of Jones and Akerman; I had the number of McDonald. We had those numbers so we could charge our calls while we were away from home. We couldn't charge the calls to our rooms, because the numbers we called might enable somebody to pinpoint where we lived or whom we dealt with by getting a copy of our room phone bill. So we were required to use a government number.

While I was in New Jersey with Fratianno, I overheard him calling a variety of locations. Each time he made a call, he gave the operator the number of a phone that she could charge the call to. I wrote that number down.

After the trial ended, I used the Fratianno numbers for five years before the phone company and the government finally caught up with me and hit me with a thousand-dollar phone bill. I figure I got off light at that, but Fratianno probably took a lot of heat for excessive telephone bills charged to the government.

On November 13, the first of three days that I had to testify at the trial, the marshals hustled me into the federal courthouse at Foley Square early in the morning, before anyone, particularly the press, had arrived.

To reach the courtrooms in the federal courthouse, you have to walk through corridors at the rear of the courtrooms themselves. These aren't public corridors; they are hallways that lead to offices, witness rooms, and the rear of the courtrooms.

As I was walking through the corridor toward the courtroom with two deputies, I spotted a Genovese soldier I knew who was called Junior. He was with Tieri and two of Funzi's granddaughters.

The sight of Junior and Funzi immediately jogged my memory to an incident at the flea market. Junior was a made member of the Genovese family, and he worked under Lou LaRocca. He had been sent to my office with a bullet in his jaw by LaRocca after he had screwed up a stickup and got shot in the process. He needed my help in getting the wound taken care of.

I made arrangements to have a doctor friend of mine take care of him. The office operation, however, caused him some pain and some temporary speech problems, so when I saw him in the court corridors, the first words out of my mouth were: "Hey, Junior, how you feeling? You talking better these days?"

Funzi didn't bat an eye, but Junior began cursing and screaming at me in the hallway. Funzi had to quiet him down.

When I took the stand, I looked at Funzi. I remember I was somewhat shocked by his appearance. I wasn't looking at the Funzi Tieri that I had known all those years. This was a different man, a shadow of the tough old boss I once knew.

The Tieri I stared down at was very ill, shaky, a hunched-up old man sitting in a wheelchair. He was still color-coordinated in the way he dressed—beige suit, shirt, and tie—but gone were the expensive diamond rings and gold and diamond-studded bracelet that he usually wore. I didn't feel a trace of emotion as I testified. There was no awe, none of the fear he generated when I was on the street. I didn't feel bad that he was ill. I felt nothing. He was just another tired old man who was paying the price for screwing people.

On November 21, four days after I finished testifying, Tieri was convicted. Two months later, on January 21, he appeared before Judge Thomas Griesa in a wheelchair, with a nurse, for sentencing. I was told he pleaded for leniency, showing the judge scars from some operations he'd just had. The judge didn't buy it. He gave Tieri ten years in jail and a sixty-thousand-dollar fine. By March 29, Funzi was dead of natural causes, and a few days later they put him in the ground at St. John's Cemetery in Middle Village, Queens, with a priest's blessing. He never served a day of the sentence in jail.

As for Louie LaRocca, the scared capo who ran the flea market with me, they never tried him. He got off by checking into a hospital long enough to show he was too sick to stand trial. The only thing he lost was some prestige. Now, he's listed as a soldier by the FBI. The new bosses demoted him.

By early April, life with Veronica had become impossible, and we separated as she filed for divorce. She was allowed to stay where she was, and I had to move without disclosing to her where I had been moved to. The rules called for my being at least two states away from her. The rules were bent a bit so I could see my sons more often. Instead of moving out of state, I was allowed to move to Idaho Falls, just two and a half hours away by car. I could not tell Veronica I was that close. Each time I came to see the boys, I drove in and left my car at the airport. Waldo would then drive me to her home and then back to the airport, so she would believe I had flown in and was flying out.

While he bent the rules for me, Waldo broke the rules for her. He got her an attorney and told the attorney she was a protected witness. That was a complete violation. He also told her I lived in Idaho Falls. That was a real no-no. Nothing happened, but as it turned out, it put me in jeopardy and cost him his job. Veronica demanded and got four hundred dollars a month support from me for the kids. I didn't fight it. I just wanted the divorce. I always intended taking care of my sons.

At the same time, I was busy working on McDonald and McNeil to get Rachel into the WITSEC Program so that we could be together permanently, without all the travel. The request dragged on for months, but on April 14, thanks to their efforts, the Main Justice in Washington approved Rachel's entrance into the witness program, and two days later a Connecticut-based WITSEC inspector for the marshals, who had helped us many times at the Red Bull, put us on a flight to Salt Lake City and then on to Boise.

Before I left, I gave him a case of his favorite Irish whisky to thank him for his help. I learned later that the gift was, like so many things I did with the marshals, a no-no, a violation of their rules and regulations. No gratuities, no socializing, no dinners, nothing with witnesses . . . but nearly all the deputies and inspectors I knew in the Marshals Service and WITSEC did such things with witnesses.

In Boise, we met Waldo, who put us up in a Holiday Inn temporarily until we could find an apartment in a new location, away from Veronica. Technically, we were each supposed to find separate apartments, because we were separately funded. We found one apartment right after Easter in Idaho Falls, and figured out a way to supply the government with separate rental bills so we wouldn't lose individual funding. Waldo knew, but he said nothing.

A month later, Waldo and his wife came to Idaho Falls for four days to party with us. Rachel and I rented the mayor's suite for them at the Stardust Hotel. That and other parties that I paid for with Waldo Belveal and others violated WITSEC rules of conduct.

There were so many rules that witnesses didn't know about, and even more that I think the deputy marshals didn't know about. They probably know more now, but in 1981 and earlier, the ship of WITSEC was loosely run, and rules were made to be broken.

An incident that took place June 9 in Kings County, Brooklyn reflects what I mean. I was back in New York to prepare for the trial of John Russo. The Brooklyn District Attorney's Office was, at the time, conducting a grand-jury investigation of loan-sharking, in particular the case that had surfaced my identity, that of Murray Berger and Anthony Scarpati. They wanted me to testify as a witness. I didn't want to particularly, but if I had to, I thought I should get paid for my troubles. After all, I was the guy who stuck his neck out, who had to change his identity, and who the federal government had to provide subsistence to.

I wasn't sure what my rights were as a protected witness, so I asked McNeil and Walsh and other deputies whether I had a right to ask the Brooklyn district attorney for some money before I agreed to testify. All of them agreed I should ask. Nothing ventured, nothing gained. So when Assistant District Attorney Robert Vinal told me he wanted me to testify before the Kings County grand jury, I told him I wanted two thousand dollars before I stuck my neck out and testified.

"You'll testify or you'll go to jail, and there will be no money involved," he snapped, when I told him what I wanted.

"Like hell," I said.

With that, he handed me a subpoena requiring me to testify or face contempt-of-court charges. I called McNeil, and I called McDonald.

"This guy says if I don't testify, he'll throw me in jail," I said excitedly. "I thought they couldn't do that to a federal witness."

"You'd better testify," McDonald said. "I can't do anything about the subpoena while you're there." McNeil said the same thing. So I went into the jury room and testified. But when I left, Vinal knew it would be the last time he'd ever see me. He'd won the battle, but not the war. He could never force the government to produce me again. He'd played fast and loose with the subpoena. That wasn't part of the deal he'd had with the government when he had asked them to let him talk to me. They had no idea he was going to hit me with a subpoena. The advice I'd been given by the marshals to ask for the money was wrong also, at least with this district attorney. On the other hand, when local prosecutors and attorneys wanted the testimony of Jimmy the Weasel, they had to pay him $250 an hour or they didn't see him. It was a screwed-up rule book they worked by, as far as I was concerned.

• • •

The Kings County grand jury wasn't the only place I tried to pick up extra bucks. During my travels as a witness, I found that organized crime, in differing forms, was in virtually every community in the country, certainly wherever the government sent witnesses. It might not be a Mafia organization, but it was organized and it was crime.

While I was in Minnesota, for example, I ran into some fair-sized bookmaking, numbers, and drug operations, and called some people in the FBI, offering to infiltrate them and help them gather evidence for a price. I wasn't just being a public-spirited citizen. I figured I could make a few bucks as an informer again. I even provided the feebs with samples of some of the merchandise. They weren't interested. It was either too small for their tastes, or wasn't important enough because the Italians weren't running it.

In Idaho Falls, I found one place, a big country-and-western club that was run by a guy who was originally from Santa Barbara, California. I'll call him Big Jim.

Now Big Jim's place was something right out of a western video, a big old barn complete with electronic, bucking riding bulls, pool tables, popular western bands, shit-kicking music, and all the "hoo-ha" stuff you want. It was also the place to go if you wanted to make the right drug deals. Eventually, the place was burned down, and Big Jim made a big buck. Tried to get the Bureau to bite on that one. They weren't moved.

In the same town was a guy I call Joe the Butcher. He had a meat business, a dairy operation, and a friend who had a disco in town that was a private club. The only way you could get in was with a special card. The card buzzed you in, and you could watch these wet T-shirt contests with young teenage girls. A cheap thrill, right? Wrong. They moved two keys of coke—that's nearly five pounds of the stuff—every week through that place. It was a big drug operation for a small town like that. I gave that information to the Bureau, figuring it had to be worth some bucks, but once again they weren't interested.

Everything came to a sudden, and violent, end in Idaho in early August. Rachel and I had been invited to go camping and boating with Belveal and his wife at Warm Lake, Idaho. Arrangements were made to meet at their home in Meridan, where, under the divorce agreement, I would meet with an insurance agent and sign a $100,000 life-insurance policy naming my kids as beneficiaries.

Unknown to me, Veronica had become suspicious of Waldo and his relationship with me. She suspected I lived a lot closer to where she lived than she was being told—that I wasn't flying in to see her and the boys, particularly since I came so often.

Once Veronica becomes suspicious, she never lets go, she becomes a detective, and in this case, she started to stake out Waldo's home every now and then to see if she could spot something wrong. It was Sunday, April 6, 1981, at about 6:00 P.M. when she hit pay dirt.

Rachel and I had returned with Waldo and Gabby after the camping trip. It had been a wonderful weekend of boating, drinking, partying, and playing cards. It cost me about four hundred dollars for the food and booze, but it was worth it. Waldo had supplied the boat and the camping equipment. I figured it was pretty much an even push. But again, it violated the rules against socializing.

Just before 6:00 P.M., Rachel and I packed our stuff in the used Thunderbird we'd just bought and headed back to Idaho Falls. That's when I spotted Veronica in the station wagon with my former mother-in-law about two blocks away, heading straight for me.

I said to Rachel, "Honey, duck down on the floor . . . right away. It's Veronica!"

With that, I pull off the side of the road and I duck down, but she's spotted me, and she is one mad female. She has a bottle in her hand, and she throws it at me, just missing me and the car.

"You son of a bitch!" she screams. "I'll fix you. You'll never see the kids again. I'll fix you and that goddamn fat marshal!"

She hadn't seen Rachel. Up to that moment, she didn't know about Rachel. She knew another woman was with me, but she didn't know it was someone from back home, a girl I knew long before I'd met her.

I shouted back, "Go to hell, Veronica. You got what you want . . . now go to hell!" Then I put the car in gear and roared off without looking back. If I had, I would have seen her driving across Waldo's lawn, blowing the horn of the car until he came out.

"I'm gonna have your goddamn job for this!" she screamed. "I'm gonna turn this goddamn Marshals Service upside down."

And she did. That night, she began calling Washington, calling top people in the Marshals Service to complain about rule violations by inspectors, beginning with Waldo Belveal and going down the list of those she knew in Minnesota and New York. It was worse than "Hell hath no fury like a woman scorned." It was a case of vengeance was going to be hers, and everybody was going to get burned.

That night, I decided that before she burned me, I'd better cover my ass, and on Monday I started taping every conversation I had with her, and every deputy, every inspector, and every prosecutor I talked to on the telephone. I was going to have proof of the things that were happening. If I knew Veronica, I was going to need that proof. She was a runaway tornado, and everything and everyone in her path were going to get sucked up in the storm she was creating.

I felt bad for Waldo. He was already certain that this was going to cost him his job in WITSEC. We never dreamed he'd be fired from the Marshals Service. "What am I going to do, Joe?" he asked. "I don't have any money. You get more money from the government than I do." He had fifteen years' good service, and he was about to lose it all.

Veronica told Waldo she was going to bury him. She was mad because he had partied with me and, she thought, neglected her and her parents. That wasn't true. When Waldo sat on one of the dining-room chairs and broke it, he made arrangements for the government to come up with seven hundred dollars for a new dining-room set. When she needed new tires for her car, Waldo had reported she'd had an accident so she could get money to pay for the tires.

When she lit the fire under his seat, he began going strictly by the rule book. It was a case of you screw me, I screw you . . . and he did, in spades. There were no more free government phone calls; she got her mail once a month; and he required her to see him monthly to get her subsistence check. Veronica blew her stack. When an inspector came out from Washington to go over the charges she had made, she was so hot she threatened to drop a dime on me.

That turned the wheels spinning again. Washington demanded I be moved. I was to leave the car—the car I'd just bought and paid for—leave everything and move again. Veronica was now considered a threat to me. I knew that wasn't true. She would never do anything like that to hurt me, no matter how she felt. It had been temper talking, not reason. I had to sign a paper to that effect, but in the meantime, they moved Rachel and me to Salt Lake City temporarily.

Things got so bad in the fading summer weeks of 1981 that in September I refused to testify at Johnny Russo's trial in Brooklyn.

The Justice Department didn't mince any words when I failed to show up to testify the first day, and it made headlines. Either testify, they said, or you and your girlfriend are off the witness program without a dime more of subsistence—and your wife and kids follow in six months. I testified. Russo was convicted. Now, I not only had the bad guys after me for being an informer, the so-called good guys—the deputies, the inspectors, Bureau agents, and prosecutors—were convinced I had done them in as well, so they weren't exactly enthusiastic protectors any longer.

All doubt ended when I was called to testify by WITSEC at a special closed hearing in Boise. The target of the hearing was Waldo Belveal. He didn't know what hit him. The government told me Rachel and I had to testify or we'd be terminated. They had statements from my wife, and they had the tapes I'd made— tapes that I had to give to Howard Safir, who was the director of the WITSEC Program and who told me that what I was doing, what he was making me do, was for the good of the witness program. Maybe it was, but a lot of people got hurt.

While Safir built his case, Veronica and the kids were moved to another area. I wasn't permitted to live near them, but arrangements were worked out for me to meet with my kids on neutral territory with deputies covering the meetings. Veronica and I, in the end, patched up our differences and became friends after our divorce became final. My regret is that my father-in-law, whom I had grown to really love and respect, died before I could ever see him again.

Rachel and I had to move to Ankeny, Iowa. Even there, I ran into an organized-crime situation at a bar where they had an interstate bookmaking operation. It wasn't Italian, but it was well organized. So was a drug operation . . . and I found a lawyer who said he had everything for sale—grenade launchers, army rockets, thousands of rounds of ammunition, and hundreds of rifles and sidearms, all stolen from armories, as well as rhinoceros tusks, which were popular and illegal as aphrodisiacs, bearer bonds, and phony identifications. All this I put on tape, and then I went to the local FBI. The agents there were hot to trot, more than willing to jump in and pay me as an informant and let me infiltrate these operations, until they found out I was a protected witness. That's when they backed off.

It's against the rules of the WITSEC Program to have protected witnesses work as confidential informants for any government agency. That ended that—and as far as I know, nothing happened to the lawyer or the rings that I had information on; they were never looked into further while I was there.

The WITSEC inspector in Des Moines kept me at arm's length, and all our contacts were strictly by the book. The word was out throughout the Marshals Service. Joe Cantalupo by any name was a pariah, and my name was to change again and again and again.

Belveal lost his job, not just in WITSEC but in the Marshals Service. A half-dozen inspectors in Minnesota, Connecticut, and New York were transferred out of WITSEC, reduced in rank, and returned to duties as deputy marshals. I didn't like it. That wasn't my intention. But in truth what Waldo did was wrong, and what his wife did was wrong.

Belveal, like so many marshals do, talked about other witnesses and where they were located and what their problems were. He and others found ways to scam the government for more money for their witnesses. Their motives were right, because witnesses can't live on what they're given for subsistence in strange communities with unfamiliar surroundings and neighbors. It was how they got that money that was wrong, from the government's point of view. They also weren't too reluctant to share the extra goodies—letting witnesses like Rachel and myself pick up their tabs. So they got nailed. It was tough, and I felt bad about it, but I wasn't left with much choice.

Once I testified against Belveal, I was forced to change my name and move again. He knew I was living in Ankeny, so the government felt I was in danger. Belveal might drop a dime. I didn't think that, but they weren't about to take chances. So we moved, not long after Rachel and I were married in March 1982, and our baby girl was born in July.

While all this was happening, there were other meetings in Washington at the Office of Professional Responsibility in the Department of Justice. I had to tell them about entertaining prosecutors at dinners and at dances in Connecticut and Utah. McDonald got a reprimand for letting me buy him dinner and giving him a bottle of booze at Christmas. Hell, I didn't intend those things as bribes; they were just gestures of friendship. The trouble was, some of it was on tape, some of it I had to tell them about. Safir made a point of saying I had to tell everything if I didn't want to be terminated and have all subsistence cut off.

Next stop was Kansas, but not before I had to fight tooth and nail against being sent to Phoenix, Arizona. Once again, no one was checking on where the mob goes, least of all the marshals. I knew that Persico had friends and associates there, and that there were members of mob families from New England, Brooklyn, New York, New Jersey, Detroit, and Chicago living and operating there. It would be only a matter of time before I'd be spotted and terminated . . . mob style.

Now there were no trials to get ready for. No hearings. There was only survival. In September 1983, the ax fell. Safir ordered me terminated from the program on the grounds that I'd violated my security by checking into a motel in Salt Lake City using one of my previous identities. It was an excuse, not a reason. It was, after all, the marshals who had breached my security so often, and forced me to move and change my identity five times.

The government is supposed to help witnesses find new jobs, train them for new occupations, place them where their talents and abilities can best be used. They don't do that. They gave me one offer—filling potholes for a highway department. I was forty-one years old. I had been a witness for five years, worked for the government for ten. I knew the real estate and insurance businesses. I was a salesman. I could do a lot of things. I would have happily taken training in computers or heavy-equipment operation. But what the marshals wanted me to do was fill potholes. As a witness with a family, I was drawing $1,347 a month. As a pothole-filler, I would net $750. When I protested, I was told by the marshals to take it or leave it. I left it.

By April 1984, all subsistence ended for Veronica and the kids and for Rachel and myself. The government had spent a total of $138,645 for subsistence and house and medical bills over a five-year period. In return, they had nailed two crime bosses, four mob soldiers, and half a dozen other criminals, saved potential victims hundreds of thousands of dollars, and cleaned up some of their witness-security problems. I was glad it was over. I would have been happier getting some help in landing a decent job, but in the long run, I was glad to be off the government's subsistence dole. I'd always hated it. It was numbing to the senses, like welfare must be.

For the moment, I was afraid, wondering if I could make it again, if I could provide for my families. I was back to the street, back to basics, using my instincts and my wits to provide for my families, stay alive, and survive. I was through with the government, through with their double deals, through with false promises . . . or was I?

23

WITNESS AGAINST THE MOB

Long before the marshals decided that pothole-filling was to be my future career, I was back in demand as a witness. This time it was investigator George Weisz of the Arizona Attorney General's Office who had asked author-reporter Tom Renner if I would be willing to be interviewed by him (Weisz). The target was Peerless Importers of New York, a wholesale liquor company run by Antonio Magliocco. Peerless had been trying to get a liquor license in Arizona through a distributors' subsidiary it had acquired, All-American Distributors.

In May 1983, Renner, who I still called regularly in hopes of writing a book, gave me Weisz's telephone number and suggested I talk to him. "It may be worth your while," he said. "They're checking on Peerless Importers and the Maglioccos."

"You trust Weisz?" I asked.

"With my life," Renner answered. "We spent seven months working together on the Arizona Project, investigating organized crime. He is the best."

By this time we both knew it would be only a matter of time before I was terminated and I would be running out of funds and options. So I called Weisz. After a series of phone calls, I arranged to sit down with him and provide his office with a sworn affidavit and testify, if need be. It wasn't a gratis deal. The

Arizona Attorney General's Office offered to pay me a $4,000 expert witness fee, plus my travel expenses. They also agreed to provide the necessary security protection under the conditions I wanted.

In February 1985, after I had given general statements to Weisz, I provided a sworn statement to the Attorney General at his office in Phoenix. In that statement, I described my life as an informer and witness and my knowledge of Peerless.

While I was still on the street and close to Anthony and Joseph Colombo Jr., I use to go with them to the Peerless warehouse in Brooklyn and pick up cases of champagne or Dewar's Scotch for their father. We'd take it from the warehouse, put it in a station wagon and put it in his garage. We did that two or three times before I suggested to them, after their father had died, that it would be a good deal to hijack one of Peerless' trucks of booze and sell ourselves.

I testified they told me that couldn't be done . . . that "good people" ran Peerless. The good people they were talking about was Antonio Magliocco Sr. who was the brother of Joseph Magliocco, the former boss of the family that Colombo ran before Colombo took it over. The Arizona Attorney General was claiming Antonio, who was chairman of the board for Peerless, was actually a member of the Colombo family as were his two late brothers, Ambrose and Joseph.

I couldn't vouch for his membership in the crime family because I wasn't around to see him sworn in as a member, but I could vouch for the fact he was an associate of the Colombos and others, that Peerless had a monopoly in the liquor business with all the families in New York. Catering halls, restaurants, liquor stores . . . whatever businesses the wiseguys ran . . . bought their booze from Peerless and they made sure their friends, even their competitors got their liquor from Peerless. They even supplied all the liquor for the wiseguys' family weddings and parties. I also testified that his first cousin, John A. (Johnny Arrow) Magliocco, was a captain in Colombo's family who regularly visited Joe Colombo Sr. at my father's real estate office while running Arrow Linen Co.

The net result of my testimony and that of other witnesses

was that Peerless pulled the plug on its attempt to get a liquor distributor's license and Magliocco Senior agreed to the demand of Arizona Attorney General Robert Corbin that he resign as chairman and sell his stock to other family members. One of those other witnesses was Henry Hill, who was the central figure of Nicholas Pileggi's book, *Wiseguy*.

The Arizona agreement was a real blow for Peerless and for Magliocco. It cost them a liquor empire they planned to build in the far west, including California. They already were operating in Connecticut, Massachusetts, New Jersey, and New York. It put a crimp in their plans for national expansion. Arizona investigators described my testimony as "devastating," the key to their stopping Peerless. Magliocco, his relatives, and his friends were furious. I had hurt the mob where it hurts the most—in business. There is nothing they hate more than losing money and all it cost Arizona was $4,000 for my expenses and my "expert" testimony.

While the Arizona case was developing, I traveled to London to appear on a Thames Television special on organized crime in the United States. I picked up another $7,000 plus expenses for that stint. I also found myself in surprising demand in August 1985 by the federal government, which suddenly realized I had value as a witness in two of the most important cases they had planned . . . the Colombo crime family racketeering case and the Commission case against the five family godfathers of New York.

Once again I learned about it through a call I made to Renner. Weisz had called him from U.S. Customs station in Alaska where he was vacationing.

"Can you reach Cantalupo?" he asked.

"He should be in touch with me in a week, or so . . . why?" Renner asked.

"Rudy Giuliani's office wants to talk to him," Weisz said. "They want him to testify in the Colombo family and the Commission cases."

"I don't know if he'll do it, but I'll tell him to call them," Renner answered. "Amazing. The feds dumped him, hung him out to dry. Now they want him to testify. I'll tell him, George."

When I called Renner a few days later, he told me to get in touch with Frank Sherman and Mike Chertoff of the Southern District of New York, giving me a number that Weisz had provided for me to call. They had been unable to locate me. The federal marshals said they didn't know where I was or how to reach me. That sounded real strange to me since the marshals had dumped me in Overland.

If ever there was an example of the left hand not knowing about the right hand! The mob got along better than federal law enforcement. Without my talking to a reporter, they might never have found me to testify in those cases.

After a lot of negotiations with Sherman and the FBI, and after a lot of soul-searching and talks with Renner and my wife, I finally agreed to testify, but not before I had called my father and found him to be unwilling to put up $15,000 to help me and my family to "disappear," to go away while the heat was on for the trials. He just told me not to testify. The danger was too great not just for me, but for him. I knew better. He was perfectly safe. He was not responsible for me. He never had been.

I would be less than honest if I didn't admit I was afraid to testify in these cases. After all, I was going up against the most powerful crime leaders in the world. This was no longer some high-level loan-shark case . . . this was numero uno in organized crime.

By this time I had a small business, selling and supplying supermarkets and stores in the Kansas City area with Italian specialties. It had taken a lot of penny-pinching to build the business and it was just starting to grow. I would now have to neglect it to some degree while I met prosecutors in cities in various parts of the country to be debriefed and go over what I was to testify in.

Before I agreed to testify, the FBI drew up an agreement to provide me with monthly expert-witness fees of $1,800 plus my travel expenses. They also agreed to pay for relocation costs if my whereabouts became known as a result of my exposure as a witness. There was one difference between this deal and the one

I had with WITSEC and the marshals. I wouldn't be dependent on federal marshals for my protection when I traveled. Only the FBI would provide me with protection when I traveled to New York, and I picked the method of travel between Kansas and New York.

We met in a lot of places—St. Louis, Minnesota, and finally New York. Whenever I came to New York to meet with Sherman or other prosecutors for a debriefing, the FBI provided agents to protect me, and, until March 1986, the site the federal government chose to use for housing witnesses scheduled to testify at these critical trials was Governor's Island. That procedure changed, at least for a while, because of an incident that occurred at the island while I was there.

Governor's Island is normally a quiet, secure location, a small friendly island with about three thousand residents, mostly U.S. Coast Guard families and personnel, sitting just a half mile from the skyscrapers of Manhattan. I've been told that at one time it had been used for a racetrack, as a quarantine station, and as a prisoner-of-war camp during the Civil War. It was also used to raise sheep, as a game preserve, and as a pleasure retreat for some New York governor before the feds turned it into a military base for the Coast Guard. More recently it was used to hold meetings between President Ronald Reagan, Vice President George Bush, and the Russian leader, Mikhail Gorbachev.

In 1986 it was a prime location to house and protect witnesses like myself whose lives were in danger. In my case, they put me up in the Coast Guard Bachelor Officers Quarters that, for nearly six days, was to be my home away from home. I lived there with an FBI agent in a two-bedroom apartment with a kitchen, dinette, living room, and bath. A duplicate apartment adjacent to it was also occupied by another team of agents sent there to provide added around-the-clock protection.

It was a pleasant place to stay and I felt totally secure there . . . secure enough to go with agents to the commissary to get food and bottles of wine and liquor to prepare meals for myself and my guardian agents. In fact, I felt the security was tight enough to allow me to jog around an open track with one of the female agents, Michele Milani, who was pregnant at the time and part of a team assigned to investigate the Colombo family.

Each day, when I had to leave for federal court at Foley Square, the agents would take me in a special van they called "the Eggshell," so-named because of its darkened windows designed to prevent the curious from seeing in. Cars with agents were stationed in the front and rear of the van while it was on the ferry that ran to the mainland—to New York—every fifteen minutes. We'd then drive from the ferry pier, along a different route each day, to Foley Square, and then directly into the courthouse through the security entrance I described earlier. We always arrived early in the morning, before the press, the spectators, and the defendants who were on trial. Once the trial began, I faced a battery of attorneys representing a whole group of Colombo-family leaders.

At the head of the class among the Colombo-family defendants was Carmine Persico, the family boss I had first met in my father's office in 1965 when he visited Joe Colombo, Sr.

Seated at the defense tables with Persico was his son, Little Allie Boy (Alphonse Junior), who was then a captain but who when I'd last seen him, in April 1977, was one of 150 mob bosses and recruits at the party at Tomasso's Restaurant. I would have to testify about that gathering and about a shylock loan of mine Little Allie Boy took over as well as his control of pinball machines at the flea market I had run.

Near him was Jerry (Lang) Langella, the underboss I'd seen both at my father's and at the Diplomat in a barber's chair. There were the captains Andrew (Andy Mush) Russo, whom I knew from my bookmaking days with Gredda; Anthony (Scappy) Scarpati, who I'd negotiated with on the Berger loan only to have Berger's son permanently disappear and have my identity surface. And there were others: captains Dominic Cataldo and John J. De Ross, and family associates Frank (the Beast) Falanga, whom I'd helped in loan-shark collections and Hugh (Apples) McIntosh, who was always bodyguarding one Persico or the other at the Diplomat and around town.

My contribution to the Colombo-family trial was both historical and firsthand. I had, after all, either dealt with them as a loan-shark victim, in the Italian-American Civil Rights League, or in my father's real estate office as they paid homage to Joe Colombo. So my testimony, while it had nothing to do with their monopoly of segments of the construction industry or other racketeering conspiracies, was significant in terms of the history of the succession of bosses from Colombo to the temporary bosses such as Vincent Aloi, Thomas DiBella, and Allie Boy Persico, and the current boss, Carmine Persico. I had met them all, and I had reported on the activities of the family to the FBI for five years. The result was, I testified about those things I had reported to the FBI about during and before the years when I served as a paid confidential informant.

On March 10, 1986, I identified Carmine Persico, Langella, McIntosh, and Falanga from the witness chair, staring them down, answering the questions put to me about loan-sharking, the flea market, my father's real estate office, and the racketeers who were in and out of that office daily for all the years I was there.

March 11 was an eventful day. Sherman produced and played tapes I had made with Michael Bolino. The tapes implicated Little Allie Boy for buying up one of the shylock loans I had with other loan sharks.

The defense objected to the use of those tapes because they hadn't received copies until two weeks before I testified. The reason, though never explained in court, was that the Justice Department had misplaced the tapes, and I had spent many, many nights months earlier trying to help them track down those tapes. It wasn't until February, the month before the trial, that the tapes were found.

For me, the most significant event was the sudden appearance of my father in the courtroom as I testified about his office and the people who appeared there to see Joe Colombo. The courtroom was packed, but somehow a space had been left near the front for him where I could see him, just as I could see wiseguys and *Godfather* movie star Jimmy Caan, a friend of Andy Mush, seated in the audience. I let Sherman know what had happened during a recess, and Sherman made a point of complaining to

District Court judge John Keenan while the jury was out of the courtroom.

This was how the court transcript recorded that incident:

JUDGE KEENAN: I understand that Mr. Sherman wanted to address the Court.

SHERMAN: Yes, your Honor.

I understand from Mr. Cantalupo that his father is in the courtroom or has been, at least, for portions of the morning.

I understand from prior discussions with defense counsel that he may be called as a defense witness, and, if that is the case, I would ask, under the sequestration order that he be excluded.

THE COURT: If Mr. Cantalupo's father is going to be a witness, I direct that he leave the courtroom.

FRANK LOPEZ [defense attorney]: I think, Your Honor, in the exercise of caution, Mr. Cantalupo Sr., should be excluded from the courtroom.

THE COURT: Well, how long has he been here?

MR. LOPEZ: I don't know. I just saw him in the hallway outside for the first time. Shall I ask the gentleman how long he has been here?

THE COURT: Let's find out how long.

[At this point Lopez walked over to my father to talk to him and then returned to the defense table.]

MR. LOPEZ: Since a quarter to 12, your Honor.

THE COURT: I see the gentleman to whom you spoke. I saw him come in. He has not been here all morning and he was not here yesterday. Mr. Cantalupo, you are directed to leave the courtroom. There is apparently a possibility you may be a witness.

With that, my father left the courtroom, and the jury was called back. He was never called as a witness. It was all part of a scheme to shake me as I testified. It didn't work.

The trial ended on June 13, 1986, after eight months. All

defendants were found guilty of being part of a racketeering conspiracy in operating the crime family. A day later, Frankie the Beast Falanga died of natural causes. The sentencing for all was delayed until November 17 to prevent influencing possible jurors who might be chosen for the Commission trial that began in September. Persico, as a boss, was one of those to stand trial in that case.

When I first appeared at the Colombo-family trial in March, I made a conscious effort to remain calm and not let them know how nervous and edgy I was. I looked at the jury as I testified, and at those I was testifying against when I had to identify them or make a point. I stared them down when I had to, and I looked out into the audience to see their thugs and friends looking me up and down. Their eyes said they would love to kill me, but I knew that most of them didn't have the guts to pull a trigger or face a man down one-on-one. Persico, people like Scappy, they were different. I knew they were already figuring their revenge. They could call up an army of hitters to stalk me until they could kill me when they were free. It was constantly in my thoughts in and out of the courtroom.

On the last day of my testimony, as I was preparing to leave Governor's Island, I felt stiff and uncomfortable, and I stepped from the FBI's "Eggshell" to the deck of the ferry to stretch for a moment. With me was my covering agent, Dominick, who took my bag to put in an FBI escort car with another agent.

As he did, out of the corner of my eye, I saw this guy standing next to a big black Mercedes, looking at me, studying me. I looked and studied him, and then I recognized him. While the two agents looked in horror, I walked over to this guy, put out my hand, and shook his.

"Tony . . . its been a long time!" I said.

Tony was known to me as Tony the Electrician when I was running the flea market in Brooklyn for Funzi Tieri and his den of thieves. He had come to our aid when we didn't have the money to pay for the electrical hookup we needed, and he had rigged the electrical connections for us so that we got all the power we wanted without paying a dime.

Tony wasn't smiling as he looked first at me and then at the agents, who looked very tense and ready to take whatever action was necessary to protect me.

"What are you doing here, Tony?" I asked.

"Me?" he asked. His voice was shaky now, uncertain, and his eyes darting from me to the agents and back. "I . . . I got a big electrical contract here . . . for the island. It's worth a couple of million bucks."

Now I don't know who's more upset, Tony the Electrician or my two agent friends, who are very, very nervous.

"I gotta go, Joe," he says. "You're looking good. I'll tell your old man how good you look the next time I see him."

"Yeah, do that, Tony," I said. "Give him my regards."

As he climbed back into his Mercedes, I knew he was having diarrhea. I was the last person he expected to see, and probably the last person he wanted to see. He was between a rock and a hard place, all because of a ferry ride. If he told friends in Brooklyn where I was and they tried something at Governor's Island, not only would all fingers point to him, but he stood a good chance of losing a multimillion-dollar contract. If he didn't tell them and the boys found out he held out on them, he would be in serious trouble.

I never did find out what happened to him, but the Bureau agents were all over me to find out who and what he was. I told them. They colored slightly. One of their best-kept secrets apparently was no longer a secret. They would have to find a new place to hide witnesses, at least for the time being.

Security for the Commission case was supposed to be tougher. Two days before I was scheduled to testify in the case, I arrived in Newark. Several agents, including Michele, met me and escorted me to a hotel where John Savarese, one of the three prosecutors in the case, met with me that afternoon. The next day, he arrived at the hotel before he was supposed to. I wasn't there. I had gone for a walk by myself. The two FBI agents who were supposed to be providing my security were still in their command-post room. I had simply walked past them, gone down the elevator, out the lobby, and taken a six-block walk. As

I returned, Savarese and the agents were running around outside the hotel, frantically looking for me.

"Where the hell have you been?" Savarese shouted.

"I took a walk," I said. "I got bored sitting in that room, so I took a walk."

"What the hell have we got agents protecting you for, if you're just gonna go off and do whatever you feel like doing?" Savarese demanded to know angrily.

"Look . . . I'm sorry," I said, "but those guys you got watching me are a pair of cold mothers. I call them one and one. They don't say a word to me, so they don't make two. Jesus . . . they didn't even ask me if I wanted a roll or some coffee for breakfast."

Savarese calmed down, and then we went over my testimony and what I was likely to face in the way of questions.

The next day was September 29, 1986, and I found myself back in a courtroom, once again facing Persico. This time, he was acting as his own attorney, ready to question me directly as I looked at him and at the other old men of the Commission.

I didn't personally know Anthony Salerno, the boss of the Genovese family, or Antonio (Ducks) Corallo, who ran the Lucchese family. There was no Gambino-family boss on trial, as I expected there to be. He had been eliminated on December 16, 1985, in front of Spark's Steak House in Manhattan, by John Gotti's hitmen. The government's plan to have me testify about his role in the Wasserman case and in other events was no longer important.

I knew Christy Tick Furnari, the Lucchese family *consigliere*, and Langella, Persico's underboss, and could testify to events involving them.

I recall being surprised at seeing attorney John Jacobs at the defense table. When I was a federal informer and a witness against Alphonse Persico, Sr., he was an assistant U.S. attorney with the Eastern District Strike Force. Instead of chasing the mob, he was now defending them. Why not? I thought. He'll make more money. That was what all this trial was all about, making money.

Savarese was my first interrogator. He took me point by

point, year by year, through my life, from the day I graduated from West Islip High School through my honorable discharge from the U.S. Army to my father's real estate office, where life with the mob began.

We revisited my first meeting with Colombo at Cantalupo Realty, and I described my role as a salesman and as office manager.

Looking straight at the jury, I told Savarese I had never been convicted of a crime, then described the illegal activities that I participated in at the office with my father, from illegal raising and lowering of contracts to the skimming of 20 percent off the top of second mortgages and the phony sales-commission scheme that we used to provide Colombo with reportable tax income.

With each question, I became more and more confidant in myself and less concerned with the consequences of what I was doing.

As I recounted Colombo's racketeering operations from the real estate office, Savarese paused and then asked, "Now, in this period of time, did you come to meet a man by the name of Carmine Persico?"

I answered, "Yes."

The questioning continued as follows:

SAVARESE: Would you look around the courtroom and tell us, Mr. Cantalupo, if you recognize the man you know as Carmine Persico?

JC: Yes, Mr. Persico is sitting to the left of Mr. Lopez.

SAVARESE: Would you describe what he is wearing, please?

JC [pointing at Persico]: He has a blue suit on and a blue tie and a white shirt.

SAVARESE: Would the record reflect he has indicated the defendant Carmine Persico.

THE COURT: It may.

SAVARESE: Did you know Mr. Persico by any nickname or any other name?

JC: Carmine Junior.

[I then went on to describe how I'd met Persico at Cantalupo Realty and seen him meeting with Colombo in the mid 1960's.]

SAVARESE: During the 1960's, when Mr. Persico came to your father's office to meet with Colombo, would you seem him accompanied by anyone else?

JC: On different occasions I would see him accompanied by Hugh McIntosh and Jerry Lang.

SAVARESE: Do you know Mr. Jerry Lang by any other name?

JC: Jerry Langella.

SAVARESE: Would you look around the court and tell us if you see Mr. Langella in court today?

JC: Yes.

SAVARESE: Would you point to where he is sitting and describe what he is wearing?

    [Once again I looked slowly across the defense tables at each of the mob leaders, their underbosses, *consiglieri,* and their attorneys before answering slowly and very deliberately, motioning to Jerry Lang.]

JC: Jerry is sitting on the right of Mr. Lopez. He is wearing a gray suit and a red tie and a white shirt.

    [Once again Savarese noted I had correctly identified the defendant Langella.]

SAVARESE: To your knowledge, during this period while you were working at Cantalupo Realty, did Mr. Persico or Mr. Langella ever purchase real estate during these visits?

JC: Not to my knowledge.

SAVARESE: Did Mr. Colombo, to your knowledge, ever take them out to look at properties for sale?

JC: No.

SAVARESE: Were they themselves, that is, Mr. Persico and Mr. Langella, involved in the real estate business or working as salesmen there?

MR. JACOBS: Objection.

THE COURT: Overruled. You may answer.

JC: No.

From that point on, Savarese drew from me the history of organized crime in my father's office, including my father's participation with Colombo in the $100,000 shylock loan to Lou DiBlasi of Moon Trucking, using me as their weekly interest collector.

Savarese questioned me about my close association with Colombo and his sons, about his requesting the use of my apartment for what turned out to be a meeting of the Commission, about my father's association with Carlo Gambino both at the office and at his home, and how I became Gambino's notary.

I identified photographs of Colombo, Gambino, and Funzi Tieri, and described my partnership with Tieri in the flea market and how it was eventually divided up between the Genovese and Colombo family, between Tieri and Allie Boy. Savarese zeroed in on the ascension of Persico as a boss, succeeding Vincent Aloi, Thomas DiBella, and his brother, Allie Boy Persico, who held the job temporarily while he was in jail.

Savarese made me focus on the story Peewee Campagna told me about the Albanese-Abbatemarco dispute with Allie Boy, and how the Commission resolved it . . . and how Sally Albanese paid with his life, although his body was never found.

At one point, Savarese took me back to the gathering of the mob at Tomasso's restaurant in April 1977.

SAVARESE: Mr. Cantalupo, let me direct your attention to April 1977 . . . did you have occasion to be present at a large gathering at that time?

JC: Yes.

SAVARESE: Where was that gathering that you observed?

JC: Tomasso's restaurant.

SAVARESE: Will you tell us where Tomasso's restaurant is located?

JC: Eighty-Sixth Street and Bay Seventh Street in Brooklyn.

SAVARESE: How did you happen to be there on that occasion?

JC: I just happened to walk into the restaurant.

SAVARESE: What time of day was it?

JC: Evening.

SAVARESE: Would you tell us what you first observed when you walked in?

JC: Lots of people standing up smoking, drinking.

SAVARESE: Was this a group of men and women, or how would you describe it?

JC: Men only.

SAVARESE: Among those men that you observed in Tomasso's restaurant, did you see any that you knew?

JC: Yes.

SAVARESE: Can you tell us who you recall seeing?

JC: I saw Michael Bolino. I saw Allie Boy Persico, Big Allie Boy. I saw Little Allie Boy.

SAVARESE: That is to say, the son of Carmine Persico, correct?

JC: Yes.

SAVARESE: Anyone else?

JC: I saw Anthony Colombo. I saw Paul Castellano. I saw Johnny Russo—not Russo, Louie LaRocca. I saw Christy Tick.

SAVARESE: Let me stop you just for a moment. When you say you saw Paul Castellano, prior to this meeting had you met Mr. Castellano before?

JC: Yes.

SAVARESE: Who did you understand Mr. Castellano to be?

JC: Paulie Castellano was the boss of the Gambino crime family.

    [At this point, Savarese showed me pictures with Gambino and Castellano in them—pictures taken at the Westchester Theater. I identified each of them. He then asked me what formal name Christy Tick was known by and I answered Christopher Furnari . . . the *consigliere* of the Lucchese crime family.]

SAVARESE: Would you look around the courtroom and tell us if you see the person you know as Christopher Furnari in the court?

JC: Christy is sitting down I think next to Mr. [James] LaRossa [defense attorney], and he has a blue suit on, blue tie, white shirt, and glasses.

SAVARESE: Would the record indicate that he has identified the defendant Furnari?

    [I then described how I first met Christy Tick at my father's office and how I'd seen him there with Colombo from time to time. I also described seeing him at the 19th Hole and two doors away, at the Hong Pan restaurant.]

SAVARESE: Returning to this party at Tomasso's that you observed, did you remain at the party?

JC: No.

SAVARESE: Had you been invited to it?

JC: No.

SAVARESE: Did you later have occasion to have a conversation with

anyone after this party in April 1977 about what the party
at Tomasso's had been for?

JC: Yes.

SAVARESE: Who did you speak with?

JC: Michael Bolino, Anthony Colombo.

SAVARESE: What did they tell you?

JC: That this was a party for the new members initiated into different families.

SAVARESE: Specifically, did you learn who it was who had been recently initiated that the party was to celebrate?

JC: Some of them.

SAVARESE: Who were some of those people?

JC: Anthony Colombo, the kid Allie Boy.

SAVARESE: By that you mean the son of Carmine Persico?

JC: Yes.

SAVARESE: Anyone else?

JC: Shorty Spero. There were different members of the Genovese
family who were made at the time, Johnny Russo, and someone
nicknamed Joey Mann.

I didn't recall any others, but Savarese followed that testimony with a tape recording I made on June 9, 1977, with
Michael Bolino while I was a confidential FBI informant. During the tape, Bolino describes how agents are swarming over
the area, searching for Sally Albanese. When I asked him
where Sally was, Bolino said, "He's gone," and Savarese had
me explain to the jury that meant Albanese had been murdered.

The tape had another segment that Savarese considered important because of the connection to Langella. It concerned the
robbery I had set up with Jerry Gordon and Gene Terra at the
home of John Scotti. Scotti was a car-leasing manager for Terragrossa who I rented my cars from.

During the robbery, they taped up and locked up a baby-sitter
in a closet and left Scotti's baby unattended.

As a result, I told the jury, Scotti was so angered he decided
to go to Jerry Lang and McIntosh to find out who had robbed
his home.

SAVARESE: Now was this something that Mr. Bolino knew about beforehand, this robbery?

JC: Yes.

SAVARESE: Why was that?

JC: I usually tell Michael what I'm going to do ahead of time.

SAVARESE: Now, when he said: 'When they see him [Scotti], they will chase him,' that's Mr. Bolino's statement, who was he referring to and what did he mean so far as you understood?

JC: That Scotti was going to go down to see McIntosh and Jerry Lang with his problem. When they saw him, they would chase him, they wouldn't want any part of him.

My direct testimony ended with some additional testimony about how the loan-shark debts of Wah On Lee, my Chinese borrower, were settled by Christy Tick at a mob sitdown, then I faced the defense attorneys and Persico.

At first the thought of being questioned by Persico upset me, but after he tried—after he stumbled and bumbled and stuttered with his questions—I knew I had nothing to be worried about. He was obviously unprepared. I stared him down. I looked at the jury as I answered his questions, and I made a point of answering him as though we knew each other. I rarely used his name. Familiarity breeds contempt. The jury knew I was familiar with Carmine—that he knew me and I knew him. His questions implied that familiarity.

He stood at the lectern, peered at me over the top of his glasses, and said with a half smile on his face, "Describe for these people [pointing to the jury] my relationship to you."

"At that particular time, or through the years?" I answered, implying that familiarity.

"At that time and any other time after," he replied.

"Our relationship was only to say hello, shake hands, goodbye . . . nothing formal."

Time and again there were questions and answers with that sense of familiarity. He was conceding to me a station in the life of the crime family that I would have normally, and tediously, had to explain.

I thought it was his biggest mistake. When other attorneys like Frank Lopez or Jacobs asked me a question, I answered them "Mr. Lopez," or "Mr. LaRossa." Not with Persico. It was always: "No . . . that's not correct," or "I met you in my father's office," or "Your brother, Alphonse." It was the language of familiarity, and I know that the jury recognized it. They knew it and they understood it.

At one point, Persico became impatient cross-examining me about various shylock loans I had had either as a victim or as a loan shark myself. The judge told him he was being repetitious, and he should move on to another subject.

THE COURT: This is repetitious. Let's move along.

PERSICO: I am sorry, Your Honor.

THE COURT: The questions are proper, but once they are answered, we should move along.

PERSICO: Can I have five minutes, Your Honor? I really need it.

THE COURT: Let's keep going, all right?

PERSICO: Jesus! Once more you were using law . . . you would use the law to pay back somebody. You did it to Gredda [the drug dealer-partner].

SAVARESE: Objection.

THE COURT: I don't know if that is a question. Let's go on to something else.

PERSICO: Could you tell us how many trials and grand juries you testified in? I don't want the names, just the amount.

JC: Eight, nine, ten . . . around there.

PERSICO: Quite a bit?

JC: Yes.

PERSICO: You are used to sitting up on that stand?

JC: Yes.

PERSICO: Have you ever lied at any of these trials?

JC: Never intentionally.

PERSICO: Unintentionally?

JC: Never unintentionally.

PERSICO: You never lied then?

JC: I tried to do my best.

PERSICO: I didn't ask you that. Did you ever lie?

JC: No.

PERSICO: I am sorry, Your Honor. I am getting a little confused with these papers.

It took several more hours of cross-examination by Persico, Lopez, who represented Langella, and James LaRossa, who represented Furnari, before my testimony ended. Persico and Lopez battered and hammered at my past criminal acts for which the government gave me immunity. They got nowhere. LaRossa tried to show that my testimony about Furnari was largely hearsay, based on conversations with others. He changed nothing. At the conclusion, I felt I ended on a high note. Savarese, on redirect questioning, asked what I thought the advantage there was for Tieri in being an off-the-books partner in the flea market.

JC: Off the books, for instance, the flea market, Funzi Tieri was my partner off the books. He put up the cash. If the business was going he would get paid back the cash.

SAVARESE: Would he have to show any of that cash as a result of his being off the books?

JC: No.

SAVARESE: What is the advantage of that?

MR. JACOBS: Objection.

MR. CARDINALE: Irrelevant.

THE COURT: I will permit it.

JC: The advantage of that is tax purposes.

SAVARESE: No further questions.

EPILOGUE:
LURE OF THE INFORMER

I left New York on October, 1, 1986, after concluding my testimony in the Commission case. Within a month, my subsistence, which had been increased to twenty-two-hundred dollars ended. The trials were over and, for the most part, so was my small business. Neglect—the constant travel, the meetings, the testifying, the stress that overwhelmed me during the period—terminated my business. I had to sell my truck and my route to raise enough money to pay my bills. I had to find a new way to survive.

In the end, I knew I would survive because organized crime flourished wherever I planted my feet. New York, Rhode Island, Minnesota, Idaho, Iowa, Utah, Kansas, Missouri, Arizona—I found organized crime in all of those states. Finding it—exposing it for law-enforcement agencies—meant money for me, a way of making a living. The only difference in the organized crime I encountered was in the size, the quality, and the ethnic background.

In Kansas, I found an unexpected variety. Not only was there a strong Italian Cosa Nostra organization built around Nick Civella and his successors, but there was a redneck mafia that used political clout and backwoods justice to peddle crime and line its pockets in a way that put the nearby city mafiosi to shame.

Drugs, prostitution, gambling, extortion, loan-sharking, and murder were all part of a way of life I found in nearby Wyandotte County. Had I made connections in other regions of the state, I am certain I would have found other versions of organized crime.

While I was still in the witness program, I met a Drug Enforcement Administration agent who somehow figured out what I was through his understanding of various government-file code numbers and through his government connections. He lived in an apartment nearby, and one day suggested I might be able to help the FBI and his agency in its investigation of the pizza connection for narcotics smuggling.

I was shaken by his knowledge about my background, but what he was asking me to do suggested that I could make some money. Unexpectedly, I felt a surge of excitement at the thought of once again doing what I had done for a decade and knew I could do best—infiltrate and spy on criminal organizations. Until that moment, I had never admitted to myself that I liked the emotional highs I got from my work as a professional informer. There was an excitement, a sense of danger, I had grown used to and now missed.

The drug agent sent me to see an FBI agent named Mike Shanahan. He supervised a group of agents and wanted my help in checking on a pizza company that had a string of shops in a number of shopping malls that I serviced with Italian specialties through a business I had set up.

The shops and the company had one thing in common—they were run by what we in Brooklyn called the greaseballs, or the zips, recently immigrated native-born Sicilians. He suspected they were part of the mob's pizza connection for drug smuggling because of their sudden expansion and heavy cash flow.

When I told him that one of the owners had come to my house with eighty thousand dollars in cash and had asked me to get him money orders for five thousand dollars made out in the name of another Sicilian in the old country, he was certain he had a drug connection. I tried to explain that the guy had used the money to buy a beautiful villa in Sicily, but he was certain it was money for drugs. I also told him one of the pizza owners wanted me to get him a gun. He couldn't buy one because he was an alien. All very suspicious, but I was certain drugs weren't involved.

As a demonstration of good faith, I gave them a list of names of people the pizza boys were dealing with and the method they were using to skim big money from their business and send it back to the old country without paying taxes. With a little work, it could make a great Internal Revenue Service or an Immigration Service case, or even more. That could mean big bucks.

Mike and his people didn't pay a dime for the information, and if they pursued it further, they didn't tell me, but they held out the hope that they might get approval from Washington to hire me as a confidential informant now that I was no longer in the witness program.

While I was checking out the pizza-skimming operation, I also located a bookmaker in Kansas City who was originally from Chicago. After betting football games and baseball games with him and winning his confidence, I convinced him I was looking for bigger and better action. He led me to a plush strip joint called the Red Apple on Minnesota Avenue, in Kansas City, and then to Wyandotte County and John "Smokey" Quinn, Jr., the son of the county sheriff.

It took a few visits, but they invited me to their casino games—big Las Vegas Nites free-for-alls they called "bachelor parties" that they ran in Wyandotte County every three months, sometimes less. I let the Bureau agents there know about the games and two twenty-five-dollar tickets I had bought to go to a game at State Avenue and 137th Street in Wyandotte on January 20. The FBI said it was interesting and they'd check it out, but there was nothing they could do about it. I was on my own.

So I went with a friend. The game was at a big barn, a place known as Auctions Unlimited. As I walked in the front door, there were two armed deputy sheriffs in uniform on duty. Whoa, I thought, what have I got myself into?

I shrugged my shoulders and with an insurance-broker friend

handed my tickets to the deputies. "John [my bookie] told me to give these to you," I said. "I'm Joe, this is my friend Jim . . . John sent us here to play."

The deputies held the tickets, and we walked in. There was a bar, there was food, there were at least seven broads walking around with their boobs and tushes hanging out so they could entertain on the dance floor or in the privacy of some Winnebagos that were parked outside, and where the entertainment was more than tossing the boobs and hips around. The hookers charged anywhere from fifty dollars for a blow job to one hundred dollars for a quick jump in the hay.

Beyond the girls were blackjack, poker, and crap tables piled high with chips and cash. White chips were a dollar, red chips five dollars. That's where I met Smokey Quinn. He was running the crap tables. The guy from the Red Apple strip joint was running a poker table, and a guy they called Rick, who controlled liquor sales, was dealing blackjack.

I stood out like a sore thumb. I had to be the only Italian there and, while they thought I was some sort of Eastern Seaboard mafioso, they weren't particularly impressed. All around me were the Heehaw boys in their cowboy hats, their cowboy boots covered with cow shit, their beards and dirty jeans and their pickup trucks. One I'll never forget. He was an albino, and he looked like Zorro, complete with a big black hat with a silver band, and a black scarf on the back of his bald head.

I introduced myself to Smokey. He was a little guy, about 5'7". Little man or not, he held all the cards. He had a big family—six brothers and three sisters. He had a club on State Avenue. And he had power, power that was amply demonstrated by the armed uniformed deputies and the protection he had against raids by state and federal authorities.

"Here's my card, Joe," he said. "Come see me anytime." With his personal card, he gave me a card to the Red Apple strip joint.

Now, the Bureau was interested, but for all the information, they were willing to pay only my expenses of a few hundred dollars a month plus the cost of leasing a Ford Taurus, which they rigged with hidden microphones to record conversations they wanted me to have with various people.

They were interested in Smokey and his redneck mafia, but they were more interested in the Kansas City Cosa Nostra and its new leadership, now that Nick Civella was dead. Because I was Italian, and because I had access to some of the clubs where mob members hung out, they decided I was going to infiltrate the Kansas City organization. To do that, they provided me with some flash money to buy dinners and drinks, and they provided me with several trays of gems—diamonds, emeralds, sapphires, rubies, garnets, and other stones—to unload. The stones, they said, had been appraised at twelve thousand dollars wholesale by a jeweler they had contacted to look at the stones in a county in Missouri. With a twelve-thousand-dollar wholesale value, the hundred gemstones the Bureau gave me to give out in any way I wanted to were probably worth thirty-six thousand dollars or more retail. I had a stake that could give me a leg up.

I thought I was back in business. Bureau agents promised to put me back on a monthly salary once they saw some results, and in the interim, they would pay my expenses, my car rental, and provide insurance for my family should something happen to me. They also guaranteed to pay the cost of moving to another area if my identity as an informer should be blown.

I got close to Smokey Quinn, close enough that he sent me to some poor business partner of his who owed him money. He wanted me to threaten to break the kid's legs unless he came up with a lousy four thousand dollars he owed Smokey. The kid lived in a shack with his wife and four kids. He didn't have enough to pay for his kids' milk, let alone pay back the business loan. I told the kid Smokey was after him and wanted his money, then I told the Bureau he was in real danger. Nothing happened. Later, someone shot him, and the Bureau got interested.

Smokey introduced me to all his redneck friends as a Mafia man from out of town. The friends weren't just saddle tramps and dirt farmers, they were state representatives, county officials, and law-enforcement people who took their orders from him. When he ran his games, he had protection from everyone, not just the deputies from his father's Sheriff's Office. Highway patrolmen, judges, prosecutors, they all reported in to Smokey, they all took care of his problems.

In May, Smokey told me the big game was set for May 6. I told the Bureau. I also took some tickets that I bought from Smokey at twenty-five dollars a piece and had fifty duplicates made. The Bureau thought I was nuts when I told them I'd counterfeited Smokey's tickets, but they didn't refuse the twenty I provided to them for agents they planned to plant at the game. The rest I sold off to friends, including people in Civella's crowd. I had to get money some way. The Bureau hadn't paid more than one thousand dollars they owed me for insurance and car-lease payments, and I was broke.

Just before the raid, I drew a map of the layout for Mike and his people. They knew exactly where to go for what. They instructed me to go to the game and play as I had in the past. When the raid came down, I would be questioned like every other player. Only Mike and several agents close to him knew I was the undercover informant.

The raid went off like greased lightning. Seventy-five agents came in like gangbusters and closed everything down at 7:30 P.M. with bullhorn announcements that this was an FBI raid. They caught two deputies at the door. They caught hookers and their johns in the Winnebegos. They cut off outside patrols before they could tip those inside the Auctions Unlimited warehouse. Agents inside playing craps and cards suddenly put on their FBI armbands and seized the pots at every table.

When all was said and done, they had seized nineteen thousand dollars in cash, took the names, addresses, and photographs of 150 attending the games, and seized all the gaming tables. When they were through, they escorted those of us inside to our cars and gave us a card that read RELEASED BY THE FBI. Then they instructed us how to leave the area, which looked like an armed camp. Without the cards, no one could have passed through the highway roadblocks they had set up all around the area of the auction house.

The next day, newspapers were filled with long headlined stories about the raid, about the sheriff's son running the games, and about the deputies who provided protection for the games. It was a full-blown scandal, but there wasn't a whisper of my role in the event, and there hasn't been until you read this.

For my role in the investigation, I got a big five thousand dollars and the news that once again my identity was probably in jeopardy. Seems the appraiser the FBI had used to put a value on the gems was at the games. He could identify the gems as Bureau property if any of the people I was dealing with took one of the gems to him for an appraisal. Rather than take a chance, I returned the trays of gems and waited for replacements.

Still the Bureau held out hopes that I would soon be employed as an informant. They kept up the car payments, they provided some expense money, and they pressed me to record conversations with Smokey—conversations in which he talked about moving pot, shooting the partner who owed him money, and transporting guns to New York. They also continued to press for infiltration of the Kansas City mob.

Infiltrating a Cosa Nostra gang is not an easy task. It takes time, it takes money, it takes careful nuturing of friendships. The Bureau in Kansas City didn't understand that. They had just come off of a successful prosecution with wiretaps and they wanted results, almost immediately. There was no way I could deliver on that timetable. I may be Italian, but to the Kansas City crew I might as well have been from the moon. To them, I was an outsider. I would have to prove myself, and that would take time. This Midwest branch of the Bureau wasn't interested in spending time . . . or money. They didn't have the smarts of New York agents.

Four months later, they cut the string. The Kansas City office called me in and told me that they would no longer pay for leasing the car. They weren't going to give me any more expense money, and they had decided they weren't going to include me on an informant payroll at two thousand dollars a month even if I could infiltrate the Kansas City mob. Three days after they cut me off, on October 20, 1987, Smokey Quinn and sixteen of his associates at the games were indicted by a federal grand jury. My immediate value had ended. Just before the indictment was returned, local Kansas City investigators raided the Red Apple and charged forty-two dancers, waitresses, and club managers with some 286 violations of city vice and morals charges. Five of them also got rapped on charges of selling cocaine.

Wyandotte County had become a hot potato all because of that raid. The Bureau had its headlines and eventually its convictions of Smokey Quinn and a number of his flunkies. It wasn't interested in going after an interstate drug deal or gunrunners. It didn't need Joe Cantalupo anymore. So what else was new?

The day of the indictment, I heard from Smokey after two weeks of ducking his calls. He wanted to meet with me, one-on-one. He was very insistent. There was no question in my mind that Smokey had figured out that I had ratted on him. I figured there had been a leak in the U.S Attorney's Office, although I had no proof. Now, hunting season was on. Between Smokey, who I knew to be a violent man with a long reach, and desertion by the FBI office, I had no alternative. Rachel, my daughter, and I would have to move again . . . and in a hurry.

This time I couldn't count on any help. I couldn't trust the so-called good guys. There were those who were bitter because I had testified against them in the WITSEC investigation. There were others who had blown my cover time and again either through stupidity or because it suited their purpose. There was no reason to think that any prosecutors would go to bat for me. The Kansas City mess wasn't their case.

Rachel and I were going to relocate on our own. I decided that neither the Bureau, nor the marshals, nor the U.S. Department of Justice, nor anyone else was going to know enough about my whereabouts to be able to blow my identity or know where I moved to.

It took some doing, but we successfully relocated in a new area of the country. We found jobs and a home and a community where we are happy. Finding what we have long dreamed about did not happen without difficulty.

In February 1988, I had to talk to a federal agent who had provided protection and help for me during the Colombo and Commission trials.

There had, it seems, been a murder in Wyandotte of the Democratic political boss, Charles W. Thompson, on December 21, 1987. Thompson, just before his murder, had been critical of Smokey Quinn and Quinn's father, as well as the Sheriff's Department. Police in Kansas were looking for me. They wanted to question me. The agent asked me to sit down with them, assuring me that I would have no problem. The Bureau, which never surfaced me during the trial, had apparently given me up to local police investigating the homicide.

Reluctantly, I made arrangements to come to New York to appear for the interview at a Long Island FBI office. During the questioning by three Kansas City detectives, it became apparent to me that I was a suspect in the homicide of Thompson, who had been gunned down by what they said was a professional killer using exploding bullets to kill Thompson in front of the Jalisco restaurant and private club on State Avenue, Wyandotte.

Why me? I was no killer. No one, not even the mob, had pointed a finger at me for something like that. I had never heard of Thompson, but I had to spend hours providing them with proof that I not only didn't know him, but I didn't know what his relationship with Smokey was, and that I was long gone from Kansas when the murder took place.

It was an emotionally draining experience. To be a mob witness—one who had testified in trials like the Colombo-family RICO and the Commission case—and now be a suspect in a murder was frightening. Who the hell was going to protect me, defend me, stand up for me and say, No, Joe Cantalupo was somewhere else when that happened; he didn't do it?

Fortunately for me, the agent who had called me to the meeting with the detectives could and did vouch for me when I produced employment records and other documentation. The detectives were not allowed to see those records, since they could have been used to trace me to my new location.

I have to feel I was put on the hot seat because Smokey Quinn found out I was the one who did a number on his operation in Wyandotte. Because of what I did, ten of the original seventeen arrested in the raid pleaded guilty to state misdemeanor gambling charges. The remainder wound up on trial in federal court, and of those, only one, Deputy Robert Huckaby, was found innocent.

A month later, on March 6, Sheriff Quinn's former chief deputy, Terry Clark, was sentenced to serve six months in jail, three years on probation, and fined twenty-five hundred dollars for "blatant abuse" of his uniform in providing protection for the games of Smokey Quinn. Four others, including the managers of the Red Apple and Bachelors III topless clubs, were sentenced to from 60 to 120 days in jail and fined two thousand dollars each for conspiring to run an illegal gambling business. They had all pleaded guilty to reduced federal charges rather than face a costly trial.

A week later, Smokey appeared in federal court and was sent to jail for a year and fined five thousand dollars for running the illegal casino. Within two months, his father, Sheriff Quinn, was indicted for mistreating prisoners. After that, I lost track of the Kansas connections, but I won't ever forget them.

When I left Long Island and New York to return to my home and family, I left with the feeling that my life on the run will probably never end. There will always be some wiseguy who thinks he knows me, some fed who talks too much, someplace I have to travel to where I may be spotted.

I've lived for more than a decade under different identities. I've had to take on different roles in life, different jobs. The job I love the most—working undercover as a paid informant—is the one I have to avoid, no matter what the temptation.

I think I have learned—at least I hope I have—that I can't trust or depend on federal agencies anymore. There are individuals who have done much to make it possible for me to survive, to live. But they work for bureaucracies that use rules and regulations that they draw up to suit themselves. Agencies are concerned only with covering their asses, avoiding criticism for the mistakes they make. If it means burning those that work for them, that's tough. It if means people lose jobs, or get hurt, or have their lives endangered, or even get killed, that's too bad. They assume no responsibility for the screw-ups, no obligation to those who get hurt.

I remember something that Mike Shanahan said to me when I told him a book was being done about my life: "When it's written, describe me as being on the team, but never playing the game." He never did. Life in the fast lane of big-time organized crime was too much for that Kansas City boy. It took players like

Ray Tallia and Frank Lazzara to grab the brass ring and shake it until goodies like Colombo, Persico, and the Commission fell out. The trouble is, they move on when their job is done, and the informer is passed on to the nonplayers. That's when the game stops.

There will be those who will still try to tap me for other jobs. When federal marshals found Persico in Connecticut after his years of hiding, agents wanted to talk to me about how he was able to hide out all those years with the help of the mob, and they wanted to know about a couple of his close associates that I knew when I was back on the streets of Brooklyn.

And when there was a possibility of a civil trial against the leadership of the International Brotherhood of Teamsters Union, I was offered a couple of thousand bucks if I'd make myself available to testify about one of the targets of the civil suit. No protection, no guarantees . . . just a quick two thousand dollars to answer some questions, expose myself again, and run some more. I said no, of course, and three days later the government settled the case—not because I wouldn't testify, but because they had cut a deal and never bothered to tell the agents who were assigned to reach out to me.

I made my bed, so I'll lie in it. I'll do my damndest to take care of my families. I'll hustle a buck the best way I can, and I'll walk on the right side of the law as best I can, because I'd never survive if I had to go to jail—if the mob didn't get me, the "good guys" might. Whatever happens, I'll always be a little bitter, a little disappointed, because I had to stop doing what I do best—exposing the mob and its activities in all its forms. There is a lure to being an informer that generates an excitement, a thrill, I'm going to miss.

MAJOR TRIALS AND CONVICTIONS

RHODE ISLAND

ANDREW F. MEROLA
> CONVICTION: July 1979, Murder
> SENTENCE: Life imprisonment
> (Reversed on appeal 1982. Pleaded guilty to second-degree murder. Resentence: June 1982 to 25 years in jail, 15 of which were suspended.)
> CRIME STATUS: Associate, Raymond Patriarca crime family.

NICHOLAS PARI
> CONVICTION: July 1979, Murder 1
> SENTENCE: Life imprisonment
> (Reversed on appeal 1982. Pleaded guilty to manslaughter. Resentence: June 1982, 20 years in jail, 13 of which were suspended.)
> CRIME STATUS: Associate, Raymond Patriarca crime family

FEDERAL 1980

ALPHONSE (ALLIE BOY) PERSICO
> CONVICTION: May 1980, Conspiracy and Extortion

SENTENCE: 25 years
(Persico was sentenced December 18, 1987, to 25 years for the 1980 conviction. He was scheduled to appear June 20, 1980 for sentencing when he disappeared and forfeited $250,000 bond. He was found by the U.S. Marshals Service fugitive squad in December 1987, and brought to court in chains for sentencing. He died in federal prison in Missouri of throat cancer on September 12, 1989.)
CRIME STATUS: Identified in 1980 as the underboss and acting boss of the Colombo crime family. He is the brother of jailed Colombo-family boss Carmine Persico, Jr., convicted of loan-sharking Joseph Cantalupo.

MICHAEL BOLINO
CONVICTION: May 1980, Conspiracy and Extortion
SENTENCE: 7 years
CRIME STATUS: Identified in 1980 as a soldier in the Colombo crime family. Closely allied with Alphonse Persico and a close friend of Joe Cantalupo, whom he shylocked.

FEDERAL 1980
(FEDERAL RACKETEERING)

FRANK (FUNZI) TIERI
CONVICTION: November 1980, Racketeering as a crime boss
SENTENCE: 10 years
CRIME STATUS: Identified in 1980 as the boss of the Genovese crime family, Tieri was a partner in a Brooklyn flea-market venture with Cantalupo. His trial was the first racketeering trial of a crime family boss, as such, and the trial spanned a decade of his criminal acts. Cantalpuo was one of

several important witnesses called in the case. Tieri died in April 1981, less than four months after being sentenced, without serving a day of his 10-year sentence.

1981: (EXPLOSIVES CONSPIRACY)

ANGELO MICHAEL MARINO
CONVICTION: PG, June 1981. Conspiracy to distribute explosives
SENTENCE: 3 years
CRIME STATUS: Colombo-family associate. Recorded selling plastic explosives to FBI agent by Cantalupo and agent.

ANTHONY BOTTIGLIO
CONVICTION: PG, March 15, 1982, Conspiracy to distribute explosives
SENTENCE: 3 years

THOMAS GUERRIO
CONVICTION: PG, June 1981, Conspiracy to distribute explosives
SENTENCE: 3 years

JOSEPH PROVOST
CONVICTION: PG, June 1981, Conspiracy to distribute explosives
SENTENCE: Six months
CRIME STATUS: Bartiglia, Guerrio, and Provost were all identified as coconspirators of Marino by Cantalupo during an undercover investigation. The case was not surfaced until after Cantalupo was identified as a protected witness.

FEDERAL 1981: (EXTORTION)

JOSEPH (MUMBLES) RUSSO
CONVICTION: September 1981, Extortion

SENTENCE: 3 years
CRIME STATUS: Russo was identified and taped by Cantalupo as a loan shark and enforcer for Frank Tieri. He was identified as a soldier of the Genovese crime family.

FEDERAL 1986: (COLOMBO RICO)

CARMINE PERSICO, JR.
CONVICTION: June 1986, Racketeering, Extortion, Gambling, Bribery, and Drug Dealing
SENTENCE (November 1986): 39 years
CRIME STATUS: Boss, Colombo crime family

GENNARO (JERRY LANG) LANGELLA
CONVICTION: June 1986, same charges as Carmine Persico, Jr.
SENTENCE (November 1986): 65 years
CRIME STATUS: Underboss.

ALPHONSE (LITTLE ALLIE BOY) PERSICO, JR.
CONVICTION: June 1986, same charges as Carmine Persico, Jr.
SENTENCE (November 1986): 12 years
CRIME STATUS: Crime captain (*Caporegime*)

DOMINIC CATALDO
CONVICTION: June 1986, same charges as Carmine Persico, Jr.
SENTENCE (November 1986): 14 years
CRIME STATUS: Crime captain (*Caporegime*)

ANDREW (MUSH) RUSSO
CONVICTION: June 1986, same charges as Carmine Persico, Jr.
SENTENCE (November 1986): 14 years
CRIME STATUS: Crime captain (*Caporegime*)

ANTHONY SCARPATI
>CONVICTION: June 1986, same charges as
Carmine Persico, Jr.
SENTENCE (November 1986): 35 years
CRIME STATUS: Crime captain *(Caporegime)*

JOHN J. DE ROSS
>CONVICTION: June 1986, same charges as
Carmine Persico, Jr.
SENTENCE (November 1986): 14 years
CRIME STATUS: Crime captain *(Caporegime)*

HUGH (APPLES) McINTOSH,
>CONVICTION: June 1986, same charges as
Carmine Persico, Jr.
SENTENCE (November 1986): 10 years
(consecutive to service of nine years for
bribery)
CRIME STATUS: Crime-family associate

FRANK (THE BEAST) FALANGA
>CONVICTION: June 1986, same charges as
Carmine Persico, Jr.
SENTENCE: Never sentenced. Died June 13,
1986, one day after being found guilty
CRIME STATUS: Crime-family associate

>NOTE: All of the above were convicted in a
1986 Colombo crime-family Rico trial at which
Cantalupo was one of several key witnesses.

FEDERAL 1986
(COMMISSION RICO)

ANTHONY (FAT TONY) SALERNO
>CONVICTION: November 1986, Racketeering.
SENTENCE (January 1987): 100 years, $250,000
fine.
CRIME STATUS: Boss, Genovese Crime Family

ANTHONY (TONY DUCKS) CORALLO
>CONVICTION: November 1986, Racketeering
>SENTENCE: 100 years, $250,000 fine
>CRIME STATUS: Boss, Lucchese Crime Family

CARMINE PERSICO, JR.
>CONVICTION: November 1986, Racketeering
>SENTENCE: 100 years, $250,000 fine
>CRIME STATUS: Boss, Colombo crime family

SALVATORE SANTORO
>CONVICTION: November 1986, Racketeering
>SENTENCE: 100 years, $250,000 fine
>CRIME STATUS: Underboss, Lucchese crime family

CHRISTOPHER (CHRISTY TICK) FURNARI
>CONVICTION: November 1986, Racketeering
>SENTENCE: 100 years, $250,000 fine
>CRIME STATUS: Consigliere (Adviser), Lucchese crime family

GENNARO (JERRY LANG) LANGELLA
>CONVICTION: November 1986, Racketeering
>SENTENCE: 100 years, $250,000 fine
>CRIME STATUS: Underboss, Colombo crime family

RALPH SCOPO
>CONVICTION: November 1986, Racketeering
>SENTENCE: 100 years, $250,000 fine
>CRIME STATUS: Soldier, labor racketeer, Colombo crime family

ANTHONY INDELICATO
>CONVICTION: November 1986, Racketeering
>SENTENCE: 40 years, $50,000 fine
>CRIME STATUS: Soldier, Bonanno crime family

>NOTE: Indelicato was charged with fewer crimes but received the maximum sentence for

the crime he committed—carrying out the
Commission's order to murder former
Bonanno family boss Carmine Galante in a
Brooklyn restaurant in 1979.

INDEX

ABOUT THE AUTHORS

JOSEPH CANTALUPO is the most effective Mafia informant since Vincent Teresa. He is now living under an assumed identity.

THOMAS C. RENNER has authored two best-sellers, the internationally acclaimed *My Life in the Mafia* with Vincent Teresa, and *Mafia Princess,* with Antoinette Giancana.

Renner is a veteran of thirty-five years on the Pulitzer Prize–winning *New York Newsday.* He has won recognition as an organized crime expert and was one of five reporters cited by the president of the United States for significant contributions in exposing organized crime. He was the first reporter in America to be assigned to investigate and write solely about organized crime and was a key member of the "Arizona Project," a prize-winning investigation of corruption and crime in the southwest. Renner was awarded the coveted Louis M. Lyons Award for Conscience and Integrity in Journalism in 1983 by the Neiman Fellows of Harvard University and the Sigma Delta Chi Distinguished Service Award for the Arizona Project. He is the recipient of numerous awards for excellence, integrity and, community service.